Peter Pál Pelbart

CARTOGRAPHY OF EXHAUSTION
NIHILISM INSIDE OUT

O AVESSO DO NIILISMO -
CARTOGRAFIAS DO ESGOTAMENTO
by Peter Pál Pelbart
© n-1 publications, 2013

Translated by John Laudenberger and Felix Rebolledo Palazuelos as
Cartography of Exhaustion: Nihilism Inside Out

First Edition
Minneapolis © 2015, Univocal Publishing

Published by Univocal
123 North 3rd Street, #202
Minneapolis, MN 55401

Designed & Printed by Jason Wagner
Distributed by the University of Minnesota Press

ISBN 9781937561512
Library of Congress Control Number 2015955620

TABLE OF CONTENTS

Life, Body, Power

Nihilism, Disaster, Community

Exhaustion, Madness, Outside

Time, Experience, Desubjectivation

Afterword

"Writing has no other goal: wind..."

Gilles Deleuze

LIFE, BODY, POWER

HOW TO LIVE ALONE?

The Populated Solitude

In the early eighties, in a class about cinema, if I remember correctly, Deleuze was interrupted by a rather fraught student, perhaps one of Guattari's patients, or a former La Borde inmate, amidst such a heterogeneous audience, composed of philosophers, architects, painters, drug addicts, vagrants…. He asked Deleuze why people were so alone, why there was such a lack of communication nowadays, and unraveled his sad story about how we are victims of abandonment and helplessness. And Deleuze, sensing that his class was being driven off track, replied politely, before proposing a small break: the problem is not that we are alone, but rather that we are not left alone enough. Indeed, Deleuze never tired of writing that we suffer from an excess of communication, that we are "riddled with pointless talk, insane quantities of words and images," so that it is no longer a question of making "people express themselves, but rather to provide small vacuoles of solitude and silence in which they might eventually find something to say." To conjure the gentleness and the right to have nothing to say is perhaps the condition "so that one might form the rare, or even rarer, thing that might be worth saying."[1]

But what is this solitude that Deleuze called for, one that he came to qualify as "absolute solitude" when referring to the creator, a condition that he finds in Nietzsche, Kafka, Melville,

---

1. Gilles Deleuze, *Negotiations*, trans. Martin Joughin, (New York: Columbia University Press, 1995), p. 129.

Godard, and so many others? It is the world's most populous solitude. "Populated not with dreams, phantasms or plans, but with encounters."[2] Because what matters is that at the bottom of that solitude we can meet people without even knowing them. Movements, ideas, events, entities. As he says: "We are deserts, but populated by tribes, flora and fauna. We pass our time in ordering these tribes, arranging them in other ways, getting rid of some and encouraging others to prosper. And all these clans, all these crowds, do not undermine the desert, which is our very own ascesis; on the contrary, they inhabit it, they pass through it, over it.... The desert, experimentation on oneself is our only identity, our single chance for all the combinations which inhabit us."[3] What fascination they exercised over him, these hybrid, solitary, desert types, and also men of groups and gangs, like Lawrence of Arabia. Deserts populated by becomings, encounters, traversed by movements of deterritorialization and depersonalization.... Even when they carried a name, this name designated first an event before a subject, more a collective assemblage than an individual, an intensity before a form. In short, the most singular point; an opening for the biggest multiplicity: rhizome. As Deleuze says, to leave the "black hole of our Ego" where we dwell with our feelings and passions, to undo one's face, to become imperceptible, and to paint ourselves in the colors of the world (D. H. Lawrence)....[4] The most absolute solitude, in favor of more radical depersonalization for a different conjugation with the flows of the world.... To become a molecule, becoming-imperceptible, to meddle in the course of things, and there proliferate, propagate everywhere.... The becoming-viral of thought, whose other name is desire. "The epitome of wishful solitude and the epitome of the socius," as Guattari wrote in his notes. Or as in Godard: being alone in order to be part of a criminal conspiracy, or a production studio, and turn into a gang; in any case, desertion, betrayal itself (of family, class, nation, the status of author), is to embrace solitude as a means for encounter, in a creative line of flight.[5]

2. Gilles Deleuze, *Dialogues*, trans. H. Tomlinson and B. Habberjam, (New York: Columbia University Press, 1987), p. 6.

3. *Ibid.*, p. 11.

4. *Ibid.*, p. 45-6.

5. *Ibid.*, p. 17.

Thus, it is anything but solipsism. Solitude is the means by which one deserts the form of the Ego and its infamous commitments to a determined totality in favor of a different combination with the flows of the socius and of the cosmos in such a way that the solitary's challenge, contrary to any autistic reclusion, is always to find or rediscover the most connections.[6] To call for a people to come. To make another community possible. To establish a different interaction between the singular and the common.

Take the figure of Bartleby, the scrivener described by Melville, who replies to every order of his boss as such: "I would prefer not to." The lawyer oscillates between fraternal compassion and indignation, between pity and repulsion, with this employee planted behind the screen, who barely speaks, barely eats, pale and thin like an irremovable lost soul. With such passivity, Bartleby empties out meaning and neutralizes the cogwheel that previously turned the gears of the world making everything run. By way of a deterritorialization of language, places, functions, and habits, he enables everything to break away in an unbridled flight. From the depths of their solitude, these individuals not only reveal the refusal of a poisoned sociability, but are the calling for a kind of new solidarity; the plea for a community to come. Not the community based on hierarchy, paternalism, or compassion, as his employer would like to offer, but the community of celibates, the society of brothers, a federation of men and goods. A community of anarchist individuals, which Deleuze often finds in American literature, as opposed to the inquisitorial utopia of the collective soul. And he asks: what remains of souls once they no longer cling to an identity, but also refuse to melt into a universal totality? What remains is precisely their "originality," that is, a sound that each one *produces* when taking to the open road, when leading life without seeking salvation, when embarking upon an incarnate voyage, without any particular aim, and then encountering other travelers, recognizing them by their sound. Against the European morality of salvation and charity, there is a morality of life in which the soul is fulfilled only by taking the road, exposed to every contact, never trying to save other souls, turning away from those who produce an overly authoritarian or groaning

---

6. Gilles Deleuze. *Essays: Critical and Clinical*, trans. D. W. Smith and M. A. Greco, (Minneapolis: University of Minnesota Press, 1997), p. 52.

sound, forming even fleeting and unresolved chords and accords. The community of the celibates is that of whichever man and his singularities that cross one another: neither individualism nor communalism.

Apparatus of Life

In light of these remarks, allow me to mention a course given by Roland Barthes many years ago on the subject of *How to Live Together*, when he confessed that the title resulted from a kind of obsession, and his research on the subject, therefore, was the fruit of a fantasy that had long been haunting him. Interestingly, Barthes only states this fantasy of living together and discards collectivist utopias where everything is meticulously regulated and shared.[7] The idea of a common life is immediately cleared of several hellish images of coexistence, from the Phalanstère to unpalatable company, from the family to the restaurant. It seems impossible to wrap up the fantasy of living together without its counterbalance, a guarantee of solitude, times of isolation, spaces of reclusion, mechanisms for escape and distancing. Barthes' original fantasy appears clearly: a human agglomeration where everyone can, at the same time, live at their own rhythm. Even if Power[8] tends to impose a homogenous rhythm on the life of a collective, as in a monastery, prayer time, meal time, rest time, each would have the right to their own rhythm, a *ruthmos*, a temporal form that is flexible, mobile, and transient; opposed to the power of a single rhythm, the call for the idiorrhythm. But, is not an idiorrhythmic community an insane utopia? From *The Magic Mountain* to Robinson Crusoe, from the life of Spinoza to the latest trend, the question that comes back is this: how to create a structure of life that is not

---

7. Barthes, Roland. *How to Live Together: Novelistic Simulations of Some Everyday Spaces*, trans. Kate Briggs, (New York: Columbia University Press, 2013). p. 119.

8. Due to the difficulty in translating the difference between Portuguese words *Poder* and *Potência*, or the French *Pouvoir* and *Puissance*, or Latin *Potestas* and *Potentia*, we have opted to follow Michael Hardt's solution by making "the distinction nominally through capitalization, rendering *Pouvoir* [poder] as 'Power' and *Puissance* [potência] as 'power'". See "Translator's Forward: The Anatomy of Power" in Antonio Negri, *The Savage Anomaly. The Power of Spinoza's Metaphysics and Politics.* trans. Michael Hardt, (Minneapolis: University of Minnesota Press, 1991), p. xii.

an apparatus of life?[9] How to live together and escape tyrannical gregariousness? How to reject forms of living together that suffocate singularity? Maybe by inventing a game made of distances and differences. A "socialism of distances," where what is shared is the asymmetry.…

But another note creeps in at the end of Barthes' course, without which this panorama could not be complete: the experience of *dépaysement,* of expatriation, of voluntary exile. To drop everything, to escape, to leave, even if the nature of this movement is internal, spiritual, imperceptible, carried out with no ostentation or vanity. As if any collective were unthinkable without a line of flight. Perhaps community itself, in the strong sense of the word — and history is full of examples — can only be born out of a desertion, an exodus, however solitary, mystical, or psychotic it may seem.

I Need to Die a Little

In a more clinical context, psychoanalyst Nathalie Zaltzman evokes the anarchist drive of the "uncompromising," beings whose lives are punctuated by dramatic ruptures, and who fight fiercely against "imprisoning organizations of life." If these lives can give off an almost epic image, we must remember that these people are caught in a "solitude that can neither be shared nor alleviated," they are devoid of what we habitually surround ourselves with in order to protect us from solitude and death. What matters above all is "to ascertain the extent to which they do not attach themselves to anyone or anything, to what extent they remain free to abandon everything, to spoil everything … to give everything. They are not worried about protecting the reasons that bind them to life; what keeps them busy is making sure they are free of any ties. For they do not go into exile from themselves, they expatriate themselves in every corner of their lives."[10] This is attested by the anarchist geographer Elisée Reclus, who was repeatedly deported, exiled, imprisoned: "I'm tired of eating and drinking, sleeping in a bed, and walking around with full pockets. *I need to die a little from hunger, to*

---

9. *Ibid*. p. 25-6. Spinoza rents a room in a boarding house and occasionally goes downstairs to talk with his hosts — a true hermit, says Barthes.

10. Nathalie Zaltzman, *A pulsão anarquista*, (São Paulo: Escuta, 1993).

sleep on the gravel...." Here is, by tortuous paths, an urgency to show that one is alive, even at the price of constantly being exposed to death. The anarchist drive is that which fights the binding intention of Eros, which is annexation, ownership, annulment of alterity — gregariousness. The libertarian impetus, with its anti-social charge, has a demoniacal, or even terroristic, halo. But what is at stake, even here, is a resistance against the "unifying domain, deceptively idyllic, sweetening and leveling of ideological love," an impulse to make the whole structure of Power, authority, connection, and their sacred fantasies fly through the air. To relieve yourself from the love that embraces and paralyzes everything is not Thanatos, but rather a vital struggle against death. I think that many of Dostoyevsky's characters are of this type; they experiment with their leeway, mobility, vitality, even if they need to flirt with the demonic. Opposed to Dostoyevsky's Grand Inquisitor, who guarantees the herd's pacified happiness by paying for their docility, the Underground Man is unwillingness personified, the refusal of the promise of narcotic quietude, the frenetic rejection of all truth, divine or scientific, in favor of an impatient freedom. Clearly we know that the Grand Inquisitor has now acquired his biotechnocapitalistic and planetary version — what remains is knowing who the underground men of today are.

What Is Mine Is My Distance

Like Thomas Bernhard, the Brazilian writer Juliano Pessanha, in his beautiful trilogy, takes it upon himself to denounce the pact of universal hypocrisy that ensures daily existence, and reveals the metaphysical cement that, at every instant, prevents us from *collapsing*.[11] However, paradoxically, in these books we see all the competent characters that guarantee the "business of the administrating life" crumble one by one, parents, educators, psychiatrists, socializers, men of culture — all of which sometimes play the part of life's jailors. From the autobiography of the character Gombro (no doubt inspired by the writer Witold Gombrowicz), we have access to the survival strategies that a child invents in order to challenge all those who prostitute the

---

11. Juliano Pessanha, *Sabedoria do Nunca* (1999); *Ignorância do Sempre* (2000); *Certeza do Agora* (2002), (São Paulo: Ateliê).

word and make it the instrument of a generalized pretense. How to avoid the assassination that is proposed to us starting at the most tender age, how to get around the obliteration of one's own face, how to escape the narrative of oneself which has always already been outsourced by those who "care" for us or "love" us? The author offers a poetic answer. Only by returning on his own to suffocation and retaliations ("I spent most of my life screaming in tunnels, windows, and alleys"), putting down in writing his early perception of death and pain. Only then is the factual linearity of a life broken, which can then be punctured by the series of questions that have characterized it: "Is anyone there? Is there some true life on the planet? Why do the so-called family life and the so-called scholastic life and the so-called social life crush the possible child? Why is it that only the frauds survive, those who identify with the dead child?" In times of "total mobilization," of "existential alcoholism," there is a voice that introduces a word of hesitation, of waiting, and presentiment. It resonates with Bartleby, but also with Saint Paul's question which Žižek has taken up. "Who is really alive nowadays?" From the lowest point of his breaking down, Gombro asks for other places to visit, where living-together and living alone are articulated in a different manner.

How many have not tried it, and in the most torturous ways. Since Barthes disclosed his personal fantasy of living together, namely, the monastery on Mount Athos, I will also allow myself to take one example, somewhat out of fashion, coming from the psychiatric field. Talking about enclosure, everyone has his own fantasy. Jean Oury, who directed the La Borde clinic with Felix Guattari, practically checked himself into the clinic along with his patients in an old, decadent castle. The question that bothered him for the rest of his life, although in a specific clinical context, is similar to that of Barthes in the monastic setting, and certainly not unlike the fate of the Gombros and Bartlebys, who we run into on every corner of this postmodern asylum of ours. How to sustain a collectivity and at the same time preserve the dimension of singularity for each and every one? How to create heterogeneous spaces, with their own tonalities, distinct atmospheres, allowing each to connect in his or her own way? How to maintain an availability that facilitates encounters, but does not impose them, an attention that allows for contact and preserves alterity? How to make room for chance, without programming it? How to sustain a "kindness" that allows for the emergence of a speaking that grows out of the affective desert? When describing La Borde, Marie Depussé referred to a community made up of smoothness, because it was softened from being massaged with pain. Example: these people need a bit of dust that protects them from the violence of the day. Even when sweeping, it must be done slowly.... "It's while you revolve around their beds, collect their crumbs, touch their blankets, their bodies, when the smoothest dialogues occur, the infinite conversation of those who fear the light with those who take upon themselves the misery of the night...."[12] Not an aseptic utopia, perhaps because the psychotic is there, fortunately or unfortunately, to remind us that there is something in the empirical world that is falsely spinning (Oury). It is true that it all seems to belong to an almost Proustian past. But even Guattari never failed to acknowledge his debt to this experience of collective life into which he also delved deeply, and the effort he invested in verifying the "mark of singularity for the smallest gestures and encounters." He confesses that out of his experience of collective life he could "dream about what life could become in the urban conglomerates, in schools, in hospitals," if the collective Assemblages were subjected to such a "baroque treatment."

But currently we are far from following such a direction, even and especially, within a networked capitalism, which exceedingly celebrates connections, and monitors them for different ends. In addition, what is seen is that in parallel to the absolute connectivity a new anguish is intensified — that of the disconnection. Not only the anguish of being disconnected from digital networks, but also from the networks of life, access to which is increasingly mediated by commercial fares, unaffordable for a large majority. Still, we should be able to distinguish this socially produced "negative solitude" from what Katz called "positive solitude," namely, that which consists in resisting a despotic socialitarianism and challenging the tyranny of productive exchanges and social circulation.[13] Sometimes within these disengagements, partial subjectivities are outlined;

12. Marie Depussé, *Dieu gît dans les détails*, (Paris: P.O.L., 1993).

13. Chaim Samuel *Katz, O coração distante: ensaio sobre a solidão positiva*, (Rio de Janeiro: Revan, 1996).

celibate machines that are resistant to a compulsory social re-enlisting.

I will allow myself to mention the theater company that I have helped to coordinate for more than seventeen years in São Paulo, the Ueinzz Theater Company, consisting mainly of mental health service users.[14] Some years ago, we were invited to the prestigious International Theater Festival in Curitiba. To our surprise, we stayed in a first class hotel. Sitting on the spinning sofa in the lobby, one of our actors places his coffee on the table, opens a newspaper, lights a cigarette. He is thin, schizo, with white hair and deep blue eyes. I watch from afar and tell myself: that could be Artaud, or some Polish actor reading the reviews in the newspaper about his play. Then I look down and see these big twisted yellow toenails sticking out from a pair of beach sandals as if to say: "not even close". Perhaps Deleuze and Guattari's beautiful saying fits here: territory is primarily the critical distance between two beings of the same species marking their distances. What is mine is primarily my distance, I possess nothing if not distances.… The animal and monstrous horde, the indomitable toenail, a sign of inhumanity, that is one's distance, one's solitude, but also one's signature.

The Argentine playwright Eduardo Pavlovsky created a character that humorously shows this claim through another type of surrounding: Poroto (which means bean). His most constant concern is to figure out how to escape any situation that might arise. Where is he going to sit at a party so that he can escape at any moment? What excuse will he come up with when he runs into someone on the street, such as Kafka, who in his diaries speaks of how to get rid of a fat Jewish lawyer? How will he get out of such and such a commitment? And he comes to exclaim a sentence that is a punch in the stomach for many psychoanalysts: "enough with bonds, just contiguity of velocities."[15] Would we not have here the outline of something peculiar to this universe of ours, so far from the time when no one would stop "defining the relationship?" A subjectivity that is more schizo, flowing, rhizomatic, having more to do with surroundings and resonances, or distances and encounters, than ties? Would it be possible to read from this perspective contemporary attitudes,

---

14. For further reading on this topic see the following chapter in the present book: "Inhuman Polyphony in the Theater of Madness."

15. Eduardo Pavlovsky, *Poroto*, (Buenos Aires: Ed. Búsqueda de Ayllú, 1996).

23

no longer dissenting against a disciplinary society and its rigid logic of belonging and affiliation, but rather against a surveillance society, with its flexible mechanisms for monitoring and conjugating flows?

Resistance

In a small book entitled *The Coming Community*, Agamben evokes a resistance, which is not like any before it such as that of a class, a party, a union, a group, or a minority, but is rather that of any singularity whatsoever, which precisely is not any one specifically, because it is "amiable" in the singularity that belongs to it.[16] For example: the anonymous man who stood up to a tank in Tiananmen Square, who is no longer defined by his belonging to a particular identity, whether of a political group or a social movement, or the Arab revolt, or the Brazilian protests, that sort of ubiquity and multitudinous resistance, without a party flag, not delegating to any leader or institutionalized movement, the leadership or the Power of representing, hence the strength of such anonymity. This is what the State cannot tolerate, the whatever singularity that refuses it without constituting a mirrored replica of the state itself, in the figure of a recognizable identitarian formation, like a party, an ideology, etc.... *Whatever singularity* — which does not claim an identity, which fails to assert a social bond, which denies all belonging, but manifests its common being — is the condition, as Agamben reiterated several years ago, of all future politics.

Sometimes we think about the collective preserving the margin of escape that would compensate for its own oppression (being able to flee from it); sometimes the collective itself is thought of as a compensation for an all too solitary escape. The community would have a function of relief, a balm, almost as a protection against unbearable solitude, while at the same time, solitude as a protection against the unbearable weight of the collective. Perhaps what is most difficult is to think about escape and the collective together, the collective itself as a line of flight, the line of flight as a collective. In other words, between living-together and living-alone there is no pacifying dialectic,

16. Giorgio Agamben, *The Coming Community*, trans. Michael Hardt (Minneapolis: University of Minnesota Press, 1993).

but a complex game, without synthesis: the disjunctive collective.[17]

Encounter

Maybe it all depends, at heart, on a strange theory of the encounter, in which the relation precedes its terms. To encounter is to affect and be affected, infect and be infected, envelop and be enveloped. Even in the extreme of solitude, encountering is not to, extrinsically, collide with someone else, but to experiment with the distance that separates us, and fly over this distance in a crazy back-and-forth: "I am Apis, I am an Egyptian. I am a red Indian. I am a Negro. I am a Chinaman. I am a Japanese. I am a foreigner, a stranger. I am a sea bird. I am a land bird. I am the tree of Tolstoy. I am the roots of Tolstoy," says Nijinski. The heterogeneous contaminate and communicate, but either of them also envelops the other that is encountered, taking possession of their strength, but without destroying them. Thus, out of this distance that Deleuze has called "politeness," Oury "kindness," Barthes "delicacy," Guattari "softness," at the same time there is a separation, a back-and-forth, a flying over, a contamination, a mutual enveloping, a reciprocal becoming. It is an overall weird connection, because it disconnects where Powers want connections, and connects where they want disconnections. Like with the schizo. One could also call it sympathy: an action at a distance, the action of one force upon another. Neither fusion, nor intersubjective dialectic, nor metaphysics of alterity, but rather an enveloping composition, a disjunctive synthesis, a polyphonic game. Hence Deleuze's question, of a Spinozist nature: "How can a being take another being into its world, but while preserving or respecting the other's own relations and world?"[18] With this, Deleuze relaunches, in an inseparable and mixed-up manner, living-together and living-alone on a large scale, pointing to another sociability, and even to a community to come. A subjective ecology would need to sustain the disparity of worlds, forms of life, points of view, rhythms, gestures, intonations, sensations, and

---

17. Fabiane Borges, *Domínios do demasiado.* (São Paulo: Hucitec, 2010).

18. Gilles Deleuze, *Spinoza: Practical Philosophy,* trans. Robert Hurley, (San Francisco: City Lights, 1988), p. 126.

encourage its proliferation rather than seize it in a universal modulation, such that each singularity preserves, not its identity, but its power of affectation and envelopment in the immense game of the world. Without that, every being sinks into the black hole of its solitude, deprived of its connections and the sympathy that makes it live.

It would be necessary to depart from the precarious lives, anonymous deserters, people suicided by society, not only to thematize the meaning of these solitudes, but also that of the evanescent gestures that reinvent sympathy, and even a solidarity in the contemporary biopolitical context. Among a Gombro, a Poroto, a Bartleby, a Walser, or an actor in our schizoscenic theater company, I see, at times, the outline of what might be called an uncertain community, not unconnected with that which has obsessed the second half of the twentieth century, from Bataille to Agamben, namely: the community of those who do not have community, the community of the celibates, the inoperative community, the impossible community, the gaming community, the coming community, or even a socialism of distances. One thing is certain: facing the terrible community that has spread across the planet, made of reciprocal monitoring and frivolity, these beings (but will it just be them?) needed their solitude in order to give rise to their crazy bifurcation, and conquer the place of their sympathies.

THE BODY OF THE FORMLESS

Giorgio Agamben recalls that literature and thought also perform experiments, just like science. But while science seeks to
prove the truth or falsity of a hypothesis, literature and thought
have a different objective. They are experiments with no truth.
Here are some examples. Avicenna proposes his experiment of
the flying man, and in his imagination he dismembers a man's
body, piece by piece, in order to prove that even though broken
and suspended in the air, he can still say "I am." Rimbaud says:
"I am other." Kleist evokes the perfect body of the marionette as
a paradigm of the absolute. Heidegger substitutes the psychosomatic self with an empty and inessential being.... According
to Agamben, it is necessary to let oneself be carried away by
such experiments. Through them we risk our convictions less
than we do our modes of existence. In the domain of our subjective history, Agamben reminds us that such experiments are
equivalent to what it was like for the primate when its hands
were freed while standing erect, or for the reptile when fore-
limbs transformed thus allowing it to become a bird. It is always
about the body, even, and principally when what's at stake is the
body of writing.[19]

---

19. Giorgio Agamben, *Bartleby ou la création.* (Circé: 1995), p. 59.

Literary Images

It is in this spirit that I would like to start from one or another literary image, and some variations around them. The first is that of the skinny body of Kafka's hunger artist, whose art interests nobody, abandoned in a cage near the stables, at the back of the circus. Kafka describes the pale man, staring into space with half-shut eyes, with extremely protruding ribs, bony arms, thin waist, emptied body, legs that, in order to keep himself on his feet, are squeezed against one another at the knee, scraping the ground — in short, a bag of bones. Amidst the rotting hay, when the circus employees find him somewhat by accident and they ask him about his reasons for fasting, he raises his excessively heavy little head by his weak neck and replies by whispering to them, before dying: "Because I couldn't find the food I liked. If I had found it, believe me, I should have made no fuss and stuffed myself like you or anyone else." We find out, in the end, that the cage where he took his last breath was subsequently used to hold a noble bodied panther, "furnished with all that it needed," and gave the impression that it carried its own freedom in its jaws.

The second image is the body of Melville's Bartleby, the copyist. From the outset, a tireless worker seated behind the folding screen, but without showing the slightest enjoyment in making copies, when suddenly he begins to answer his boss' orders with "I would prefer not to." The narrator thus describes him: his face thin and gaunt, sucked in and calm, his gray eyes still and pale, at times dull and glazed. His haggard body, which eats ginger nuts, his pale silhouette, sometimes in his shirt sleeves and strange and tattered homemade suit, a cavalier and cadaverous indifference. In short, debris from a shipwreck in the middle of the Atlantic. And the most intolerable in the attorney's eyes: passive resistance. Impossible to "frighten his immobility into compliance." Even in prison, there is Bartleby, alone on the most isolated patio, facing a high wall, or languishing, lying on his side, refusing to eat. Upon discovering that this man with no past had at one time worked with lost letters, the narrator begins to compassionately refer to these lost men....

Body and Gesture

We shall refuse the humanist interpretations, full of meaning or piety for these lost men with their immobile and inert bodies, emptied and squalid. We would have every reason, indeed, to associate them with an endless chain of defiled bodies, in the cruelty and indifference of the genocides that populated the iconography of the last century. But I insist, let us initially stay with these strange postures, this "standing in front of the wall," this "lying" amidst the hay, this fallen little head but speaking in one's ear, this being seated behind the folding screen, these gestures devoid of traditional supports, as Walter Benjamin says in his essay on Kafka, but still preserving a certain leeway that the War would come to abort. A gesture is a means without an end; it is enough, as in dance. That is why, says Agamben, it opens the sphere of ethics, belonging to man. Further still when it happens starting from an inert or undone body, at the impossible conjunction between the dying and the embryonic, as is the case in the literary characters mentioned.

Let us consider the fragility of these bodies, nearly inhumane, in postures that touch upon death, and which nonetheless embody a strange obstinacy, an unwavering refusal. In this renunciation of the world we sense the sign of resistance. Thus it states something essential of the world itself. In these beings we are confronted with a deafness that hears, a blindness that sees, a numbness that is an exacerbated sensibility, an apathy that is pure pathos, a frailty that is indicative of a superior vitality. To describe the life of the writer, Deleuze uses a similar image: "[the writer] possesses an irresistible and delicate health that stems from what he has seen and heard of things too big for him, too strong for him, suffocating things whose passage exhausts him, while nonetheless giving him the becomings that a dominant and substantial health would render impossible."[20] What the writer refuses, just like the faster or the scrivener, is this fat-dominant health, gorging, stuffing oneself full, the pregnancy of an all-too categorical world, the panther's jaw.

Let us understand: the writer's weakness and exhaustion are due to the fact that he or she has seen too much, heard too much, and been overwhelmed by what has been seen and heard. He has been marred, it is too much for him and so he

---

20. Gilles Deleuze, *Essays: Critical and Clinical*, p. 3.

collapsed, but as for that, he can only be kept permeable if he remains in a condition of frailty, of imperfection. This deformity, this incompleteness, might even be a condition of literature, hence it is where *life is found in the most embryonic state*, where form has not yet "taken" entirely, as Gombrowicz says. There is no way, therefore, to preserve this freedom of "beings yet to be born" so dear to so many authors, in an excessively muscular body, amidst an athletic self-sufficiency, overly excited, plugged in, obscene. Perhaps the characters we mentioned need their immobility, deflation, pallor, on the limits of the dead body in order to make way for different strengths that an "armored" body would not allow.

Is it necessary to produce a dead body so that different forces pass through the body? José Gil observed the process through which, in contemporary dance, the body takes over itself like a bundle of forces and disinvests its organs, disentangling itself from the "internalized sensory-motor models," as Cunningham says. A body "that can be deserted, emptied, robbed of its soul," to then be able to "be traversed by the most exuberant fluxes of life." It is there, says Gil, that this body, which is already a body without organs, constitutes around itself an intensive domain, a virtual cloud, a type of affective atmosphere, with its own density, texture, and viscosity, as if the body exhaled and liberated unconscious forces that circulate at the surface, projecting around itself a type of "white shadow."[21]

Through entirely different existential and aesthetic means, we find again among some actors of the Ueinzz Theater Company, "carriers of psychological distress," postures that are "lost," inhumane, misshapen, and solitary, with their impalpable presence and lead weight, in their own weirdness and sparkle, surrounded by their "white shadow," or immersed in a "zone of offensive opacity," according to the expression coined by a recent magazine, in a different context. Is it not this that we see surrounding the postures of Bartleby or some of Kafka's characters? But why does it seem so difficult to embrace these postures bereft of meaning, intention, and ends, surrounded by their white shadow, their zone of offensive opacity?

---

21. José Gil, *Metamorphoses of the Body*, (Minneapolis: University of Minnesota Press, 1998), p. 28.

The Body That Can't Take Anymore

Perhaps owing to that which David Lapoujade, in Deleuze's wake, and especially Beckett's, defined in the most colloquial and lapidary manner possible: it deals with a body *qui n'en peut plus*, a body that cannot take any more. "We are like Beckett's characters, for whom it is already difficult to ride a bicycle, then, difficult to walk, then, difficult to simply drag oneself, and further still, to remain seated. Even in increasingly elementary situations, which require less and less effort, the body cannot take any more. Everything happens as if it could no longer move, no longer respond [...] the body is that which cannot take any more," by definition.[22]

However, the author asks, what is it that the body can no longer take? It cannot take any more of that which coerces, from the outside and from the inside. Coercion outside of the body from time immemorial was described by Nietzsche in the admirable pages of *On the Genealogy of Morality*; it is the progressive "civilizing" training of the animal-man, by sword and fire, which resulted in the man-form that we now know. In Nietzsche's wake, Foucault described the shaping of the modern body, its taming through disciplinary technology that has optimized man's strengths since the industrial revolution — and from this we also have some echoes in Kafka. Well, more precisely, the body cannot take the *training* and the *discipline*. In addition, it also cannot take more of the system of martyrdom and narcosis that Christianity — in the first place, and subsequently Medicine — developed to deal with pain: blame and the pathologization of suffering, desensitizing and the negation of the body.

Therefore, we should reclaim the body in that which is most its own, its pain by way of the encounter with the outside, its condition of a body *affected* by the forces of the world. As Barbara Stiegler notes in a remarkable study on Nietzsche, for him every living subject is first an affected subject, a body that suffers from its affections, its encounters, the alterity that strikes it, the throng of stimuli and excitement, and it is up to it to select, avoid, choose, or embrace.... [23] In order to continue to be

---

22. David Lapoujade, "O corpo que não agüenta mais", in *Nietzsche e Deleuze, Que pode o corpo*, org. D. Lins, (Rio de Janeiro: Relume-Dumará, 2002), p. 82.

23. Barbara Stiegler, *Nietzsche et la biologie*, (Paris: PUF, 2001), p. 38.

affected, more and better, the affected subject needs to be attentive to the excitations that affect it and filter them, rejecting those that are too threatening. The ability of a living being to remain open to affections and alterity, to the stranger, also depends on its capacity to avoid the violence that would destroy it altogether.

Following this line of thought, Deleuze also insists that a body never ceases to be subjected to encounters, with light, oxygen, food, sounds, and cutting words — a body is first an encounter with other bodies. But how could the body protect itself from serious wounds in order to embrace the more subtle ones, or as Nietzsche says in *Ecce Homo*, to use "self-defense" in order to preserve "open hands?" How does the body have the force to be at the height of his weakness, instead of remaining in the weakness of just cultivating the force? That is how Lapoujade defines this paradox: "like being at the height of the protoplasm or the embryo, being at the height of one's fatigue instead of overcoming it through a voluntary hardening…?"

Thus, the body is synonymous with a certain powerlessness, and it is from this powerlessness that it now extracts a superior power, freed from form, the act, the agent, even from "posture.…"

The Post-Organic Body

But perhaps the contemporary picture makes all of this much more complex, keeping in mind new decompositions of the material body. In the context of universal digitization, in which a new bioinformatics metaphor has besieged our bodies, the old human body, so primitive in its organicity, already seems obsolete. Given the new techno-scientific array, where virtual utopia sees in the materiality of the body an uncomfortable viscosity, an obstacle to immaterial liberation, we are all somewhat handicapped. From this gnostical-informatics perspective, we long for the loss of carnal support, we yearn for a fluid and disembodied immateriality. Hi-tech neo-Cartesianism, incorporeal aspiration, resuscitated Platonism, the fact is that there is a techno-demiurgism that responds to a new sociopolitical, post-organic, and post-human utopia, as Paula Sibilia says in a recent study....[24] There is no reason to cry because a certain kind of humanism has indeed been surpassed, but that does not mean that a rising unrest can be avoided. Perhaps the most difficult part is knowing which relation exists between that which some call the post-organic body — that is, the digitized, virtualized, immaterialized body, reduced to a combination of finite and recombinable elements according to a limitless plasticity— and what others have called the conquest of a body without organs.... Indeed both configure an overcoming of the human form and an overcoming of humanism, which had served the human form as a support, but would these bodies (despite being in such a provocative proximity that Deleuze and Guattari's thought never tired of exploring in so many areas) not be the opposite of each other, different by way of a certain critical tradition, be it Marxist or Frankfurtian, always more dichotomous? Similar to Nietzsche, where what is the most horrifying can bring with it the most promising. Nietzsche, who referred to the vivisection operated upon ourselves, and to the risks and promises embedded therein.

How does one differentiate Spinoza's perplexity — the fact that we do not yet know what **the body can do** — from the technoscientific challenge that precisely continues to experiment with **what can be done with the body**? How does one differentiate the body's necessary decomposition and disfiguration so that the forces that traverse it invent new connections and liberate new powers, a tendency that characterized part of our culture over the last few decades, in its diverse experiments, from dances, to drugs, and to literature itself, how does one not confuse this with the decomposition and disfiguration that biotechnological manipulation conjures and stimulates? On the one hand we have the Powers of life which need a body without organs in order to experiment, on the other hand, we have Power over life that needs a post-organic body to annex it to the capitalistic axiomatic.

Perhaps this opposition refers to two aspects present in Nietzsche, in the paradoxical form that was taken on at the end of his existence, according to Stiegler's analysis. "The subject that receives power does not walk away unharmed. Wounded, suffering from these wounds, after painfully experiencing such suffering, the question of the fortune of such wounds is

24. Paula Sibília, *O homem pós-orgânico*, (Rio de Janeiro: Relume-Dumará, 2002).

increasingly posed to the subject more clearly: should he mend them through vigorous therapeutic measures, or leave them to chance, at the risk of infection? Here is the force of the aporia with which one confronts the living human, the only one who is aware of his wounds: all suffering should invoke acting, but acting that does not impede suffering; the pathologies of the living call for medicine, but medicine that respects pathologies as a condition of life."[25] Thus, the body's status appears inseparable from a frailty, a pain, even a certain "passivity," however these conditions become necessary for a vital affirmation of a different order, despite the many inflections to the contrary, as seen in the case for Nietzsche, for Artaud, for Beckett, for Deleuze, and in certain circumstances as well for Kafka.

Kafka's Body

In Kafka we initially uncover the singular characteristic of him often referring to his own body, be it in his diary or in his letters, and always in a negative manner. "I write this very decidedly out of despair over my body and over a future with this body" (1910); "It is certain that a major obstacle to my progress is my physical condition. Nothing can be accomplished with such a body. I shall have to get used to its perpetual balking" (21/Nov/1910); "At the junction with Bergstein I once more thought about the distant future. How would I live through it with this body picked up in a lumberyard?" (24/Nov/1910).

Similarly, he speaks of the strengths he lacks to bring his literary work to fruition, or the outside forces which seem welcome, whether from listeners at a conference, or from Felice. However, in a complete reversal, he also mentions a bit of the strength that is left over and that he will save in refusing marriage or any other commitments. "All I possess are certain powers which, at a depth almost inaccessible under normal conditions, shape themselves into literature, powers to which, however, in my present professional as well as physical state, I dare not commit myself...." (Letter to F, 16/Jun/1913) "The connection with F. will give my existence more strength to resist"; "It is easy to recognize a concentration in me of all my forces on writing. When it became clear in my organism that writing was the most

---

25. Barbara Stiegler, *Nietzsche et la biologie*, (Paris: PUF, 2001).

productive direction for my being to take, everything rushed in that direction and left empty all those abilities which were directed toward the joys of sex, eating, drinking, philosophical reflection and above all music. This was necessary because the totality of my strengths was so slight that only together could they even halfway serve the purpose of my writing...."; "incapable of being known by whoever, incapable of supporting knowledge, at bottom full of infinite astonishment facing a happy society or facing their children (in the hotel, naturally, there is not much happiness, it wouldn't come to saying that I am the cause, in my quality of 'the man with too big a shadow,' but effectively my shadow is too big, and with new astonishment I find the strength to resist, the obstinacy of certain beings in wanting to live 'in spite of everything' in this shadow, precisely in it....); besides that, abandoned not only here, but in general, even in Prague, my 'homeland,' and not abandoned by men, that would not be the worst, while I live I could be able to run after them, but abandoned by me in relation to the beings, by my strength, in relation to the beings." (27/Feb/22) In all of these quotations one observes what the critic Luiz Costa Lima has noted: "Saddled with a weak, ungainly body, a most inadequate tool to ensure his own future, Kafka tries to find powers that might animate him, dispel uncertainty, confusion, and apathy."[26]

But amidst this strange energetic accounting, in which it is not yet known if what comes from the outside merely wounds or also nourishes the weak body, one sentence stands out: "A push is not in fact necessary; simply a withdrawal from the last force that was applied on me and I will attain a desperation that will tear me apart." (11/Dec/1913) This is where the friction with the world seems just as painful as it is necessary, almost a proof of existence, indicating an intrinsic relationship between resisting and existing in the chest of a weakened body.

Perhaps such a relationship, not only in Kafka, but also in the previously mentioned authors, allows for a glimpse within the body of the centrality of a *strength to resist in the face of suffering*. In other words, defending itself from the most vulgar wounds, it opens itself to embracing the array of subtle affections. And concurrently, it becomes active out of its primary *suffering*, the elementary *sensibility*, the pains and

26. Luiz Costa Lima, *Limites da voz: Kafka*, (Rio de Janeiro: Rocco, 1993), ch. 2.

wounds and the originating affectation. In other words, it becomes active out of this constitutive passivity, without denying it, making from it an event, as in *The Hunger Artist*. That this sometimes ends in death is almost a necessity. "The best things I have written have their basis in this capacity of mine to meet death with contentment. All these very fine and very convincing passages always deal with the fact that someone is dying, that it is hard for him to do, that it seems unjust to him, or at least harsh, and the reader is moved by this, or at least he should be. But for me, who believes that I shall be able to lie contentedly on my deathbed, such scenes are secretly a game; indeed, in the death enacted I rejoice in my own death" ... (13/Dec/1914).

Beyond every possible reflection here on death as part of his own literary work, like that which Blanchot demonstrated in an insurmountable manner, perhaps here we have the evidence of what Peter Sloterdijk has called a different ecology of pain and pleasure. When contrasting the silencing of the body and suffering proposed by Western metaphysics since its beginning, either in its philosophical, religious, or medical version, beginning with Nietzsche we see the emergence of a different economy of pain, that is, a different relationship with *physis* and with *pathos*, free of an aseptic utopia of a painless and immaterial future. Pain is reinserted into the "immanence of a life that no longer requires redemption," in such a way that here one may achieve "the endurance of the unendurable."[27]

The Dying and the Newborn

Perhaps a final note might fit before moving on to my meager conclusions. In an enigmatic article, Deleuze recalls what Nietzsche, Lawrence, Artaud, and Kafka had in common: an aversion to the insatiable thirst for judging. Against the system of infinite judgment they pitted a system of affects, each in his own way, where debt is no longer inscribed abstractly in an autonomous book that escapes our gaze, but marks finite bodies in their collisions. No longer the endless delays, unpayable debt, apparent acquittal, or ubiquitous judge, but rather

27. Peter Sloterdijk, *Thinker on Stage: Nietzsche's Materialism*, trans. Jamie Owen Daniel (Minneapolis: University of Minnesota Press, 1989), p. 102.

combat among bodies. To the body of judgment, says Deleuze, with its organization, hierarchy, segments, and differentiations, Kafka would oppose the "affective, intensive, anarchist body that consists solely of poles, zones, thresholds, and gradients." With it, the hierarchies are undone and thrown into confusion, retaining "nothing but intensities that make up uncertain zones, that traverse these zones at full speed and confront the powers in them ... on this anarchist body restored to itself,"[28] even if it is that of a coleopteron. "The way to escape judgment is to make yourself a body without organs, to find your body without organs." This is how, at least, Gregor escapes his father. However, more than that, he tries to "find an escape where his father didn't know to find one, in order to flee the director, the business, and the bureaucrats."[29] Here, insist the authors, in this undone and intensive body that flees from the system of judgment or taming and that of discipline, as we have shown above, there is a strange non-organic, inhuman vitality.

Such a body is always in combat: "All gestures are defenses or even attacks, evasions, ripostes, anticipations of a blow one does not always see coming, or of an enemy one is not always able to identify: hence the importance of the body's postures."[30] But the goal of combat, distinct from war, does not consist of destroying the Other, but rather of escaping from or taking hold of the Other's force. Even in the love letters, which are a "combat against the fiancee, whose disquieting carnivorous forces they seek to repel. But they are also a combat *between* the fiancee's forces and the animal forces he joins with so as to better flee the force he fears falling prey to, or the vampiric forces he will use to suck the woman's blood before she devours him. All these associations of forces constitute so many becomings — a becoming-animal, a becoming-vampire, perhaps even a becoming-woman — that can only be obtained through combat." In short, combat as a "powerful, nonorganic vitality that supplements force with force, and enriches whatever it takes hold of."

We could close this enigmatic mention of Deleuze here, but we would not have sufficiently reached the strangeness of this essay if we do not complete it with the double reference

28. Gilles Deleuze, *Essays: Critical and Clinical*, p. 131.

29. Gilles Deleuze and Félix Guattari, *Kafka: Toward a Minor Literature*, trans. Dana Polan, (Minneapolis, University of Minnesota Press, 1986), p. 13.

30. Gilles Deleuze, *Essays: Critical and Clinical*, p. 132.

to that which best embodies such a nonorganic vitality. In *Immanence: A Life*, there is an example — that of Dickens. The rogue, Riderhood, is about to die from almost drowning, and at this moment he shows a "spark of life inside of him" that seems to be capable of ushering the rogue that he is into light; a spark with which all those around him sympathize, as much as they hate him — here is *a life*, a pure event, in suspension, impersonal, singular, neutral, beyond good and evil, a "sort of beatitude," says Deleuze.[31] The other example is at the extreme opposite end of existence: newborns, who, "through all their sufferings and weaknesses, are infused with an immanent life that is pure power and even bliss." The baby, like the dying, are both traversed by *a life*. This is how Deleuze defines it in his essay "To Have Done with Judgment": "this obstinate, stubborn, and indomitable will to live that differs from all organic life. With a young child, one already has an organic, personal relationship, but not with a baby, who concentrates in its smallness the same energy that shatters paving stones (Lawrence's baby tortoise). With a baby, one has nothing but an affective, athletic, impersonal, and vital relationship. The will to power certainly appears in an infinitely more exact manner in a baby than in a man of war. For the baby is combat, and the *small* is an irreducible locus of forces, the most revealing test of forces." Hence the reference to minor-becoming in Kafka.[32]

A surprising essay that goes from the system of judgment to newborns in a dizzying sequence of somersaults, scrutinizing the other side of the body and of the individuated life, as if Deleuze were looking for — not only in Kafka, Lawrence, Artaud, and Nietzsche, but also throughout his own work — that vital threshold, from which all distributed lots, by gods or men, falsely spin and skid, lose their meaningfulness, no longer "take" in the body, allowing for the most unusual redistributions of affect. This threshold between life and death, between man and animal, between madness and sanity, where being born and perishing mutually reverberate, question the divisions bequeathed by our tradition — and between them one of the most difficult to be thought.

---

31. Gilles Deleuze, *Pure Immanence: Essays on a Life*, trans. Anne Boyman, (New York: Zone Books, 2001), p. 29.

32. Gilles Deleuze, *Essays: Critical and Clinical*, p. 133.

Life Without Form, Form of Life

Hence we return to Agamben. He recalls that the Greeks referred to life with two different words. *Zoè* referred to life as a fact, the fact of life; natural, biological, "bare life." *Bios* designated qualified life, a form-of-life, a mode of life of an individual or group. We shall skip all the author's important mediations regarding the relationship between bare life and sovereign power, in order to simply say the following: the contemporary context reduces the forms-of-life to bare life, from what is done with the Al-Qaeda prisoners at Guantánamo, or with the resistance in Palestine, or with detainees in Brazilian prisons, even what is perpetrated in biotechnological experiments, passing through the anesthetic excitation en masse to which we are subjected to daily, reduced as we are to meek cybernetic cattle or cyberzombies, as Gilles Châtelet noted in *To Live and Think Like Pigs*.[33] Facing the biopolitical reduction of the forms-of-life to bare life, it opens an array of challenges. One of them could be formulated in the following manner: how does one extract forms-of-life from bare life when the very form is undone, and how does one do it without re-invoking ready-made forms, which are the instrument of the reduction to bare life? It deals with, in short, rethinking the body of the formless, in its diverse dimensions. If the characters that I mentioned, together with their squalid bodies, their inert gesturing, their white, or too large shadow, their offensive opacity, their originating passivity, amidst the "neutral" space of literature in which they arose, if all that makes some sense, it is because from the interior of what could seem like bare life to what was reduced by the Powers, be they sovereign, disciplinary or biopolitical, in these characters *a life* is expressed, singular, impersonal, neutral, that does not belong to a subject and is situated beyond good and evil. "A sort of beatitude," Deleuze notes, perhaps because they lack nothing, because they enjoy themselves, in their full power — an absolutely immanent life.

In any case, we could risk the hypothesis that in these "angelic" characters, as Benjamin would say, one can still hear the demand for a form-of-life, but a form-of-life without form, and precisely, without thirst for form, without thirst for truth,

---

33. Gilles Châtelet, *To Live and Think Like Pigs: The Incitement of Envy and Boredom in Market Democracies*, trans. Robin Mackay. (Falmouth: Urbanomic, 2014).

without thirst for judging or being judged. As we said earlier, these are some literary experiments "without truth" that call into question our modes of existence, and that are perhaps, in the subjective domain, equivalent to what it was like for primates to have their hands freed upon acquiring an upright posture.

* * *

Perhaps this is the paradox that is proposed to us in the present times: to extrapolate from the field of literaure for the benefit of a variety of fields, from art to politics, from the clinic to thought, in its effort to regain the forces of the body and the body of the formless, besides the crystallized forms that are intent on molding it or representing it, beyond the traditional supports that seem to give them meaning, contrary to the current logic of domination. In the terms we suggested above, from Agamben to Deleuze, in our current times this would mean the following: in the same way biopolitical power focuses itself on life reduced to bare life, today it is a question of regaining *a life*, both in its beatitude and in its inherent capacity for making its forms vary.

BARE LIFE, BEASTLY LIFE, A LIFE

I would like to begin with the most extreme form of life — the *muselmann* — and do so by returning briefly to Giorgio Agamben's description of those who, in concentration camps, received this terminal designation.[34] The *muselmann* was the vagrant corpse, a bundle of physical functions in their final gasps.[35] Curved upon himself, this vile being, without will, had an opaque gaze, an indifferent expression, a pale gray skin that was both thin and as hard as peeled paper, a slow respiration, a very low pitched speech, undertaken at great cost.... The *muselmann* was the detained one who had given up, indifferent to everything that surrounded him, too exhausted to understand that which awaited him shortly: death. This non-human life had been emptied to such an extent that it could no longer suffer.[36] But why *muselmann*, if what was at stake were mainly Jews? Because the *muselmann* handed his life over to destiny, in line with the banal, prejudiced and certainly unjust image of a supposed Islamic fatalism: the Muslim as the one who submits without reserve to divine will. In any case, when life is reduced to the contour of a mere silhouette, as the Nazis would themselves say in referring to prisoners as *Figuren* (figures,

34. Giorgio Agamben, *Remnants of Auschwitz: The Witness and the Archive,* trans. Daniel Heller-Roazen, (New York: Zone Books, 2002).

35. Jean Améry, *At the Mind's Limits: Contemplations by a Survivor of Auschwitz and Its Realities,* trans. Sidney and Stella P. Rosenfeld; (Bloomington: Indiana University Press, 1980).

36. Primo Levi, *If This Is a Man,* trans. Stuart Woolf, (New York: Orion Press, 1959).

mannequins), what appears is the perversion of a power which does not eliminate the body, but maintains it in the intermediary zone between life and death, between the human and the inhuman: the survivor. Contemporary bioPower, Agamben concludes while twisting Foucault's conception, reduces life to a biological afterlife; it *produces survivors*. From Guantanamo to Africa, this is confirmed every day. The incumbency of contemporary bioPower is no longer to produce death, as in the regime of sovereignty, or to make live as in the regime of bioPower, but *to produce survivors*, and, with them, the *afterlife*. [37] For the moment, let us stick to this odd postulate. BioPower makes survivors, produces the state of a biological afterlife, reduces man to a residual, non-human dimension, incarnated in two complementary extremes: with the *muselmann* in the camp on the one hand and the neo-dead of intensive therapy rooms on the other. The afterlife is a human life reduced to its biological minimum, to its ultimate bareness, to a life without form, to the mere fact of life, to what Agamben calls *bare life*. But those who see bare life merely in the extreme figure of the concentration camp *muselmann*, or the refugees in Rwanda, are misled without understanding what is most terrifying: that in a certain way *we are all in this terminal condition*. Even Bruno Bettelheim, a survivor of Dachau, in describing the camp's chieftain, qualifies him as a type of "*muselmann*," "well fed and well dressed." The executioner is equally a living corpse, inhabiting that intermediary zone between the human and the inhuman, the biological machine deprived of sensibility and nervous excitation. The condition of survivor is a generalized effect of contemporary bioPower, not being restricted to totalitarian regimes, and fully including Western democracies, the society of consumption, of mass hedonism, of medicalized existence, that is, of the biological approach to life in an all encompassing scale, even in a context of luxury and biotechnological sophistication.

---

37. Giorgio Agamben, *Remnants of Auschwitz*, p. 156.

The Self Is the Body

Let us take as an example the over-investment in the body which characterizes our contemporaneity. For a few decades, the focus on the subject has been shifted from psychic intimacy to the body itself. Today, the self is the body. Subjectivity has been reduced to the body, to its appearance, its image, its performance, its health, its longevity. The predominance of the bodily dimension in the constitution of identity allows for talk of a bio-identity. We no longer face a body made docile by disciplinary institutions, a body striated by the panoptical machine, the body of the factory, the army, the school. Today in gyms or in cosmetic surgery clinics, everyone voluntarily submits him or herself to an ascesis following the scientific and aesthetic precept.[38] This is also what Francisco Ortega, following Foucault, calls bioascesis. On the one hand, we find the adequation of the body to the norms of show business, according to the celebrity-type format. Given the infinite possibilities to transform the body genetically, chemically, and electronically, the obsession for physical perfection, and the compulsion of the self to arouse the other's desire, even at the cost of one's own well-being, ultimately substitutes the promised erotic satisfaction with a self-imposed mortification.[39] The fact is that we voluntarily embrace the tyranny of a perfect body in favor of a sensorial enjoyment whose immediacy makes the suffering undergone even more surprising. Bioascesis is a care of the self, but different from the ancients, whose care was directed at the good life, something which Foucault also called an aesthetics of existence. Our care aims at the body itself, its longevity, health, beauty, good shape, scientific and aesthetic happiness, or what Deleuze would call fat-dominant health. We shall not hesitate in calling it, even under the modulating conditions of contemporary coercion, a fascist body — in face of such an unattainable model a large part of the population is thrown into a condition of sub-human inferiority. Moreover, in the domain of biosociality the body becomes an information packet, a genetic reservoir, a statistical dividual (I belong to the group of the hypertensive,

---

38. Denise Bernuzzi de Sant'Anna, *Políticas do corpo*, (São Paulo: Estação Liberdade, 1995), and *Corpos de passagem,* (São Paulo: Estação Liberdade, 2001).

39. Jurandir Freire Costa, *O vestígio e a aura: corpo e consumismo na moral do espetáculo*, (Rio de Janeiro: Garamond, 2004).

of HIV-AIDS, etc.), which only heightens the risks of eugenics. That any weekly magazine with its health, beauty, sex, and nutrition slogans are adopted happily as scientific precepts, and therefore, as imperatives, only illustrates this context. We are, in any case, surrounded by the register of a biologized life.… While identified to the mere body, to the excitable and manipulable body, from show business to the moldable body, we are reduced to the domain of bare life. We continue in the sphere of the afterlife, of the mass production of "survivors" in the broad sense of the term.

Survivalism

Allow me to broaden the notion of survivor. In his analysis of September 11, Slavoj Žižek contested the use of the adjective coward to describe the terrorists. After all, they weren't afraid of death, contrary to the Westerners who not only praise life but want to preserve and prolong it at all costs. We are slaves of survival, even in a Hegelian sense: we don't risk our lives. Our culture aims above all at this: survivalism, no matter the cost. We are Nietzsche's Last Men, who don't want to perish, and who prolong their agony "immersed in the stupidity of daily pleasures" — *Homo Sucker*. Žižek's question is also Saint Paul's: "Who is really alive today? […] What if we are 'really alive' only if we commit ourselves with an excessive intensity which puts us beyond '[bare] life?' What if, when we focus on mere survival, even if it is qualified as 'having a good time', what we ultimately lose is life itself? What if the Palestinian suicide bomber on the point of blowing him- or herself (and others) up is, in an emphatic sense, 'more alive' […]? What if a hysteric is truly alive in his or her permanent excessive questioning of his or her existence, while an obsessional is the very model of choosing a 'life in death' […] to prevent [some] 'thing' from happening?"[40] Obviously, at stake here is not any incitement of terrorism, but a caustic criticism of what Žižek calls the "post-metaphysical" survivalist posture of the Last Men, and the anemic spectacle of life dragging itself as a shadow of itself, where an aseptic, painless existence is prolonged to the fullest in a biopolitical context. Even pleasures are controlled and artificial: coffee

40. Slavoj Žižek, *Welcome to the Desert of the Real*. (New York: Verso, 2002), pp. 88-89.

without caffeine, beer without alcohol, sex without sex, war without casualties, politics without politics — a virtualized reality. For Žižek, death and life do not designate objective facts, but subjective existential positions, and in this sense, he plays with the provocative idea that there would be more life on the side of those who, without concessions, and in an explosion of enjoyment, reintroduced the dimension of absolute negativity into our daily lives with 9/11 than on the side of the Last Men, which include all those who drag their shadows of life as living dead; postmodern zombies. It is against the backdrop of this desolation that the terrorist act inscribes itself, giving the appearance that vitality has migrated to the side of those who, in a lust for death, managed to defy our cadaverous survivalism. Baudrillard also calls attention to the contrast between systems like our own, which are "disenchanted," "without intensity," and include "protected existences" and "captive lives," and cultures of "high intensity," even in their sacrificial aspects. Baudrillard reminds us that what we detest in ourselves is that which Dostoyevsky's Great Inquisitor promises the domesticated masses: an excess of reality, of comfort, of accomplishment, the kingdom of God on earth. All of which Nietzsche, moreover, would judge, in the historical process of *décadence* he analyzed incessantly, as a gregarious abasement of humanity. In any case, the present context in the West for Žižek is fertile for the evocation of the Last Man's passive nihilism, or even for detecting among us the fulfillment of the capitalistic and biopolitical belief in the Great Inquisitor, where bread, servitude and tepid happiness would free us from disquiet and revolt.

We can say that in the post-political spectacle, and with the respective abduction of social vitality, we are all reduced to biological survivalism at the mercy of biopolitical management, worshipping low-intensity forms of life, submitted to a tepid hypnosis, even when the sensorial anesthesia is disguised as hyper-excitation. As Gilles Châtelet put it in *To Live and Think Like Pigs*, we face the existence of cyberzombies, grazing indolently between services and commodities. It is *beastly*[41] *life* as a global abasement of existence, a depreciation of life, its reduction to bare life, to an afterlife, the final stage of contemporary nihilism.

---

41. "Beastly" here is translated from the Portuguese word *besta*, which besides referring to beast or animal, also implies a certain amount of stupidity. [TN].

Giorgio Agamben retrieved the Roman notion of *Homo Sacer* to indicate those who were excluded from the sphere of human rights, but also from the divine. Banished from political community and exposed to a relation of exception by the sovereign power, they were also put to death, which did not constitute a crime.[42] If this notion leads us to think that the logic of the concentration camp is now a present political paradigm, then the zones in which this state of exception has become commonplace, in a larger sense, are found within representative democracies themselves. Insofar as their political space has been abducted and emptied, with politics being restricted to administrative policies, then this would lead us to the fact that we would all be *Homo Sacer*, reduced to biological survivalism, to bare life, at the mercy of biopolitical management and its strategic contrivances. When life is reduced to beastly life on a planetary scale, when nihilism becomes itself so visible in our own laxity, in the consuming hypnosis of *Homo Sucker* or in a fat-dominant health, it is worth asking first, what could still shake off this state of lethargy, and second, whether catastrophe is not installed in our everyday ("the most sinister of guests") rather than in the sudden irruption of the spectacular event of a terrorist attack against the Empire's capital.

Bloom: this is the name the journal *Tiqqun* gave, in today's nihilism, to formless life of the common man.[43] Inspired by one of Joyce's characters, it would be a human type that appeared recently on the planet, and which designates the pale, thin existence of the common, anonymous man, although perhaps a man agitated with the illusion that his existence may overshadow his boredom, solitude, separation, incompleteness, contingency — his nothingness. Bloom designates this affective tonality which characterizes our age of nihilistic decomposition, the moment in which it rises to the surface, because it is accomplished in a pure state, the metaphysical fact of our strangeness and inoperativeness, beyond the social problems of misery, precariousness, unemployment, etc. Bloom is the figure that represents the death of the subject and its world, where everything fluctuates in indifference devoid of qualities, where no one recognizes themselves in the triviality of a world of

---

42. Giorgio Agamben, *Homo Sacer: Sovereign Power and Bare Life*, trans. Daniel Heller-Roazen, (Stanford, CA: Stanford University Press, 1998).

43. Tiqqun, *Théorie du Bloom*, (Paris: La Fabrique, 2000), and *Tiqqun*, 2001.

infinitely exchangeable and replaceable commodities. It matters little how the contents of life, which we visit in our existential tourism, alternate. Bloom is already incapable of joy as well as suffering, in an illiteracy to emotions of which he only collects diffracted echoes.

The Body That Can't Take Anymore

If we accept David Lapoujade's captivating definition of the body: "The body is that which can't take anymore,"[44] we could say that, in a broader sense, what the body can't take anymore is a survivalist mortification, be it in the state of exception or in everyday banality. The "muselmann," the "cyberzombie," the "show business body," "fat-dominant health," the Homo Sucker and "Bloom" (however extreme their differences may appear), resonate in their anesthetic and narcotic effect, configuring, in the context of a terminal nihilism, the impermeability of an "armored body."[45]

Confronted with this, it would be necessary to retrieve that which is most proper to the body, its pain in the encounter with exteriority, its condition of a body affected by the forces of the world and its capacity to be affected by them: its affectability. At stake here is the introduction of another relation with life, with life "before" it has received a form, or as it frees itself from these forms, or even, with a dimension of life below or beyond the form which it tends to acquire. This is what Deleuze called *a life*. *A life* is not at all abstract, it is the most elementary, life in its immanence and positivity, stripped of all that wants to represent or contain it. The entire problematic of the body without organs is preeminently a variation around this biopolitical theme, life undoing itself from what imprisons it, from the organism, the organs, the inscription of diverse powers upon the body. *A life* is entirely contrary to bare, dead, mummified, shelled life. If life has to free itself from social, historical, political moorings, isn't it to regain something of its denuded, dispossessed animality? No one saw this better than Artaud. Kuniichi Uno, the Japanese translator of Artaud as well as Deleuze and Guattari, put it like

---

44. David Lapoujade, "O corpo que não agüenta mais," in *Nietzsche e Deleuze, Que pode o corpo*, org. D. Lins, (Rio de Janeiro: Relume Dumará, 2002), p. 82.

45. Juliano Pessanha, *A Certeza do Agora*. (São Paulo: Ateliê, 2002).

this: "But he [Artaud] never lost the intense sense of life and of the body as a genesis, or auto-genesis, as an intense force, impermeable, a mobility without limits which doesn't let itself be determined even by the terms *bios* or *zoè*. Life for Artaud is indeterminable, in all senses, while society is made up of infamy, bootlegging, commerce, which do not cease to satiate life and, above all else, the body."[46]

It would be enough to meditate on Artaud's enigmatic phrase: "I am innately genital, and if we examine closely what that means, it means that I have never made the most of myself. There are some fools who think of themselves as beings, as innately being. I am he who, in order to be, must whip his innateness." Uno says that someone innately genital is someone who tries to be born through himself, who creates a second birth, beyond given biological nature. We could say, with Artaud, that we are innate but that we have not yet been born, in the strong sense of the term. Let us listen to what Beckett heard Jung say about one of his patients: the fact is that she has never been born. Transporting this sentence to his work, Beckett creates an "I" who has never been born, and it is precisely this "I" who writes about the other "I" who has already been born. This refusal of biological birth does not mean a refusal to live, but it is rather a claim to continue to be born without end. The innately genital is the story of a body which questions its body as something which has been born, with its functions and all its organs as representatives of orders, institutions, visible or invisible technologies, all of which aim at managing the body. It is a body which has the courage to challenge that sociopolitical complex which Artaud called the Judgment of God, and which we call bioPower, a power which falls upon our body.... Nor does this refusal of birth in favor of a self-birth mean the desire to dominate one's own beginning, but, as Uno says, to recreate the body which has in it the power to begin. The life of this body, he insists, as long as it, on the one hand, discovers in the body the power of genesis, and on the other, liberates itself from the determination which weighs upon it — means war on biopolitics.... Perhaps this is one of the few points where we agree with Badiou, as he affirms that for Deleuze the name of

46. Kuniichi Uno, "Artaud's Slipper according to Hijikata", in *Leituras da morte*, (São Paulo: Annablume, 2007), orgzanized by Christine Greiner and Claudia Amorim; See also Kuniichi Uno, *The Genesis of an Unknown Body*, (São Paulo/Helsinki: n-1 publications, 2012).

being is life itself, but not life understood as a gift or treasure, or as an afterlife, but instead as a neuter which rejects all categories. As he puts it: "All life is bare. All life is becoming bare, the abandoning of garments, of codes and organs; not that we are headed for a nihilist black hole, on the contrary, all this is in order to sustain the point where actualization and virtualization interchange, in order to become creators."[47] But is Badiou right in designating this life as bare? The life to which he refers cannot be, as Uno had already noted, *zoè*, the name given by the Greeks to designate the fact of life, as a mere biological or animal fact, or as a life reduced to biological bareness by the state of exception's juridical order, or even, as the technoscientific manipulation of nihilist movement brought about by capital. *A life*, as Deleuze conceives it, is life as virtuality, difference, invention of forms, impersonal power, beatitude. *Bare life*, on the contrary, as Agamben has already made evident, is life reduced to its state of mere actuality, indifference, deformity, powerlessness, biological banality. And not to mention *beastly life*, the entropic exacerbation and dissemination of bare life at its nihilist limit. If these lives are so opposed, and at the same time so overlapping, it is because in the biopolitical context it is life itself which is at stake, life itself as a battlefield. In any case, as Foucault said, it is at the point where Power is most concentrated in life and will from then on be that which resistance is anchored to, but only on the condition that the signals are changed…. In other words, at times it is in the extreme of *bare life* that *a life* is found.

If, from Nietzsche and Artaud to the present-day youth, with their experimentations and research, a diagnosis of beastly life has been generated, precisely where the body retrieves its affectability and even its power to begin, is it not because in them beastly life has become intolerable? Maybe there is something in the extortion of life that should be brought to its end so that this life may arise all together differently…. Something must be exhausted, as Deleuze sensed in *The Exhausted,* so that a different game may be conceivable….

47. Alain Badiou, "De la Vie comme nom de l'Être," in *Rue Descartes,* n. 20, (Paris: PUF, 1998), p. 32.

NIHILISM, DISASTER, COMMUNITY

CROSSING NIHILISM

Nihilism in Nietzsche is equivocal. On the one hand, it is a symptom of decadence and aversion to existence, on the other, and at the same time, it is an expression of increased force, a condition for a new beginning, perhaps even a promise. This ambivalence in dealing with cultural phenomena is characteristic of the Nietzschean approach, but here it seems to reach a point of tension where many wagers put forth in his philosophy converge. Part of what continues to awaken interest in the harbinger of *transvaluation* is due to the contemporary aspect of his thought, in which decline and ascent, collapse and emergence, end and beginning all coexist in an irresolute tension. Some can object that this conjunction is not Nietzsche's invention, and is instead rooted in the German philosophical tradition and its renewed promises of a new beginning, characterizing Modernity itself and its consciousness of time.[48] That seems possible. In any case, I would like to show that the paradoxical logic dominating Nietzsche's approach to nihilism pulls his thought as a whole in a very unique direction.

The fact is that the reader of Nietzsche feels baffled when confronted with his analyses regarding nihilism. At times one gets the impression that he is about to diagnose a nihilism which he condemns, at other times one can be sure that, on the contrary, Nietzsche himself is a nihilist, and that according

---

48. Jürgen Habermas, *The Philosophical Discourse of Modernity*, trans. Frederick Lawrence, (Cambridge, MA: The MIT Press, 1987).

to him it is necessary to bring this movement to its end. Such duplicity in reading is not due to a mere zigzagging by Nietzsche himself, or simply a change in perspective that is so peculiar to him, which fits entirely into his philosophical logic; nor should it be attributed to any intrinsic incoherence. Ambiguity is constitutive of the concept, and only reflects the fact that this thematization, and Nietzsche's very philosophical trajectory as a whole, is conceived as a *crossing through nihilism*. Thus, I would like to insist upon two main aspects: on the one hand, nihilism's historical and philosophical necessity that Nietzsche detects, and on the other, the way by which he feels himself to be a participant of this movement that behooves him to diagnose, hasten, combat, and surpass, all at the same time.

Now, we know that the full consciousness of this second aspect appeared to Nietzsche with a certain tardiness in his work. In 1887, he writes: "It is only late that one musters the courage for what one really knows. That I have hitherto been a thorough-going nihilist, I have admitted to myself only recently."[49] Thus my choosing to privilege, in this brief commentary, some writings from this time period, above all those from autumn of 1887 to the beginning of 1888. Even though these fragments were not originally intended for publication, it is known that Nietzsche saw in them an initial outline of the planned and aborted work, *The Will to Power*. He thus numbered them 1 to 372, and even sketched out a table of contents.[50] The variety of topics extends from Socrates to Stendhal, from Buddhism to Offenbach, from the lascivious melancholy of Moorish dance to Christian castrati. The ensemble is irregular, both in style and in content, alternating sketches of ideas, commentaries on authors, reading quotations, finished aphorisms, some of which were reused in subsequent works, such as *The Case of Wagner*, *Twilight of the Idols*, and *The Anti-Christ*. However, the preface that outlines the entire work leaves no doubt as to the gravity of these fragments. "I describe what is coming [...]: *the advent of nihilism*."[51] In fact, that is where we find some of Nietzsche's crucial passages regarding the theme, in its already mature, yet ever unfinished formulation. However,

49. Friedrich Nietzsche, *The Will to Power*, [25], ed. and trans. Walter Kaufmann, (New York: Vintage, 1968), p. 18.

50. Whenever one of these fragments are cited, they will be indicated between parentheses by the number attributed to them by Nietzsche.

51. Friedrich Nietzsche, *Nietzsche's Notebook of 1887-1888*, 11[119], trans. Daniel Fidel Ferrer, (US Archives online, 2012).

in order to acquire their full meaning, it is important to consider what Nietzsche sees as the function of theory. "Every doctrine is superfluous unless everything lies ready for it, all the accumulated forces, the dynamite. A revaluation of values is achieved only when there is a tension of new needs, of new needers who suffer under the old valuation without becoming aware."[52]

The Death of God

My point of departure will be a small phrase extracted from *The Anti-Christ*. "When the center of gravity of life is placed, *not* in life itself, but in 'the beyond' — in *nothingness* — then one has taken away its center of gravity altogether."[53] What is exposed here is the logic that bundles a good part of Nietzsche's thought with regard to nihilism. Nihilism begins with a displacement from life's center of gravity toward a different sphere which is not itself — the rest is consequence. To say it in a more direct manner: nihilism consists of a metaphysical depreciation of life, starting from a position where values are considered superior to life itself, wherein life becomes reduced to a value of nothing. Previously, these same values had already appeared (according to the process of devaluation) as they were from the outset — "nothing." Here we have several moments on top of one another. And indeed, with the term nihilism Nietzsche embraces a very long philosophical-historical arc, in which he reads the ascension of moral values, the way in which these values came to have their worth in the course of our Socratic-Christian culture, assuring existence with a finality and a meaning but at the same time denigrating it, and the process by which they fell into disbelief, letting us see that the truth of such values were of a fictitious nature from the very beginning. If we think about it radically, Nietzsche means that Western history was built upon nihilist foundations, and that the nihilism of such foundations could not fail to come to the surface sooner or later, in the course of history, thus questioning the construction as a whole and the very idea of fundament.

52. Friedrich Nietzsche, *Writings from the Late Notebooks*, 9[77], trans. Kate Sturge (Cambridge: Cambridge University Press, 2003), p. 152.

53. Friedrich Nietzsche, *The Anti-Christ*, [43] in *The Anti-Christ, Ecce Homo, Twilight of the Idols and Other Writings*, trans. Judith Norman, (Cambridge: Cambridge University Press, 2005), p. 39.

We can already postulate that the term "nihilism," as described with such a wide scope, roughly covers the history of philosophy and the entirety of Western Culture, in its two successive and contradictory movements. The first movement corresponds to the metaphysical shift that had taken place in Antiquity, beginning with Plato, and prolonged into Christianity, and the second, inverse movement corresponds to the loss of this metaphysical axis, most of all in Modernity. The further he advances in his work, the further Nietzsche addresses the second moment of this sequence, leaving the impression that the term nihilism relates mainly to this period, or at least it is the most concurrent meaning of his time, in consonance with his circulation among the Russians, especially Turgenev and Dostoyevsky, whose work Nietzsche deeply admired.

How does Nietzsche describe this nihilism of Modernity? "Since Copernicus, man seems to have been on a downward path — now he seems to be rolling faster and faster away from the center — where to? Into nothingness? Into the '*piercing* sensation of his nothingness'?"[54] However, perhaps the work in which such perplexity finds its most finished and dramatic formulation is the well-known fragment dated from 1882, in which the lunatic looks for God with a lantern in the full morning light, to then announce that God is dead: "What were we doing when we unchained this earth from its sun? Where is it moving to now? Where are we moving to? Away from all suns? Are we not continually falling? And backwards, sideways, forwards, in all directions? Is there still an up and a down? Aren't we straying as though through an infinite nothing? Isn't empty space breathing at us?"[55]

As is known, this is Nietzsche's first explicit formulation of the death of God. The novelty of this formula is not in announcing that the Christian God has died, but in showing that the supra-sensible world in general, which gave man's existence a meaning and reason, has fallen into disbelief. Since this belief has lost its efficacy, as well as its anchoring function, man no longer knows what to grab onto, and nothing seems to drive him or motivate him anymore. We go from an extreme

54. Friedrich Nietzsche, *On the Genealogy of Morality*, [25], trans. Carol Diethe, (Cambridge: Cambridge University Press, 2006), p. 115.

55. Friedrich Nietzsche, *The Gay Science*, [125], trans. Josefine Nauckhoff, (Cambridge: Cambridge University Press, 2001), p. 120.

experience of belief, in which we orbited around a center, a sun, a light, a truth, to the extreme opposite, disbelief, where we wander aimlessly in the dark. We no longer have the coordinates of high and low, the sacred and the profane, the center and the periphery in such a way that in this flattened topography, without beacons or references, we wander adrift. Nietzsche is not pleased in describing this vertigo, because what is essential is detecting the reasons for such a loss. For if what is lacking is a goal and a reason, where this feeling of "everything is in vain" tends to grow, and the fear that goes along with it, it's not merely due to the fact that "the highest values devaluate themselves." More specifically, it is due to the fact that after metaphysical evaluation and its moral permeation collapsed, any kind of value now seems impossible. Nihilism, Nietzsche categorically says, is a "sequela of the moralist interpretation of the world."[56] A good portion of Nietzsche's work is dedicated to the analysis of this moralist interpretation of the world which lasted for millennia, which filled it with finality and meaning, as well as its growing unraveling. Nietzsche states: "The time is coming when we have to *pay* for having been *Christians* for two thousand years: the *weight* that allowed us to live is gone - for a while we don't know which way to turn. We rush headlong into the *opposite* valuations, with the same degree of energy with which we used to be Christians.…"[57]

Thus, upon announcing the downfall of the supra-sensible world of the metaphysical tradition, whereby the figure of God is nothing more than a historico-religious concretion, Nietzsche takes the trouble to point out its modern substitutes, which in vain fill a similar function, offering themselves as centers of gravity and attempting to establish objectives and ensure meanings with the authority previously equivalent which was attributed to the supra-human sphere. Whether it be Consciousness, Reason, History, the Collective, and at times reflecting the mirage of the Moral Imperative, of Progress, of Happiness, or of Civilization, from a strictly genealogical point of view, as we shall see, there is no discontinuity among these modern figures and the metaphysical tradition that they intend to contest. Even Science, insists Nietzsche, when opposed to divine truth, presupposes a faith in the truth, and an

---

56. Friedrich Nietzsche, Posthumous fragment, Spring 1887, p. 7 [43].

57. Friedrich Nietzsche, *Nietzsche's Notebook of 1887-1888,* p. 11[148].

overall metaphysical belief that truth is divine. Therefore, even the most unconditional atheism, which prohibits "the lie of believing in God," still preserves its assumption, faith in the truth, which is nothing more than one of the final forms and necessary consequences of this story of truth and the exigency for veracity inherited from its predecessors and the moral necessity upon which it sits. The most extreme nihilism, and soon we will have to situate this modality in relation to what was mentioned above, concludes Nietzsche, consists of recognizing that the essence of truth is a consideration of value — this value, whose utility for life was demonstrated by experience, could already no longer be necessary, could even be harmful, could no longer have such value.… Perhaps this is the only point upon which we can follow Heidegger without hesitating: in rereading the history of metaphysics as a history of values, in converting truth, finality, and being itself into value, Nietzsche had already single-handedly carried out the most iconoclastic and nihilistic of gestures, and in doing so, he brings about a transvaluation that he had only intended to announce.[58]

Values

Without going into all the details of this long history of truth that Nietzsche reconstructs by linking Platonism, Christianity, and modern science, it is sufficient to explain, from a genealogical point of view, what according to him, these historically produced values — the substitution of some for others, and their progressive devaluation — respond to ... Nietzsche's method states that in respect to a determined value, one will no longer ask about intrinsic truth, validity, legitimacy, but rather about its conditions of production. It's not about asking "*What is* justice?", but rather what do those who defend it want? Who needs this or that conviction, credence, value, in order to conserve himself, in order to impose his kind, in order to spread his dominion? For a value is just a symptom of a kind of life, of a formation of

58. Martin Heidegger, *Nietzsche, Volume IV: Nihilism* trans. F. A. Capuzzi. (New York: Harper & Row, 1982), p. 70. "Properly thought, the transvaluation carried out by Nietzsche does not consist in the fact that he posits new values in the place of the highest values hitherto, but that he conceives of 'Being,' 'purpose,' and 'truth' as values and *only* as values. Nietzsche's 'transvaluation' is at bottom the rethinking of all determinations of the being on the basis of values."

dominion.... With this, Nietzsche shows the set of perspectives before they were transformed into beliefs, convictions, ideals. It's the historical sense that he doesn't tire of demanding from philosophers. Thus, truth, virtue, beauty, progress, every one of these values should be conceived as a perspective produced in the time before it became universal, a point of view that is much more victorious when it insists on hiding the fact of being a point of view. A value, by definition, always results from an evaluation, that's why the expression "estimation of value," or "appreciation of value" is capable of defetishizing the idea of value in itself and returning it to the operation of evaluation which is in the origin of value. After all, man is the evaluating animal par excellence, the being that measures, that fixes prices, that imagines equivalencies, that establishes hierarchies, that privileges such and such element over another, attributing to it a superior weight, and deriving from it a specific measurement.

But an evaluation is not just a point of view on the world, it expresses psycho-physiological requirements, it is inseparable from the body which generated it, from the instinctive hierarchy thus present, from the interpretative processes of the organism itself, that is, its modes of appropriation, metabolizing, domination, and incorporation of an exteriority. An evaluation sprouts from a manner of being that it expresses and claims. In respect to a value, Nietzsche asks what mode of existence or what style of life does it imply? A heavy, light, low, high, slave, or noble existence? A value always has a genealogy upon which the nobility and baseness which it invites us to believe in, feel, and think with depends, as Deleuze clarifies.[59]

A value is an instrument through which a type of life imposes itself, conserves itself, or attempts to be expanded. Nietzsche expressed it in the following terms: "The viewpoint of 'value' is the viewpoint of conditions of preservation and enhancement in regard to complex structures that have relatively lasting life within becoming."[60] Thus we can add, explicating Nietzsche's last direction with regard to this subject: values are conditions for exercising the will to power, they are placed by the will to power itself, and also discarded by it when they no longer serve

59. Gilles Deleuze, *Nietzsche and Philosophy*, (London: Continuum, 1983), p. 73: "What a will wants, depending on its quality, is to affirm its difference. [...] Only qualities are ever willed: the heavy, the light. [...] What a will wants is not an object but a type, the type of the one that speaks, of the one that thinks, that acts, that does not act, that reacts, etc."

60. Friedrich Nietzsche, *Writings from the Late Notebooks*, p. 11[73], 212.

its requirements, be they of conservation or expansion. The consequence for any project of transvaluation of values is that it is only when the will to power is recognized as a source of values that the institution of new values can be originally exercised. But such reversion — and this is the paradox to which Nietzsche refers so often — is only possible when the depreciation of values is carried to its end, because only such a concluded process is capable of showing the value of prevailing values up to now (i.e., the value of nothing) and the negativity from which they result. Consequently, only in the tracks of this declining movement can one unravel the exigency for reversion. In other words, the counter-movement claimed by Nietzsche is only thinkable from the position of nihilism from which it is spawned, and that which he intends to overcome, and bring to fruition. As sketched out in the preface:

> For one should make no mistake about the meaning of the title that this gospel of the future wants to bear. '*The Will to Power:* Attempt at a Transvaluation of All Values' — in this formulation a countermovement finds expression, regarding both principle and task; a movement that in some future will take the place of this perfect nihilism — but presupposes it, logically and psychologically, and certainly can come only after and out of it.
>
> For why has the advent of nihilism become *necessary*? Because the values we have had hitherto thus draw their final consequence; because nihilism represents the ultimate logical conclusion of our great values and ideals — because we must experience nihilism before we can find out what value these 'values' really had. We will require, sometime, *new values*.[61]

Disbelief

Before a reversal can be possible and thinkable, many oscillations and zigzags are foreseeable and even inevitable. Beginning with the fact that the destruction of a dominant interpretation seems to impede, for a time at least, any other interpretation, making space for the realm of everything is vain, for a Buddhist characteristic, for the aspiring for nothing.[62] "Here

---

61. Friedrich Nietzsche, *The Will to Power*, Preface, pp. 3-4.

62. Friedrich Nietzsche, *Writings from the Late Notebooks*, (Cambridge, 2003), p. 2 [127], 83.

there is snow, here life is silenced; the last crows heard here are called 'what for?', 'in vain', '*nada*' — here nothing flourishes or grows any more, except, perhaps, for St. Petersburg metapolitics and Tolstoy's 'compassion.'"[63] Nietzsche claimed it's the most paralyzing kind of thought. It is born within those who, when confronted with the exhaustion of Christian morality and the vanishing of its place as a guaranteed value within the metaphysical order, are unable to conform to its absence. If disbelief seems to indicate a vital exhaustion, Nietzsche also sees an opportunity here, and even an exigency for being at the height of this disbelief, in order to sustain it and carry it to its ultimate consequences. But it's as if, as Nietzsche sometimes remarks, a "superior species" was lacking that would be capable of forever giving up belief in the truth — this exquisite expression of the impotence of the will — in order to be able to finally undertake creative acts.[64] Only a tired species needs belief, truth, and instances of authority that legitimate and sanction it in order to live, instead of being itself legislative, establishing, and creative. Only a tired man, when he doesn't find support in these beliefs or instances, becomes a nihilist in a way that Nietzsche calls passive. In other words, the person who becomes paralyzed is the one who, upon realizing that the world should *not* be as it is, and that the world as it should be doesn't exist, is one who believes it doesn't make sense to act, suffer, want, feel. In short, they believe everything is in vain. This is the nihilist pathos that Nietzsche attempts to dissect and combat, but also, in following passive nihilim's lack of consequences, figures out what can turn it upside down. For it is Nietzsche's very particular stance of proclaiming that there is nothing condemnable in recognizing a world without meaning. This recognition only leads to a paralysis of wanting and a depleted will precisely from the fact that on the contrary, underneath it a superabundant life supports and even necessitates this emptying of meaning in order to vent its interpretative strength: that which doesn't look for sense in things, for it imposes meaning upon them. At bottom, belief and will are in an inversely proportional relationship: "Faith is always most desired and most urgently needed where will is lacking; for will, as the affect of command, is the decisive mark of sovereignty and strength. That is, the less

---

63. Friedrich Nietzsche, *On the Genealogy of Morality*, III, 26 (Cambridge, 1994), p.123.
64. Friedrich Nietzsche, *The Will to Power*, p. [585], 318.

someone knows how to command, the more urgently does he desire someone who commands, who commands severely — a god, prince, the social order, doctor, father confessor, dogma, or party conscience."[65] In this need for belief and veneration, Nietzsche detects a sickening of the will, the source of religions and fanaticisms. In contradistinction to the believer, Nietzsche calls for a spirit that "takes leave of all faith and every wish for certainty, practiced as it is in maintaining itself on light ropes and possibilities and dancing even beside abysses."

Now we can define this transition from veneration to command as being the passing from "you should" to "I want." Through this metamorphosis of the spirit from camel into lion, what is being dramatized is the act through which the will frees itself not only of its submission, but of its inclination to veneration, to the abnegation and to the negation of itself. Such a transition, moreover, is not given, it is a crossing, and has its price and its very own vertigo. It's called nihilism.[66] The transition from "you should" to "I want" cannot, therefore, skip over this intermediate, problematic state, in which disbelief still cannot find the will that sustains it, or the growing will still hasn't found a path that is clear enough for being able to want what behooves it, though it has already gotten rid of its venerations.… This is the ambiguity found in modernity's nihilism, in which the decline of morality and the ascent of a will that still doesn't know what it came for both coexist.… It can even be a period of lucidity, as Nietzsche says, where an antagonism between the old and the new is identified, and where *all the old ideals* are identified as hostile to life, resulting from *decadence* and culminating in it, but where life lacks the strength for the new. It's the moment of the greatest promise and biggest danger. Because precisely "now when the *greatest strength of will would be necessary, it is weakest and least confident.*"[67]

65. Nietzsche, *The Gay Science*, p. 205-206 [347].

66. Karl Jaspers, *Nietzsche*, trans. Charles F. Wallraff and Frederick J. Schmitz (Baltimore: Johns Hopkins University Press, 1965).

67. Friedrich Nietzsche, *The Will to Power*, p. 17 [20].

Double Meaning

We can now evoke the double meaning of nihilism that the writings from this period allow us to glimpse, or the double movement embedded in the very notion of nihilism. On the one hand, nihilism is a symptom of growing weakness, on the other, rising strength. At times it is an expression of a decrease in creative force, where the deception facing an absence of meaning or general direction leads to the feeling that everything is in vain, at other times it signals a rise in the force of creating, of wanting, to such an extent that conventional interpretations are no longer necessary in order to provide meaning to a worldly existence.[68] You can't think about nihilism in the way that Nietzsche elaborated it without such duplicity, without this equivocal, ambivalent character, at the intersection of antagonistic directions, a downward and upward movement of life. "Biologically, modern man represents a contradiction of values; he sits between two chairs, he says Yes and No in the same breath."[69]

When the reader of Nietzsche asks, within these contradictory writings, whether ultimately nihilism for Nietzsche is something desirable or nefarious *per se*, and how he situates himself in relation to what it is that he diagnoses, one must keep the preparatory fragment from the preface in mind: "I describe what is coming: the advent of nihilism [...] I praise, I don't here reproach *the fact that* it is coming [...] knowing if man will recover, if he will dominate this crisis, it is a question that depends on his force: it is *possible*."[70] And in the more elaborated version of the preface, we see Nietzsche himself confessing to be the first perfect nihilist of Europe, having lived nihilism in his soul to its end — and having already overcome it — he already has it behind him, below him, outside of him....[71] Therefore, Nietzsche's position is not extrinsic to the theme, and the perfection seems to refer to the fact of having plunged into nihilism and having traversed it in all of its states, "as a spirit of daring and experiment that has already lost its

68. Friedrich Nietzsche, *The Will to Power*, p. 312 [580].

69. Friedrich Nietzsche, *The Case of Wagner*, in *The Anti-Christ, Ecce Homo, Twilight of the Idols and Other Writings*, op. cit., p. 262.

70. Friedrich Nietzsche, *Nietzsche's Notebook of 1887-1888*, p. 11 [411].

71. *Ibid.*

way in every labyrinth of the future," until coming out on the other side — and by way of its "augural" nature looks back and says what is to come. Nietzsche was at once the patient who lived through the sickness until its end, and by way of his astute self-observation, the doctor who was able to sustain it and intensify it to the point of its exhaustion, enduring it like a "homeopathic" cure. So it was that, as a doctor, he could already diagnose it in his contemporaries and even prevent its necessary and possible unfoldings, though the outcome is always undetermined.

In less personal terms, as said above, nihilism appears to Nietzsche as a historical necessity to the extent that it results from those values whose supremacy finds itself in question, carrying the internal logic of such values to its end, to the extent that these values are turned against themselves, in a dynamic of self-suppression. "All great things bring about their own destruction through an act of self-overcoming: thus the law of life will have it, the law of the necessity of "self-overcoming" in the nature of life — the lawgiver himself eventually receives the call: *"patere legem, quam ipse tulisti."*[Submit to the law you yourself proposed.][72] For example, "the sense of truthfulness, highly developed by Christianity, is disgusted at the falseness and mendacity of the whole Christian interpretation of world and history."[73] The excess of the valuation of truth is pitted against the belief in illusions taken as truths, resulting in a suspicion in relation to everything and whatever is taken-as-true, that is, pitted against every value, and therefore against the very possibility of evaluation and valuation....

Types of Nihilism

However, how is this framework of nihilism presented in Nietzsche, with all these oscillations of the concept with regard to its extension and coloring? We should start from a form prior to nihilism, a certain pessimism of Schopenhauer's inspiration present among the Greeks as referred to in *The Birth of Tragedy*, and which subsequently Nietzsche would call theoretical and practical nihilism, or first nihilism. It deals with an inherent

72. Friedrich Nietzsche, *On the Genealogy of Morality*, p.161.

73. Friedrich Nietzsche, *Writings from the Late Notebooks*, p. 2, 83 [127].

suffering of life, and when faced with it someone from Ancient Greece would run the risk of aspiring to a Buddhist negation of existence, if he didn't precisely interpose an artistic, divine, or Apollonian shield, apt to seduce all creatures to live life and guard them from metaphysical disgust. But nihilism properly stated, as developed by Nietzsche in the last period of his work, owes nothing to Schopenhauer — except as a symptomatic example of one of the most effectuated types of nihilism.

It would be necessary, then, to begin going through *negative nihilism*, the most encompassing, so as to practically refer to the history of metaphysics as a whole, with its theoretical, moral, and rational appreciations of value, and its simultaneous disregard for the sensorial world. It's the kingdom of the spirit of vengeance and of depreciation, which turns against life. More than a metaphysical structure, it deals with a psychological structure, in the sense that Nietzsche understands it, as morphology of the will to power: the will to power reduced to its power of negating.

Modernity, however, facing such a process of devaluation of supreme values, proposes successive substitutes (the Moral Imperative, Progress, Happiness, Culture), without the place from which they emanate undergoing any alteration, even if it has lost its power of caution. It is under this sign that modern man lives, God's assassin, but wrapped in the dead God's shadow.[74]

What could result from this, if not deception? "We see that we cannot reach the sphere in which we have placed our values; but this does not by any means confer any value on that other sphere in which we live: on the contrary, we are *weary* because we have lost the main stimulus. 'In vain so far!'[75] *Passive nihilism* comes from this great weariness whereby it prevailing over the sensation that 'everything is the same, nothing is worth the effort.'"[76] It's the nausea for this repetitive existence without meaning, symbolized by the horrifying image of the pastor with a black snake hanging from his mouth, in *Zarathustra*. It's the end of moral optimism, the awareness that in a world without God and without purpose there is nothing more to expect. It's

74. Roberto Machado, *Zaratustra, tragédia nietzschiana*, (Rio de Janeiro: J. Zahar, 1997).

75. Friedrich Nietzsche, *The Will to Power*, p. [8], 11.

76. With some variations, in *Thus Spoke Zarathustra*: II, "The Soothsayer,"; III, "On the Three Evils," part 2, and "On Old and New Tablets," parts 13 and 16; IV, "The Cry of Distress."

also the stage in which the unity of culture is dissolved, according to the logic of *décadence*, and the different elements that constitute it enter into war, intensifying the expedients which are compensatory, tranquilizing, curing, inebriating, hedonist, comforting, as well as their moral, religious, political, and aesthetic disguises.[77] It concerns a "*pathological* transient state."

The three figures of nihilism mentioned above could thus be translated in terms of the position of values: superior values, substitutive values, the nothingness of values. Negative nihilism, reactive nihilism, passive nihilism — whichever the case may be, it is always an incomplete nihilism. The most interesting in this progression is the terminal point, the most afflicting stage, the most pathological, most paradoxical — it is precisely here where a conversion is possible.

The paradox of passive nihilism lies in the fact that the same symptoms could signify opposite directions. Even the extreme pessimism of the modern world could be the indication of a growth in force, and of a transition to new conditions of existence that our conservative moral feeling judges negatively, because it is not able to understand what new conditions it accompanies....[78] From this point of view, nihilist sentiment could be the sign of a broadened power of the spirit, which needs new values, since previous ones are incapable of expressing the current state of force.

In the conversion from passive to active nihilism, one perceives that the prevailing goals up until then (convictions, articles of faith) are not up to the task given to them by the present forces at play, and therefore one is compelled to actively destroy them. "Nihilism is not just a contemplation of the 'In vain!', and not just the belief that everything deserves to perish: one puts one's hand to it, one makes it perish...."[79] But Nietzsche distinguishes two types of destruction: "The desire for destruction, for change and for becoming can be the

---

77. *Decadence* is a central and recurrent idea from this period, which recalls a process of disaggregation proper to life, even from a physiological point of view, which puts an end on the formations of dominion, once having exhausted its possibilities and completed its cycle. See Oswaldo Giacóia Jr., *Labirintos da Alma*, (Campinas: Ed. Unicamp, 1997); Wolfgang Müller-Lauter, "*Décadence* artística enquanto *décadence* fisiológica", in "Cadernos Nietzsche" n. 6, 1999; and mainly, Paul Bourget, *Essais de Psychologie Contemporaine*, (Paris: Gallimard, 1993).

78. Friedrich Nietzsche, *Writings from the Late Notebooks*, p. 10[22], 180.

79. *Ibid.*, p. 11[123], 225.

expression of an overflowing energy pregnant with the future [...], but it can also be the hatred of the ill-constituted, deprived, and underprivileged one who destroys and must destroy because what exists, indeed all existence, all being, outrages and provokes him."[80] The destruction of morality, religion, and metaphysics, and of the forces that propagate them, advocated by Nietzsche for active nihilism, cannot come from a hatred of failure, from the poison of the resented, from the reactive impulse of a negativist aspiration, but should be the necessary consequence of an affirmative will.[81] Nietzsche is very clear about the statute of its destruction. "But we who are different, we immoralists. [...] We do not negate easily, we stake our honor on being affirmative."[82] When praising criticism, Nietzsche reveals the logic embedded therein: "When we criticize [...] it is, at least very often, proof that there are living, active forces within us shedding skin. We negate and have to negate because something in us wants to live and affirm itself, something we might not yet know or see!"[83] Or as he says in a preparatory fragment for *Zarathustra*: "Creators are the most hated: indeed, they are the most radical destroyers."[84] Or: "The creator should always be a destroyer."[85] Or: "I speak of a great synthesis of the creator, of the lover, and of the destroyer." At the limit, it is the preponderance of Yes: "I want to be, someday, just someone who says Yes!" We could use this assessment as a criterion for a differential diagnostic of nihilisms....

As such, it is precisely at this extreme point of destruction and affirmation that complete nihilism can intervene, suppressing the very place of values in order to place them in a different way. Finished nihilism, "classic," perfect, from which

---

80. Friedrich Nietzsche, *The Gay Science*, p. [370], 234-6.

81. Leon Kossovitch, *Signos e Poderes em Nietzsche*, (São Paulo: Ática, 2004), p. 127: "The virulence of active nihilism is in its destructive Power. Not to think it takes values into account: the opposite is true, to annihilate the forces that propagate it. By saying that '*it must begin by hanging the* moralists,' Nietzsche accuses them not only of vile values, but, beyond these, the preservation, through these values, of the forces that ought to commit suicide."

82. Friedrich Nietzsche, "Morality as Anti-Nature," in *Twilight of the Idols*, in *The Anti-Christ, Ecce Homo, Twilight of the Idols and Other Writings*, op. cit., p. 175.

83. Friedrich Nietzsche, *The Gay Science*, p. 174-5 [307].

84. Friedrich Nietzsche, *Posthumous fragment, Summer-Autumn 1882*, p. 3[1].

85. Friedrich Nietzsche, *Posthumous fragment, November, 1882 — February, 1883*, p. 5[1].

Nietzsche seems to make himself the mouthpiece, requires the establishment of values starting from a different matter situated in life itself, the will to power, and of a different element, affirmativeness.

We can already, before we direct ourselves to some conclusive notes, try to synthesize some general features gathered from the consulted writings and some interpretations. Nihilism can express itself as philosophy, as religion, as morality, as aesthetics, as a social movement, as political convulsion, as revolutionary violence.[86] Nihilism traverses all these phenomena like a diffuse awareness that supreme values in Western culture are devalued, and they, thereby, reveal its value of nothing, and the nothing appears like the truth of such values. With Nietzsche, it's as if this movement ascends to philosophical self-comprehension.

There is a vacuum of meaning, which is lived as a "psychological" experience, and where devaluation reaches a level of representation. But in an extensive paragraph about nihilism as a psychological state, Nietzsche desubstantializes this "nothing," reminding us, in part, of Bergson's arguments to that respect. For the nothing appears as a result of an expectation of finding a finality, a totality, a truth in the flow of the world, and the consequent deception due to these categories of reason which don't find equivalence in reality. We again find what Nietzsche never ceases to rework, since his writing *On Truth and Lies in a Nonmoral Sense*: the failure of anthropomorphic projection transformed into metaphysical postulate. As he says: "all the values by means of which up to now we first tried to make the world estimable to us and with which, once they proved inapplicable, we then devaluated it — all these values are, calculated psychologically, the results of particular perspectives of usefulness for the preservation and enhancement of human formations of rule, and only falsely projected into the essence of things. It's still the hyperbolic naivety of man, positing himself as the meaning of things and the measure of their value."[87]

---

86. Oswaldo Giacóia Jr., *Os Labritintos da Alma*, op. cit.op. cit. I follow closely the first part of this book in this paragraph.

87. Friedrich Nietzsche, *Writings from the Late Notebooks*, p. 11, 219 [99].

Counter-Movement

It would be necessary now, briefly, to situate the way through which Nietzsche understands counterpoising himself to these anthropomorphic mechanisms of projection and nihilist negation. Upon a first reading, it seems that the philosopher of transvaluation directs himself toward a re-appropriation, recalling Hegel's heroes. "All the beauty and sublimity we've lent to real and imagined things I want to demand back, as the property and product of man: as his most splendid vindication. Man as poet, as thinker, as God, as love, as power — oh, the kingly prodigality with which he has given gifts to things, only to impoverish himself and himself feel miserable! That has been man's greatest selflessness so far, that he admired and worshipped and knew how to conceal from himself the fact that it was he who created what he admired."[88] But a more attentive reading of some fragments reveals that a twilight of idols is not enough for overcoming nihilism, as in suppressing the supra-sensible sphere, and the humanist re-appropriation; different from Feuerbach, what becomes necessary is the deconstruction of man himself who projected his needs and categories in this sphere, with his debility and inclination to reverence. It is not enough, therefore, to put man in place of God or return divine attributes to man, or even a creation of values, without dismantling man himself in his slavish, resentful, guilty, reactive configuration. In other words, axiology cannot be rooted in anthropology, whose relation to theology is its unconfessed origin. The nihilist who destroys the world without destroying himself prolongs anthropocentrism, decadence, and the metaphysics that he thinks he is opposing. In short, voluntary suicide would consequently be the end of nihilism, its most extreme gesture. The death of God implies the death of man, but as Deleuze says, both still await the forces that can give them the most elevated meaning.

88. *Ibid*, p.11, 215 [87].

Force

In order for this final trajectory of Nietzsche's thought to acquire its full meaning, it is necessary to situate it in relation to an array of criteria that reappear in several writings from this period, but which are already present throughout a large portion of his work. In particular, notions like great style, great health, superabundance, elevation, plenitude, and activity, rise in force, intensification of power, pathos of distance, always in comparison with the supposed "improvement" of man, his domestication, mediocrization, debasement, and gregariousness. Nietzsche claims that these criteria allow for the assessment and even classification of a value, a culture, a philosophy, a life, or even a modality of detected nihilism. Let's take the well-known Prologue to *The Gay Science*: "In some, it is their weaknesses that philosophize; in others, their riches and strengths. [...] What is at stake in all philosophizing hitherto was not at all 'truth' but rather something else — let us say health, future, growth, power, life...."[89] And further on he insists upon asking, in each case, if it is "hunger or superabundance that have become creative here?"[90] In the fragments from the later period, Nietzsche returns countless times to outline his criterion: "I assess a man by the quantum of power and abundance of his will: not by its enfeeblement and extinction; I regard a philosophy which teaches denial of the will as a teaching of defamation and slander"[91]; in a fragment about hierarchy: "one must have a **Criterion**: I distinguish the *grand style*; I distinguish *activity* and reactivity; I distinguish the excessive, the squandering from the *suffering* who are passionate (– the idealists)"[92] "a rich and self-assured nature [...] doesn't give a damn about whether it will achieve bliss — it has no such interest in happiness in any form whatsoever, it is force, deed, desire...."[93] "Viewpoints for my values: whether out of plenitude or hunger [...] whether one observes or intervenes [...] or looks away, moves aside [...] whether animated, stimulated 'spontaneously' out of the build-up of force or merely

89. Friedrich Nietzsche, *The Gay Science*, Preface, p. 4-5.

90. *Ibid*, p. 235 [370].

91. Friedrich Nietzsche, *The Will to Power*, p. 206 [382].

92. *Ibid*. footnote, p. 471 [881].

93. Friedrich Nietzsche, *Writings from the Late Notebooks*, p. 10[127], 196.

reactively."[94] In other words: "What is good? — All that heightens the feeling of power, the will to power, the power increases, even in humans. […] / What is happiness? The feeling that power increases — that resistance is overcome. / Not contentment, but more power, not peace at all, but war; not virtue, but efficiency (virtue in the Renaissance style, *virtù, virtue moraline*)"[95] "the goal is not the increase of consciousness but the enhancement of power."[96] Even when he speaks of suffering, it is still the same criterion: "But there are two types of sufferers: first, those who suffer from a superabundance of life — they want a Dionysian art as well as a tragic outlook and insight into life — then, those who suffer from an impoverishment of life and demand quiet, stillness, calm seas or else intoxication, paroxysm, stupor from art and philosophy."[97] In order for this observation to become fully comprehensible, it would be necessary to take a lengthy detour through the Greeks, to whom Nietzsche increasingly recognizes his debt, and who in effect seem to elucidate this list. Because the criteria listed above, in one way or another, are already present in what Nietzsche calls the Hellenic instinct: the excess of force, the agonistic dimension, reckless immoralism, the will to power, in short, the "will to life," *eternal* life. But contrary to Christian eternity, the eternal return of life translates here, beyond death and change, with all the suffering coming from it, a triumphant yes to life connected to the eternal pleasure of creation, to the eternal "martyrdom of the parturient." In short, Dionysus. Tragedy as an antidote, as refusal of pessimism, as counter-instance, and tragic thought as an overcoming of all pessimism. "Saying yes to life, even in its strangest and harshest problems; the will to life rejoicing in its own inexhaustibility […] over and above all horror and pity, so that you yourself may be the eternal joy in becoming — the joy that includes even the eternal joy in negating." Nietzsche recognizes having touched, at this last extreme of his thought,

---

94. *Ibid.*, p. 10[145], 199-200. The active/reactive pair shows up often in Nietzsche, and Deleuze made this a capital criteria in his redescription of Nietzsche's Philosophy.

95. Friedrich Nietzsche, *Nietzsche's Notebook of 1887-1888,* p.11[414], vol. 13.

96. Friedrich Nietzsche, *Writings from the Late Notebooks*, p. 11[74], 213.

97. Friedrich Nietzsche, "We Antipodes" in *Nietzsche Contra Wagner*, in *Twilight of the Idols*, in *The Anti-Christ, Ecce Homo, Twilight of the Idols and Other Writings*, op. cit., pp. 271-272.

the point of which he had started with *The Birth of Tragedy*, his "first transvaluation of all values."[98]

In any case, when Nietzsche re-encounters his debt to the Greeks at the same time his own work seems to reach its most daring extremity, Nietzsche does not move regressively or melancholically, he just throws another dart at the future. As he confessed in the *Second Untimely Meditation* (and it is my understanding that this is where Nietzsche formulated the exemplary logic of his undertaking as a whole): what would the utility of a having a familiarity with Greek antiquity be, if not that of working against his time, hence it would also be a question of dealing with his own time, and, as he expects, "in favor of a time to come."[99]

The Time to Come

Some words, therefore, regarding this "time to come." Contemporary nihilism, as Zarathustra points out, presents two possibilities of the future, one that's positive or one that's negative, symbolized respectively by the last man and by the overman. The last man is he who, when substituting God, remains in re-activity, in the absence of meaning and value, lacking eagerness and creation, and (according to Deleuze's commentary) prefers, contrary to a will to nothing, an embrace of the lack of will — that's why he gives himself over to passive extinction. However, the over-man sees in this collapse of meaning and value a *possibility*, an *opening*, a *stimulus*. If Deleuze had reason to conceive the overman as a new way of feeling, thinking, evaluating, as a new form of life, and even another type of subjectivity, contrary to Heidegger, to whom he is the realization of the metaphysics of subjectivity and its continuity in techno-science, in a reading whose political logic Jean-Pierre Faye painfully elucidated for us,[100] it is because, as we have already said, for Nietzsche the

98. Friedrich Nietzsche, "What I Owe the Ancients," in *The Anti-Christ, Ecce Homo, Twilight of the Idols and Other Writings*, op. cit., pp. 228-229.

99. Friedrich Nietzsche, Foreword to "On the Uses and Disadvantages of History for Life," in *Untimely Meditations*, trans. Reginald John Hollingdale, (Cambridge: Cambridge University Press, 1997), pp. 59-60.

100 Jean-Pierre Faye, *Le vrai Nietzsche* (Paris: Hermann, 1998), 49. Faye raises the hypothesis that, upon being accused by Kriek, then rector of the University of Frankfurt and high-ranking official of the SS, of "metaphysical nihilism," Heidegger would shielded

death of God necessarily signifies the death of man, thought under the mode of an ethical challenge, and not under the mode of an empirical or metaphysical event.

The death of man is a frequent theme in contemporary philosophy, which has evoked no fewer misunderstandings than the theme of the death of God in Nietzsche. This is particularly the case regarding the ambiguity that is made evident by way of this theme. And because of this ambiguity and its dimension of pathos, we should occasionally grant ourselves the right to laugh at it. At any rate, in both cases, one does not always perceive the melancholic exhaustion of a promise, or the opening of a possibility whose design is entirely unknown to us. It is probable that the contemporary condition, including the mistaken deviation through the postmodern, or even the ambiguous condition of biopolitics, is characterized precisely by the schizophrenic conjunction between these two affective tonalities, corresponding to disparate movements, though simultaneous, in which we don't already know if we are on the verge of dying or being born, of lamenting or celebrating. Of this, Nietzsche had a very strong awareness, and expressed it in the first line of his autobiography. "The good fortune of my existence, its uniqueness perhaps, lies in its fatality: I am, to express it in the form of a riddle, already dead as my father, while as my mother I am still living and becoming old. This dual descent, as it were, both from the highest and the lowest rung on the ladder of life, at the same time a *decline* and a *beginning* — this, if anything, explains that neutrality, that freedom from all partiality in relation to the total problem of life, that perhaps distinguishes me. I have a subtler sense of smell for the signs of ascent and decline than any other human being before me; I am the teacher *par excellence* for this — I know both, I am both."[101]

It would be the case to ask if the lucidity that Nietzsche demonstrated regarding the amphibious condition of his trajectory is not a characteristic of contemporary thought itself or even of philosophy as such. Would it be too much to risk

himself with Nietzsche in order to later sacrifice him, accusing him of that which was attributed to him: "The dear Heidegger, who contributed to the rehabilitation of Nietzsche in popular opinion, buries him in philosophical thought by placing him where the Nazis wanted to place Heidegger himself." Cf. additionally, the acid text "Le transformat, le littoral", *Concepts*, n. 7, Mons, (Belgium: Ed. Sils Maria, 2004).

101. Friedrich Nietzsche, "Why I am So Wise," in *The Anti-Christ, Ecce Homo, Twilight of the Idols and Other Writings*, op. cit., p. 222.

the hypothesis that philosophy today carries this double attribution, that of detecting what is on the verge of perishing and, at the same time, what is on the verge of being born, reinventing in each case the relation between them? There are sufficient indications, in Nietzsche at least, to corroborate such a hypothesis. On the one hand, and from very early on, Nietzsche made a caustic inventory from that which in our culture is declining, exsanguine, or dying, claiming that such a process of disintegration is realized, according to a conception of justice that finds in Goethe's maxim his notable expression: "For all that is born *deserves* to perish." Was it not that which his work carried out with uncommon causticity, and that from the beginning, when it defended that man "cannot live if he does not have the strength to break and dissolve a part of his past, and if he doesn't from time to time make use of this strength?"

But whoever sees in Nietzsche only a merciless and barbarous destroyer does not perceive that such demolition is always at the service of a primary affirmativity, from the desire of a founding time, whose foreshadowing he ceaselessly detects here and there, at times in resonance with a supposedly exemplary antiquity, in any case a founding time whose necessity he increasingly invokes: "Every great growth indeed brings with it a tremendous crumbling and falling into ruin: suffering, the symptoms of decline, belong to the periods of great advances; every fruitful and powerful movement of mankind has also produced alongside it a nihilistic movement; it would perhaps be the sign of a decisive and most essential growth, of the transition into new conditions of existence, that the most extreme form of pessimism, real nihilism, would be born. This I have understood."[102]

The most difficult task in engaging with Nietzsche's work, is to think the conjunction between these two movements, traveling along on a Moebius strip, and in the process of this traversal recognizing the cause of its reciprocal co-extensiveness, but at the same time preserving dissymmetry, heterogeneity, and disparity of regimes between the two sides. On the one hand, there is a type of historical necessity in the advent of nihilism, since nihilism is not an accident of history, but its internal logic, history as the history of an error, "of the longest error," and of a negation of the world that only now comes to an end and reveals

---

102. Friedrich Nietzsche, *Writings from the Late Notebooks*, p. 10[22], 180.

the bacillus of revenge that moved it since the beginning. On the other hand, Nietzsche defends a *counter-movement*, which cannot be thought of independently from the nihilism which he surpasses, because this counter-movement presupposes nihilism and therefore proceeds it, as Nietzsche states in the preparatory writings to the preface. Nevertheless, despite his initial comments, this counter-movement doesn't receive a necessary direction and unfolding — since this counter-movement is uncertain, for it is without truth, without teleology, without determinism, without dialectics.

However, contrary to what it might seem like — the world evacuated of a supposed or awaited finality — we don't end up at axiological indifferentiation. Philosophizing with a hammer, which Nietzsche writes about, takes "anything goes" or "everything is equivalent" (and what is more "contemporary" than that?) to be major symptoms of the great nihilist danger. Therefore, the whole challenge consists of *not making a nihilistic reading of nihilism....*

In short, as in the case of the eternal return, nihilism can also be read with a double meaning: as the most despicable form of thought, but also the most divine. It depends, ultimately, on who announces it, or to use Nietzsche's terms, it depends on the accumulated force, on the explosive material, on the new necessities and the new unsatisfied who claim it.

DELEUZE, NIHILISM, CAPITALISM

"Nietzsche presents the aim of his philosophy as the freeing of thought from nihilism and its various forms."[103] Is this not one of the meanings of Gilles Deleuze's philosophical endeavor? It remains to be known what inflections he attributes to nihilism, in his interpretation which privileges negativity as a principle, and resentment as a greater expression. In fact, in refusing the dialectic and combating reactivity, Deleuze's critical extension is revealed, as well as his reliance on the work of Nietzsche: tragic thought, which affirms the innocence of becoming, of the past and of the future, of will, of chance. "The dice throw is tragic. All the rest is nihilism, Christian and dialectic pathos, caricature of the tragic, comedy of bad conscience."[104] Just another game, another way of playing, can reject the "little bacillus" of vengeance....

We can now return to this scenario and stress some points. In maintaining a strict fidelity to Nietzsche, Deleuze understands Nihilism as "the enterprise of denying life and depreciating existence."[105] Since Socrates, life "crushed *by the weight* of the negative, is unworthy of being desired for itself, experienced in itself."[106] Whether submitted to values superior to it,

---

103. Gilles Deleuze, *Nietzsche and Philosophy,* trans. Hugh Tomlinson (New York: Columbia University Press, 1983), p. 35.

104. *Ibid*, p. 36.

105. *Ibid*, p. 34.

106. *Ibid*, p. 14.

impregnated with reactive values that substitute for them, or devoid of values, "it is expressed in values superior to life, but also in the reactive values which take their place and again in the world without values of the last man,"[107] life always has the element of depreciation or of negation, it is trapped by a will to deny. Negation "has dominated our thought, our ways of feeling and evaluating, up to the present day," but "it is constitutive of man. And with man the whole world sinks and sickens, the whole world is depreciated, everything known slides toward its own nothingness."[108] If negation is Deleuze's ultimate philosophical target, his most recurrent adversary, it is because this is the element that most clearly reveals the core of nihilism. Nihilism, more than the empire of nothing, is the realm of negation, negation directed against life in its entirety, with all the groans that go along with it, from anguish to lack, from the cult of death to the apology of renunciation, from finitude to castration — this is what is meant by combating, from its speculative figures to its historical concretions. Deleuze follows the adventures of nihilism — negative, reactive, passive — in order to highlight what remains unaltered in them: the type of life: "it is always the same type of life which benefits from the depreciation of the whole of life in the first place, the type of life which took advantage of the will to nothingness in order to obtain its victory, the type of life which triumphed in the temples of God, in the shadow of higher values. Then, secondly, the type of life which puts itself in God's place, which turns against the *principle* of its own triumph and no longer recognizes values other than its own. Finally, the exhausted life which prefers to not will, to fade away passively, rather than being animated by a will which goes beyond it. This still is and will always remain the same type of life; life depreciated, reduced to its reactive form. Values can change, be renewed or even disappear. What does not change *and does not disappear is the nihilistic perspective* which governs this history from beginning to end and from which all these values (as well as their absence) arise. This is why Nietzsche can think that nihilism is not an event in history but the motor of the history of man as universal history."[109]

---

107. *Ibid*, p. 171.

108. *Ibid*, pp. 176-7.

109. *Ibid*, pp. 151-2.

Let's stop for a second on this notion that is so precious to Deleuze, the notion of life. It cannot be taken abstractly, for it is inseparable from the nature of the force that qualifies it, active or reactive, and of the quality of the will to power that is in its origin, affirmative or negative. Thus, quite summarily, and depending on this combination of the quality of force and of the will to power, we have an active or reactive life that is amorous or vengeful, aggressive or resentful, creative or full of believe, evaluative or interpretive, legislative or adaptive, forgetful or memorial, innocent or guilty, sick or healthy, happy or suffering, light or heavy, high or low. We know the care that is necessary to handle these pairs, and the complex cost by which health is conquered, a lightness, an innocence. If all of this still sounds excessively anthropomorphic, it is necessary to insist upon the degree within animality itself that man and his science refuse to take note of this plastic and metamorphic force, a force of variation and of differentiation, in short — of difference.[110] Science prioritizes quantity, equalizing quantities, compensation of inequalities, in other words, undifferentiation, adiaphoria. "The attempt to deny differences is a part of the more general enterprise of denying life, depreciating existence and promising it a death ("heat" or otherwise) where the universe sinks into the undiffentiated." It is because science, "by inclination, understands phenomena in terms of reactive forces and interprets them from this standpoint."[111]

Thus, if nihilism is equivalent to the predominance of negation, and the negation of life, and the negation of inequalities, we can therefore add Deleuze's conceptual inflection with regard to Nietzsche, in a somewhat abrupt formulation: nihilism is defined, in its ultimate instance, by the negation … of difference. From Plato to Hegel and Heidegger, that is what is always at stake, in relatively all of Deleuze's philosophical evaluations of the philosophers whom he rejects: the debasement of difference, its strangling, its emptying or its inversion. From the point of view of the figures that command thought and Western subjectivity, whether in regard to Being, Good, the Idea, God, the Self, the Signifier, Oedipus, the State, or Capital, we are always dealing with modalities of debasing or negating difference, with greater

---

110. *Ibid*, pp. 55-56. "Only active force asserts itself, it affirms its difference and makes its difference an object of enjoyment and affirmation."

111. *Ibid*, p. 45.

or lesser doses of transcendence, vengeance, leveling, emptiness. Against the demon of nihilism and its disregard throughout the world, Zarathustra manifests his disregard for disregard, his negation of negation. As Deleuze says: "We can see what Nietzsche is driving at and what he is opposed to. He is opposed to every form of thought which trusts in the power of the negative. He is opposed to all thought which moves in the element of the negative, which makes use of negation as a motor, a power and a quality."[112] Nietzsche would have substituted the work of the negative with the joy of difference ("and who tells us that there is more thought in work than in joy?"). A transvaluation is only possible if the element from which it derives the value of values comes to be, instead of negation, affirmation. Only as such will there be appreciation instead of depreciation, activity instead of reactivity. "As long as we remain in the element of the negative it is no use changing values or even suppressing them, it is no use killing God: the place and the predicate remain [...]"[113] Transmutation is the point in which the negative is converted into a "warlike play of difference, affirmation and the joy of destruction."[114] Transmutation corresponds to the point in which incomplete nihilism is converted into complete nihilism, in which nihilism turns against itself, the will to nothingness, already disconnected from reactive man and from the reactive forces that he previously promoted, turning around against himself, inspiring man with a new taste, that of destroying himself actively. Active destruction has nothing to do with the passive extinction of the last man, but with the man who wants to perish. It is the will to nothingness in the service of a power to affirm, the conversion from the negative into the active, such that "negation has broken everything which still held it back, it has defeated itself, it has become power of affirming, a power which is already superhuman."[115] Change in the quality of the will to power, conversion of the element of the will to power. "Negation is no longer the form under which life conserves all that is reactive in itself, but is, on the contrary, the act by which it sacrifices all its reactive forms."[116]

112. *Ibid*, p. 179.

113. *Ibid*, p. 171.

114. *Ibid*, p. 191.

115. *Ibid*, p. 175.

116. *Ibid*, p. 176.

Capitalism and Counternihilism

In Nietzsche as well as in Deleuze, the struggle against nihilism cannot take place unless it begins from within the nihilism that it intends to surpass, turning it around against itself, as a kind of suicide of the negating will. In other words: the counter-movement does not mean to halt, to brake, to block the escalation of nihilism — but precisely to intensify it, to exhaust it, to bring it to its end, to make it so it is completed and turn it around against itself. Counternihilism is, radically thought, nihilism brought to its suicidal limit.… Counternihilism corresponds to nihilism turned active, complete, finished. Not that which is dragged by a decadence, but that which is propelled by an active destruction, in which the active forces are taken in an active-becoming and the will to nothingness is thrown against itself, freeing up other forces.

So that all of this does not sound abstract, and assuming the risks of this deviation, let's think of the leveling that capitalism promotes out of the generalized deterritorialization that is part of it, as exposed in *Anti-Oedipus*: "perhaps the flows are not yet deterritorialized enough, not decoded enough, from the viewpoint of a theory and a practice of a highly schizophrenic character. Not to withdraw from the process, but to go further, to 'accelerate the process,' as Nietzsche put it: in this matter, the truth is that we haven't seen anything yet."[117] Capitalism, as equivalent to the decodification of flows as it is, "It axiomatizes with one hand what it decodes with the other."[118] It seeks to bind "the schizophrenic charges and energies into a world axiomatic that always opposes the revolutionary potential of decoded flows with new interior limits. And it is impossible in

117. Gilles Deleuze and Félix Guattari, *Anti-Oedipus: Capitalism and Schizophrenia*, trans. Robert Hurley, Mark Seem and Helen R. Lane (New York: Viking Press, 1977), pp. 239-240. Or, when commenting on Foucault about the era in which madness would cease to exist, for "it would receive the support of all the other flows, including science and art — because the exterior limit designated by madness would be overcome by means of other flows escaping control on all sides, and carrying us along," and they add: "It should therefore be said that one can never go far enough in the direction of deterritorialization: you haven't seen anything yet — an irreversible process. And when we consider what there is of a profoundly artificial nature in the perverted reterritorializations, but also in the psychotic reterritorializations of the hospital, or even the familial neurotic reterritorializations, we cry out, 'More perversion! More artifice!' — to a point where the earth becomes so artificial that the movement of deterritorialization creates of necessity and by itself a new earth." *Ibid*, p. 321.

118. *Ibid*, p. 246.

such a regime to distinguish, even in two phases, between decoding and the axiomatization that comes to replace the vanished codes. The flows are decoded *and* axiomatized by capitalism at the same time."[119] In such a way that the challenge, even in the so-called harshest conflict of classes, consists of discriminating the decoded flows "that enter into a class axiomatic on the full body of capital, and on the other hand, the decoded flows that free themselves from this axiomatic just as they free themselves from the despotic signifier, that break through this wall, and this wall of a wall, and begin flowing on the full body without organs."[120] As Jean-François Lyotard said: "Capitalism approaches this schizophrenic limit, through the multiplication of metamorphic principles, through the annulment of the codes that regulate the flow. As we approach this limit, it places us on the other side [...] desire effectively destroys the limit field, and its action is not to transgress the limit, but to pulverize the very field on the libidinal surface. [...] Destroying can only result from an even more liquid liquidation, from an even bigger *clinamen* and from a smaller free fall, from more dance and from less piety. What we need: that variations of intensity become more unforeseeable, stronger: that in 'social life' the highs and lows of desiring production can be inscribed without objective, without justification, without origin as in the strong times of 'affective' or 'creative' life; ceasing the resentment and bad conscience (*always equal to themselves, always depressed*) of the identities of functions engendered by the service of paranoid machines, by technology, and by the bureaucracies of Kapital."[121] In referring to the power of disorganizing which comes from force, in its piercing energy, Lyotard adds: "Now, this is virtuality of an alterity that is ready to multiply itself in the breast of the capitalistic 'organism' and from the value device, that is ready to *critique* without touching upon it, ready to *forget* the law of exchange, of lathing it and making from it an antiquated and crude illusion, a disaffected device. Who will be able to calculate the time that the new device is going to take in order to destroy with its unknown, transparent organs,

---

119. *Ibid.*

120. *Ibid*, p. 255.

121. Jean-François Lyotard, "Capitalismo Energúmeno," in M. M. Carrilho (org.), *Capitalismo e Esquizofrenia*, Dossier Anti-Édipo, trans. José A. Furtado, (Lisboa: Assírio & Alvim, 1976), p. 129.

the surface of our bodies and that of the social body, liberating them from the bustle of interests and from the preoccupation of saving, spending and counting? It's a different figure that is raised, the libido removes itself from the capitalist device, desire makes itself available in a different way, according to a different figure, formless, ramified in a thousand propositions and attempts throughout the world, bastard, disguised with the rags of this and that, with the words of Marx, and with the words of Jesus and Mohammed, and with the words of Nietzsche and Mao, […] and with the practices of the happening and demusicalized songs and with the practices of the sit-in and the sit-out, and of the 'trip' and light-shows, and with the liberation practices of pederasts and lesbians and 'lunatics' and delinquents, and with the practices of gratuity unilaterally decided. What is capitalism capable of against this disaffection which grows in its interior (under the form, among others, of disaffected 'youth'), against this thing that is the new libidinal device, and of which *Anti-Oedipus* is the enormous production--inscription in language?"[122]

We know that capitalism is quite capable against this and much more than what was believed at the time, but perhaps, much less — in any case, nowadays such an evaluation would demand a thorough "update."[123] For example, Christian Marazzi writes: "It was thought that capitalism, destroying all the *belongers*, would have created the conditions for beatitude: nomadism of the rootless individual, absolute, resulting from 'deterritorialization' inherent to the development of the world economy. And, instead of this, precisely where globalization culminates, capitalist 'deterritorialization,' everything returns: the family, the national State, religious fundamentalisms. Everything returns, but, as the philosopher teaches, in a perverse, reactionary, conservative manner. Precisely when the 'vacuum of meaning' is approached from the threshold of an era in which people seem to be able to speak among themselves in a manner of free communicative access, here is where the idea of ethnicity returns, the myth of the origin and of belonging. Possible

---

122. *Ibid*, p. 128. Translated by C. Brayton.

123. It is, for example, what has been attempted according to several inflections by Julián Ferreyra in *Ontologie du capitalisme chez Gilles Deleuze*, (Paris: L'Harmattan, 2010), Guillaume Sibertin-Blanc in *Politique et État chez Deleuze et Guattari: Essai sur le matérialisme historico-machinique*, (Paris: Puf, 2013), Virtanen Akseli in *Critique of the Biopolitical Economy*, to soon be released by n-1 publications.

freedom from 'transparent society' is reverted into its opposite."[124] And thus nihilism is referred back to capitalism itself: "The vacuum of meaning, understood as absence of a 'symbolic order,' is certainly the crowning of the historical development of capitalism, of its vocation to everything, in order to decode everything. Nothing before the economy was globalized resetting old rituals and ceremonies like today, emptying nation-States of their efficacy, disaggregating the traditional family. Also, ethnicities disappear, 'immersed' as they are in the immaterial productive processes, in which colors and perfumes of actors can be reproduced artificially."[125]

Subjective Subjection and Machinic Servitude

Maurizio Lazzarato, in his own way, has insisted on a double movement formulated by Guattari in the domain of relations between capitalistic deterritorialization and the forms of subjective subjugation.[126] On the one hand, we have subjection through attribution or reiteration of roles, functions, places (sex, profession, nationality, race), semiotic traps through which we "recognize" ourselves as subjects, with the equivalent illusion of autonomy and self-dominion — that is, the more well-known processes of subjectification. On the other hand, we are entangled within a machinic servitude, in the very sense that, as "dividuals," and no longer as individuals, we are "treated" machinically (as statistics, as a database, whether it is through genetic, informational, consumer, or based of one's interest), and also "affected" machinically, in other words, no longer "influenced" by ideological or political content, signification or meaning, and indeed affected by a-signifying signs (algorithms, equations, graphics) that are not directed to consciousness or to the will, but are imposed as modes of semiotization in a pre-subjective plane. If in the first case the subject/object dichotomy is strengthened, in the second it is already difficult to even sustain the man/machine distinction.

124. Christian Marazzi, *Capital and Affects: the politics of the language economy*, (Los Angeles: Semiotext(e), 2011).

125. *Ibid.*

126. Mauricio Lazzarato, *Signs, Machines, Subjectivities*, (São Paulo n-1 publications, 2014).

In any case, subjective subjection and machinic servitude, subjectivation, and desubjectivation complement one another and even form a continuous circuit. The force of capitalism, however, is more prevalent in this a-signifying machinic dimension that does not even pass for representation or consciousness — that's why Guattari always defended the efficacy of retaliations in the modes of semiotization, in a-signifying ruptures, in a-subjective deterritorializations. Thus it's not a question of demonizing this machinic configuration, but rather it is also a matter of accepting such a context by way of the new possibilities that it opens up, including in the area of what Guattari called "machinic animism." Different from the technophobia that is inferred from other theoretical or political perspectives, the machinic conception is immediately installed in the hybridism of the realms, in which one wouldn't be able to think human subjectivity isolated from the rhizome in which it emerges, in a properly ecosophic conception (environmental, social, mental). Critical discourse should not base itself on a universalist humanism, lest they miss what contemporary assemblages constitute.

Of course in recent decades we have witnessed an even more disturbing inflection. In his analysis of financialization, Lazzarato regains the nature most proper to capital (M-M', instead of M-C-M'). Independent of the qualified flows that he conjugates and subjugates (work, information, sex), financial capital is an abstract machine entirely indifferent to production, to employment or to wealth, since what matters to it, by definition even, is solely and exclusively the accumulation by accumulation, in an infinite movement, provided that it reiterates social and political asymmetries. If in the Fordist period of the Welfare State, the forms of unionization offered a codified and compensatory subjectivity to the deterritorialization undertaken by capital (however compatible with its infinitization), everything changes when the dominating financialization specifically decodes these instances that previously served it and with which it is composed.

But Lazzarato insists: as much as capitalism yearns to function blindly, "automatically," as if it were an autonomous technical machine, it is indissociable from a "social machine" composed of relationships of domination and exploitation of all sorts, and by the innumerous subjectivations that incessantly redesign their game. For example, the new subjective figure of the indebted man, based on the crisis of the derivatives, transversally cuts through social struggles and can give rise to other modalities of subjectivation and combat, for example in favor of the annulment of *all* debts, getting at the heart of one of the most unspeakable capitalistic axioms — here we have a "subjective conversion" that would make us exit the "morality of debt" in favor of a second innocence, in a Nietzschean inspiration — a transvaluation of values.[127]

From a more distinct angle, Isabelle Stengers and Philippe Pignarre defined capitalism as a sorcery system without sorcerers, or with sorcerers who don't consider themselves as such, precisely in a world that disqualifies sorcery, and consequently, the need to protect itself against it.[128] Now, if Marx's categories sought to "disenchant" that which seemed to be enchanted, namely, merchandise, tracking the genesis of the fetish inherent in it, according to Stengers and Pignarre the Marxian bet continues to be valid, though some of its terms have been altered. Sorcery technologies in contemporary capitalism have greatly increased, whether through bioinformatic devices of capturing souls and bodies, of integral mobilization of vital energy, of self-accountability, of the regime of "control of engagement," and this list is very extensive. But this doesn't blindly take place, for it circulates through millions of "little hands" that guarantee its efficacy, with varying degrees of success, maintaining the "conjugation" of an infinity of connections, laws, regulations, definitions, ways of thinking. Confronted with this, the lines of fracture can also be read as counter-sorceries, artificial unbewitchings that mobilize not "the truth," or "science," in contradistinction to sorcery (whereas in Marx's time it still seemed plausible, given the status attributed to "conscience"), but something that could be called counter-performativity, given the machinic and a-signifying functioning of capitalism. In Guattari's wake, Franco Berardi had already called attention to the "neuromagmatic" dimension of the new psychic landscape which no longer has as a support, or as an antidote, conscious

127. Maurizio Lazzarato, "The Making of the Indebted Man: Essay on the Neoliberal Condition", trans. Joashua David Jordan, Cambridge: semiotext(e), p. 2012

128. Isabelle Stengers and Philippe Pignarre, *La sorcellerie capitaliste*, (Paris: La Découverte, 2005-7), p. 59.

or scientific rationality."[129] Thus the singular modalities of deviation. When invoking the example of ethnopsychiatrist Tobie Nathan, Stengers and Pignarre refer to the estrangement that provoked his method for treating immigrants in Paris, allowing the "entities" with which the patients live — gods, ancestors, dead people, spirits — to enter the consultation room and "negotiate" with them, helping the patients, occasionally, creating supports, instead of ignoring all of this "superstition," based on a supposed scientific neutrality that precisely would leave them at the mercy of the "beings" that surround them. Thus, instead of "undoing" the sorcery in the name of a "scientificity" whose neutrality is our modern fiction, it deals with creating collective devices of "protection" which, in articulating voices, actions, intensities, create a "common means" apt to increase the collective "empowerment" in an entirely opposite direction to the meaning that this term has acquired in management, the end result being businesses.

In any case, it is important to insist upon the fact that in the very movement of capitalistic deterritorialization, conjugated to the axiomatics that capitalism multiplies, the "monster" can change its nature. Despite the extent to which capitalism and biopolitics seem to monopolize the totality of space, time, life, bodies, and souls, of virtuality itself, it contains in the same impulse of its extensive and intensive expansion, the most unusual lines of flight. In this sense, Beatriz Preciado's work is exemplar. In denouncing the pharmacopornographic regime (biomolecular and semiotic-technical at the same time), she shows how throughout the 20th century the psyche, the libido, the conscience, even heterosexuality or homosexuality "were being transformed into tangible realities, into chemical substances, into marketable molecules, into bodies, into human biotypes, into manageable goods of exchange by the pharmaceutical multinationals."[130] The success of science would be the transformation of depression into Prozac, masculinity into testosterone, erections into Viagra, etc. Facing this molecularization of biopower, and although recognizing the value of the Italians' theorizing, she considers that their descriptions stop at waist level. Hence the question: "But what if they were in reality the

129. Franco Berardi, *Neuromagma*, (Roma: Castelvecchi, 1995).

130. Beatriz Preciado, *Texto yonqui*, (Madrid: Espasa, 2008), p. 32. *Testo Junkie: Sex, Drugs, and Biopolitics in the Pharmacopornographic Era*, (New York: CUNY, 2013).

insatiable bodies of the multitude, their dicks and clitorises, their anuses, their hormones, their neurosexual synapses, what if desire, excitation, sexuality, seduction and pleasure of the multitude were the motors of value creation in the contemporary economy, what if cooperation were a 'masturbatory cooperation' and not simply a cooperation of brains?"[131] Or, more radically, the question expands: "We dare the hypothesis: the true raw materials of the current productive process are excitation, erection, ejaculation, pleasure, and the feeling of self-complacency and omnipotent control. The true motor of current capitalism is the pharmacopornographic control of subjectivity, whose products would be serotonin, testosterone, antacids, cortisone, antibiotics, estradiol, alcohol and tobacco, morphine, insulin, cocaine, sildenofil citrate (Viagra) and all that complex virtual-material that can help in the production of mental and psychosomatic states of excitation, relaxation and discharge, of total omnipotence of control. Here, even money becomes a significant psychotropic abstract. The addicted and sexual body, sex and all of its semiotic-technical derivatives are today the principal resource of post-Fordist capitalism."[132]

It would be hard to find a more provocative description of biopolitical nihilism and contemporary capitalism. Not by chance, rigorously faithful to the Moebius logic that we highlight at other moments of this book, the author at the same time calls attention to the "material" that is thus being vampirized — orgasmic force: this *potentia gaudendi*, the power of global excitation of every living molecule that tends toward expansion in a Spinozist manner despite the fact that conceptions of event, relationship, practice, becoming, can hardly be reduced to a private object, given its expansive and common nature. Now, if bioPower monopolizes something, it is not life, but rather the techno-living body, "techno-eros," adds Preciado. What is at stake in this confrontation is orgasmic force — which precisely cannot be thought of as inert or passive material, except in its pharmacopornographic reduction, where it is entirely expropriated as "bare life."

It is obvious that Preciado's description sinks its teeth into the flesh of the present, and runs through the latitude of the biobody coming and going with what she calls ejaculating

131. *Ibid*, p. 34.
132. *Ibid*, p. 37.

profit, which for now, excludes large portions of the population of the entire planet, for good or bad. In any case, beyond the living description of a context that our shame has a hard time naming, Preciado deserves credit for offering her own body as a laboratory in which to voluntarily experiment, the driftings of sensibility and erotism by way of a protocol of voluntary intoxication with testosterone gel. She clarifies that her book *Testo Junkie* can be read as a bioterrorism manual of gender on the molecular scale, or a point in a cartography of the extinction of genders, or simply as an exercise of disassembling and reassembling a subjectivity. In any case, there is an effort to go as far as possible in capitalistic deterritorialization and how one experiments with those points in which its axiomatic blocks it, or where it is reterritorialized on taboo-codes. From within the pharmacopornobioPower, she is able to discern new modalities as well as possible reversions.

We can now return to the theme of nihilism in a more generic key. If Vattimo could write that the consumption of nihilism rests upon the hegemony of the value of exchange, of the general equivalent, of the generalized indifferentiation, it is because before him Marx had postulated that in capitalism there are no longer values, but only "value."[133] However, we shouldn't dissolve such an analysis into an epochal history of being, ignoring its extremely material dimension which Preciado has shown with such acuity. In the same way that Deleuze and Guattari insist that production increasingly approaches antiproduction (it is the power of "self-destruction" of capitalism — growing production of scarcity, of debt, of catastrophe, but also of "bullshit"), this process should also not be read as "destinal."[134] In all of these cases, it is the nature of the assemblage that should be made evident. And the assemblage is, for these authors, always an assemblage of desire, as *A Thousand Plateaus* shows.

That is one of the challenges which, in its way, Guillaume Sibertin-Blanc confronts, in designating *Capitalism and Schizophrenia*'s method as "historical-machinic materialism," stressing the relevance of the "unconscious" dimension in this whole sequence. In the original reading that he proposes, the fascism of the interwar period would have impelled Deleuze and

---

133. Gianni Vattimo, *The End of Modernity: Nihilism and Hermeneutics in Postmodern Culture*, trans. John R. Snyder, (Baltimore: Polity Press, 1991).

134. Maurizio Lazzarato, *Idem*.

Guattari to rethink a "conjuncture marked by a manipulation of the unconscious on a mass scale, by which political space itself is destroyed." As such, political struggle should also take place within this "analytic" space, in this "different scene of the unconscious" where impasses and crises are inscribed that traverse their agents. That such symptoms, theorized as "desiring machines" and then as "becomings, unintegrable into a political, strategic, or even ethico-social rationality [...] can however return brutally at the level of the relationship to the body and to language, to art, and to sexuality, to space and to history, forming other features of self-heterogeneity from the subjects of political intervention, here is what is called the construction of an analytic space *sui generis*."[135]

Given the uneven elements listed in this short zigzag through such different authors, we can now say: in the diabolical flow that drags everything, the demon can suffer a transmutation, and the process of being able to create "a new earth."[136] "Not a promised and a pre-existing land, but a world created in the process of its tendency, its coming undone, its deterritorialization [...] where the flows cross the threshold of deterritorialization and produce the new land. [...] An active point of escape where the revolutionary machine, the artistic machine, the scientific machine, and the (schizo) analytic machine become parts and pieces of one another."[137] As the authors of *Anti-Oedipus* say, "the negative or destructive task of schizoanalysis is in no way separable from its positive tasks," and at the end of the book it is reiterated: "We have seen how the negative task of schizoanalysis must be violent, brutal: defamiliarizing, de-oedipalizing, decastrating; undoing theater, dream, and fantasy; decoding, deterritorializing — a terrible curettage, a malevolent activity. But everything happens at the same time. For at the same time the process is liberated — the process of desiring-production, following its molecular lines of escape – [...] Completes the process and does not arrest it, not making it turn about in the void, nor assigning it a goal. We'll never go too far with the deterritorialization, the decoding of flows." However, it is in the light of Zarathustra that such a conclusion

135. Guillaume Sibertin-Blanc, *Politique et État chez Deleuze et Guattari: Essai sur le matérialisme historico-machinique*, op. cit. p. 237.

136. *Anti-Oedipus*, p. 321.

137. *Ibid*, p. 322.

acquires an affirmative meaning: "In truth, the earth will one day become a place of healing."[138]

As for those who can see in this ending a dithyrambic tone, without historical or scientific basis, the authors anticipate their objection. "Those who have read us this far will perhaps find many reasons for reproaching us: for believing too much in the pure potentialities of art and even of science; for denying or minimizing the role of classes and class struggle; for militating in favor of an irrationalism of desire; for identifying the revolutionary with the schizo."[139] We are not here taking up the set of responses, what matters to us is briefly evoking one of them — with regard to the supposed irrationality of desire and its role of an eventual inflection in the logic of capitalism. Desire, Deleuze and Guattari remind us, is the "irrational of every form of rationality," because it implies a "rupture with causality," it "breaks with causes and aims" and brings the *socius* to "reveal its other side." Its only cause is a "rupture with causality," and "even though one can and must assign the objective factors, such as the weakest links, within causal series that made such a rupture possible, only what is of the order of desire and its irruption accounts for the reality this rupture assumes at a given moment, in a given place."[140] A position that is taken up in an even more categorical way in the following formulation: "The actualization of a revolutionary potentiality is explained less by the preconscious state of causality in which it is nonetheless included, than by the efficacy of a libidinal break at a precise moment, a schiz whose sole cause is desire — which is to say the rupture with causality that forces a rewriting of history on a level with the real, and produces this strangely polyvocal moment when everything is possible. Of course the schiz has been prepared by a subterranean labor of causes, aims, and interests working together; of course this order of causes runs the risk of closing and cementing the breach in the name of the new socius and its interests. Of course one can always say after the

---

138. *Ibid*, 381-382, with the pertinent clarification of the Brazilian translator of *Anti-Oedipus*, Luiz Orlandi, regarding the origin of Nietzsche's phrase. In this perspective, deterritorialization cannot be identified in worshipping an overcoming governed by a will to will, nor its technoscientific translation — its ontological reach is different, as Julián Ferreyra has shown recently in *L'ontologie du capitalisme chez Gilles Deleuze*, (Paris: L'Harmattan, 2010).

139. *Ibid*, p. 378-9.

140. *Ibid*, p. 377.

fact that history has never ceased being governed by the same laws of aggregates and large numbers. The fact remains that the schiz came into existence only by means of a desire without aim or cause that charted it and sided with it. While the schiz is possible without the order of causes, it becomes real only by means of something of another order: Desire, the desert-desire, the revolutionary investment of desire."[141]

It's true that the landscape of *A Thousand Plateaus* is distinct: ten years after the publication of *Anti-Oedipus*, the sparks of 1968 having settled down, in a neo-liberal context, new problems emerged and theoretical sobriety was imposed. However, there it persists, always and forever, the force of the untimely, be it in the minor-becomings, in the many war machines, in the events that cannot be reduced to the history from which they deviate, in the nomadology which confronts the State-form, in the body without organs, and in the assemblages of desire that make them burst upon the scene of the *socius*. The modalities in which the "bacillus of vengeance" engenders its antidotes are multiplied in the same proportion in which the biopolitical forms that it takes on are diversified.

---

141. *Ibid*, p. 378.

THE COMMUNITY OF THOSE
WHO DO NOT HAVE A COMMUNITY

A trivial affirmation is insistently evoked by several contemporary thinkers, among them Toni Negri, Giorgio Agamben, Paolo Virno, Jean-Luc Nancy, or even Maurice Blanchot: we live in a crisis of the "common." The forms that previously seemed to guarantee men a common surrounding, and assured social ties with some consistency, have lost their significance and collapsed for good, from the so-called public sphere, to the consecrated ways of associating: communitarian, national, ideological, partisan, syndicalist. We wander amidst specters of the common: the media, the political theater, consecrated economic consensus, but also wander amidst ethical or religious relapses, a civilizing invocation grounded in panic, a militarization of existence to defend "life" that is supposedly "common," or more precisely, to defend a so-called "common" way-of-life. However, we know very well that this "life" or this "form-of-life" is not really "common," that when we partake in these consensuses, these wars, these panics, these political circuses, these expired ways of assembly, or even this language that speaks in our name, we are victims or accomplices of a kidnapping.

Today, if there is in fact a kidnapping of the common under consenting, unitary, spectacularized, totalized, transcendentalized forms, we need to recognize that, at the same time and paradoxically, such figurations of the "common" start to finally appear for what they are: pure specter. In a different context, Deleuze recalls that above all, after World War II, clichés started to appear for what they are: mere clichés, clichés of relation, clichés of love, clichés of the people, clichés of politics or revolution, clichés of that which connects us to the world — and as such, they are emptied of their meaningfulness when they are revealed as clichés, that is, ready-made images, pre-fabricated, recognizable schemata, mere tracings of the empirical, only then can thought free itself from them in order to find that which is "real" and effective with aesthetic and political consequences that can be subsequently determined.

Today, such a perception of a kidnapping of the common — as the revelation of the spectral character of this transcendentalized common — comes about under very specific conditions. That is to say, precisely at the moment when, given the new current productive and biopolitical context, the common (and not its image) becomes central. In other words: unlike several decades ago, when the common was defined but also lived as the abstract public space, which joined individualities and was placed over them (whether as public space or as politics), today the common is the productive space par excellence. The contemporary context has been unveiled in an unforeseen manner since it occurs at its own economic and biopolitical core: the prevalence of the "common." So-called immaterial work, post-Fordist production, cognitive capitalism, all of these are coextensive with the emergence of the common: they all require the faculties which are connected to what is most common to us, that is, language, and its correlating bundle, intelligence, knowledge, cognition, memory, imagination, and, consequently, common inventiveness. But also subjective requirements attached to language, such as the capacity to communicate, to interact, to associate, to cooperate, to share memory, to forge new connections and make networks proliferate. In this context of a network, or connectionist capitalism, which some call rhizomatic, at least ideally, that which is common is put to work in common. It couldn't be any different: after all, what would a private language be? What meaning would exclusively self-referential knowledge have? Putting in common that which is common, placing in circulation that which is already everyone's patrimony, making proliferate that which is in everyone and is everywhere, whether it be language, life, or inventiveness. But this dynamic, thus described, only partially corresponds to what in fact happens, since it goes along with

the appropriation, expropriation, privatization and vampiriza-
tion of the common undertaken by so many corporations, ma-
fias, states, and institutions with goals that Capitalism cannot
conceal, even in its most rhizomatic versions.

Expanded Sensorium

If language — that which since Heraclitus has been considered
to be the most common good — has today become the very core
of production, one must keep in mind that the contemporary
common is wider than mere language. Given the context of the
expanded sensorium of the uninterrupted circulation of flows,
of collective synergy, of affective plurality and of the resulting
collective subjectivity, today the common passes through the
social *bios*, through the assemblages that are vital, material and
immaterial, biophysical and semiotic. Today, all of these constitute the core of economic production but also the production
of common life. That is, it is the multitude's power of life, in
its mix of collective intelligence, of the circulation of affects, of
the production of bonds, of the capacity for invention of new
desires and new beliefs, of new associations and new forms of
cooperation, as Maurizio Lazzarato says in Tarde's wake.[142] In
fact, this is increasingly the primordial source of wealth for that
very capitalism, which is the reason why this common is the
aim of capitalistic captures and kidnappings, but paradoxically
it is also precisely this common that extrapolates them, fleeing
in every direction and out of every pore.

Given this situation, we might be tempted to redefine the
common out of this exact context. Paraphrasing Paolo Virno, it
would be a case of postulating the common more as a premise
than as a promise, more as a shared reservoir made of multiplicity and singularity, more as an already real virtuality than
as a lost or future ideal unity. We could say that the common is
a reservoir of singularities in continual variation, an inorganic
matter, a body without organs, an unlimited (*apeiron*) apt to
the most diverse individuations.

It is clear that when the common is conceived as a virtual
bottom, as pre-individual social vitality, as pure non-totalizable

---

142. Maurizio Lazzarato, *Puissance de L'invention*, (Paris: Les Empêcheurs de penser en
rond, 2002).

heterogeneity, it has nothing to do with the media, political, imperial figures that try to hypostatize it, represent it, or expropriate it. Therefore, today's resistance is undertaking an exodus in relation to these instances that transcendentalize the common, and above all through the immanent experimentation of the compositions and recompositions that comprise it.

Ethics and Ethology

Perhaps the work in which Deleuze (together with Guattari) has best traversed these two directions, that of refusing transcendentalized instances and that of experimenting this immanent common, is *Capitalism and Schizophrenia*. Against Oedipus or the State-form, against the plane of transcendent organization, the authors simply invoke the plane of consistency, the plane of composition, the plane of immanence. In a plane of composition, one deals with variable connections, relations of speed and slowness, anonymous and impalpable matter dissolving forms and people, stratum and subjects, liberating movements, extracting particles and affects. It's a plane of proliferation, of population, and contagion. In a plane of composition, what's at stake is the consistency with which it gathers heterogeneous, disparate elements. As mentioned in the practically unintelligible conclusion of *A Thousand Plateaus*, what is inscribed on a plane of composition are the events, the incorporeal transformations, the nomad essences, intense variations, becomings, smooth spaces — it's always a body without organs. Call it what you like, Body without organs, Mecanosphere, Plane of Consistency, Plane of Immanence, the Spinozist lineage here is very clear, and entirely embraced.

In a short text by Deleuze about Spinoza from 1978, this connection or single Nature is conceived as a *common plane of immanence*, where all bodies, all souls, all individuals are to be found. When explaining this plane, Deleuze insists upon a paradox: it is already completely given, and yet must be constructed, in order to live in a Spinozist way.

Behold the argument. What is a body, or an individual, or a living being, if not a composition of speeds and slownesses on a plane of immanence? Now, to each body thus defined corresponds a power to affect and be affected, such that we can define

104

an individual, be it animal or man, by the affects it is capable of. Deleuze insists on the following: no one knows beforehand of what affects he is capable, we still don't know what a body or a soul can do, it's a question of experimentation, but also of prudence. This is Deleuze's ethological interpretation: Ethics would be a study of compositions, of the composition between relations, of the composition between powers. The question is knowing if relations can compose themselves in order to form a new, more "extended" relation, or if powers can be composed as such in order to constitute a more "intense" power. It then deals with, as Deleuze states, "sociabilities and communities. How do individuals enter into composition with one another in order to form a higher individual, ad infinitum? How can a being take another being into its world, but while preserving or respecting the other's own relations and world?"[143]

The question, the most ardent of all, could be translated like this: In what way do you go from the common to the community, in light of this theory of compositions and the double optics that it implies? And, to what extent does this community respond to both the common and the singularities that inflect it?

Nostalgias for Community

Before taking a stab at some of Deleuze's indications regarding this subject, I propose a deviation in order to situate the question of the community in a broader context. Jean-Luc Nancy, in *The Inoperative Community*, recalls that according to the occidental theoretical tradition, wherever society exists, community has been lost. Whoever speaks of society is speaking of the loss or degradation of a communitarian intimacy, in such a way that the community is that which society has destroyed. That's how the solitary figure must have been born, the one who on the inside of society wants to be a citizen of a free and sovereign community, precisely the community that society has ruined. Rousseau, for instance, would be the first thinker of community, who had the "consciousness of a

---

143. Gilles Deleuze, *Spinoza: Practical Philosophy,* trans. Robert Hurley, (San Francisco: City Lights, 1988), p. 126.

(perhaps irreparable) rupture in this community."[144] He was followed by the Romantics, by Hegel.... "Until this day," says Nancy, "history has been thought on the basis of a lost community — one to be regained or reconstituted."[145] The lost, or broken, community can be exemplified in several ways, such as the natural family, the Athenian city, the Roman Republic, the first Christian community, corporations, communes, or brotherhoods.... Always referring to a lost age in which community was woven of tight, harmonious bonds and sustained a representation of its own unity, whether through institutions, rituals, or symbols. "Distinct from society ... community is not only intimate communication between its members, but also its organic communion with its own essence."[146] It is constituted by way of sharing an identity, according to the model of the family and of love.

Nancy concludes that we should be suspicious of such a retrospective consciousness of the lost community and its identity, as well as a prospective ideal that such nostalgia produces, since it has accompanied the West from its outset. At every moment in its history, it has given itself over to the nostalgia of a lost, disappeared, archaic community, deploring the loss of familiarity, fraternity, and conviviality. What's curious is that the true consciousness of the loss of community is Christian: the community pined for by Rousseau, Schlegel, Hegel, Bakunin, Marx, Wagner, or Mallarmé is understood as communion, at the heart of the mystical body of Christ. The community would be the modern myth of humanity's partaking of divine life. The desire for community could be a belated invention that tried to respond to the harsh reality of the modern experience, from which divinity was infinitely withdrawing (as shown by Hölderlin). The death of God would be a way to refer to the death of community, and would carry that implicit promise of a possible resurrection, in a common immanence between humanity and God. All Christian, modern, and humanist consciousness of the loss of community goes in this direction.

---

144. Jean-Luc Nancy, *The Inoperative Community*, ed. Peter Connor, (Minneapolis: University of Minnesota Press, 1991), p. 9.

145. *Ibid.*

146. *Ibid.*

Community Has Not Taken Place

To which Nancy simply responds: *Community has not taken place*. Neither for the Ache-Guayaki Indians, nor for the Hegelian spirit of a people, nor for Christianity. "No *Gesellschaft* (society) has come along to help the State, industry, and capital dissolve a prior *Gemeinschaft* (community)." It would be more accurate to say that "society," understood as the dissociating association of forces, needs, and signs, has taken the place of something for which we have no name, or concept, and which maintains much more extensive communication than that of the social bond (with the gods, the cosmos, animals, the dead, the unknown), and at the same time a much more defined segmentation, with harsher effects (solitude, helplessness, rejection, etc.). "Society was not built on the ruins of a *community* [...] community, far from being what society has crushed or lost, is *what happens to us* — question, waiting, event, imperative — *in the wake of* society. [...] Nothing, therefore, has been lost, and for this reason nothing is lost. We alone are lost, we upon whom the 'social bond' (relations, communication), our own invention, now descends heavily."[147]

Namely, the lost community is nothing more than a phantasm. Or, what this "community" supposedly has lost, that communion, unity, co-pertinence, such a loss is precisely constitutive of community. In other words, and in a more paradoxical approach, community can only be thought of as a negation of fusion, of homogeneity, of identity with itself. The necessary conditions for community are heterogeneity, plurality and distance. Hence the categorical condemnation of the desire for communal fusion, since it always implies death or suicide, of which Nazism would be an extreme example. The desire for unitary fusion presupposes unitary purity, and the resulting exclusions can always be carried further and further, until culminating in collective suicide. Moreover, for a certain time, the very term community, which the Nazis sought to steal with their praise of the "community of the people," unleashed a reflexive hostility on the German left. Several years were needed so that the term could be disconnected from Nazism and reconnected with the word communism.[148] In any case, this national

---

147. *Ibid*, p. 11.

148. Jean-Luc Nancy, *The Confronted Community*, trans. Amanda MacDonald,

immolation, by means of, or in the name of community, made death become reabsorbed by community, with which death became full of meaning, values, ends, history. It is the reabsorbed negativity (the death of each and every one reabsorbed in the life of the Infinite). But the work of death, insists Nancy, cannot establish a community. Quite the contrary: it is solely the impossibility of creating a work from death that could establish one.

Another vision of community is counterpoised to fusing desire, or that which creates a work from death, and it runs in the opposite direction of all nostalgia, of all communal metaphysics. According to Nancy, such a form of community has yet to emerge. The idea is not to shape a communitarian essence, but rather to think the insistent and unusual demand for community, beyond the totalitarianisms which are insinuated everywhere and the techno-economic projects that have substituted for communitarian-communist-humanist projects. In this way, the demand for community would still be unknown to us; why should this demand for community, even with its childish concerns that are at times confusing, be unknown to us? Because community, contrary to the fusing dream, is made of interruption, fragmentation, suspense, of singular beings and their encounters. Therefore, the very idea of a social bond that is insinuated in the reflection on community is crafty, because it precisely omits this *between*. Community as the sharing of a separation given by singularity.

We now come to a curious idea. If community is the opposite of society, it is not because it is the space of an intimacy that society has destroyed, but almost the opposite, because it is the space of distance which society, in its inclination for totalization, never stops evoking. In other words, as Blanchot says in *The Unavowable Community*, community is not about a relationship between the Same and the Same, but a relationship in which the Other intervenes, and he is always irreducible, in dissymmetry. He *introduces* the dissymmetry. On the one hand, then, the infinite of alterity incarnated by the Other devastates the integrity of the subject, making its centered and isolated identity collapse, opening it to an irrevocable exteriority, in a constitutive incompleteness. On the other hand, this dissymmetry impedes everyone from being reabsorbed into a totality

Postcolonial Studies, Vol. 6, No. 1, (2003), pp. 23–36.

that would constitute a widened individuality, which customarily happens when, for example, monks give up everything in order to join a community, but once they give it up they become possessors of everything, as in the Kibbutz, or in real or utopian forms of communism. On the other hand, there is that which we would hardly dare call community, because it is not a community of equals, and would first be an absence of community in the sense that it is an absence of reciprocity, fusion, unity, communion, and possession. This negative community, as Georges Bataille called it, the community of those who do not have a community, assumes the impossibility of coinciding with itself. For it is founded, as he would say, on the absolute of the separation which needs to affirm itself in order to break itself down until it becomes a relation, a paradoxical, senseless relation. A senselessness in such a refusal that Melville's character, Bartleby, perhaps dramatizes in the most extreme manner: the refusal to do work. This is what the community serves for ... nothing. And this, perhaps, is where it starts to become sovereign.

Community and Sovereignty

What is the sovereign, strictly speaking? It is that which exists in a sovereign manner, independent of any utility, of any usefulness, of any necessity, of any finality.[149] The sovereign serves for nothing, and its ends are not driven by a productive logic. Literally, the sovereign is one who lives from the extorted surplus, and whose existence opens up without limit, apart from his own death. The sovereign is the opposite of the slave, the servile, the subjected, whether it be regarding necessity, work, production, accumulation, limits, or death. The sovereign can freely make use of time and the world, and the world's resources. The sovereign's present is not subordinated to the future, and the instant shines autonomously. He or she who lives sovereignly, if we are to radically consider it, lives and dies in the same way as animals, or a god. The sovereign is of the order of play, not work. Sexuality, for example, is useful, thus servile, while eroticism is useless, and in this sense, sovereign. This

---

149. Georges Bataille, *The Accursed Share,* Vol. III, trans. Robert Hurley, (New York: Zone Books, 1991).

implies a gratuitous expenditure. In the same way as laughter, parties, tears, outbursts, everything that has a surplus. Bataille, in his *Essay on Sovereignty*, affirms that this surplus is in some way miraculous, and even divine. Bataille comes to agree with the Gospel, according to which man does not only need bread, he is hungry for miracles. Because the desire for sovereignty, according to Bataille, is in all of us, even in the worker, who with his glass of beer participates to some degree, at least for a moment, in this gratuitous and miraculous element, in this useless, and therefore glorious, expenditure. This can happen with anyone, to the same extent, facing beauty, mournful sadness, the sacred, or even violence. For Bataille, what is most difficult to understand is that these sovereignties, which interrupt the sequential continuity of time, have no object or objective, they come to Nothing, they are Nothing (*Rien*, not *Néant*).

Well, it is clear that the world we live in, says Bataille, is that of utility, accumulation, sequential duration, subordinated operation, useful work, in contradistinction to this dose of chance, arbitrariness, useless splendor, grace or disgrace, that no longer outwardly appears in consecrated ritual forms, as in other times, but rather in diffuse and subjective moments and states, of non-servility, miraculous gratuity, expenditure or merely dissipation. What is at stake in this sovereignty is a loss of self, behind which a refusal of servitude is voiced. Playing with words, we could say: Involuntary Non-Servitude. It is something of this order that is at stake in the notion of sovereignty as it was thought in Bataille, a conception that Habermas considers to be an inheritance from Nietzsche and a precursor to Foucault.[150]

May '68 and the Desire for Community

Let us now return to the topic of community with this non-conventional idea as a backdrop, because it would oppose our productivist and communicational tradition, as much of sovereignty as of community. Perhaps we could accompany the beautiful commentary made by Maurice Blanchot regarding May '68, shortly after his observations on Bataille's work on

---

150. Jürgen Habermas, *The Philosophical Discourse of Modernity*, trans. Frederick Lawrence, (Cambridge, MA: The MIT Press, 1987).

the impossible community, the absent community, the negative community, the community of those who do not have a community.

After a description of the atmosphere of May 1968, which includes the explosive communication, the effervescence, the freedom of speech, the pleasure of being together, a certain innocence, the absence of project, Blanchot refers to the refusal of taking power to which something could be delegated — it is as if it were a declaration of powerlessness. Like a presence that, in order to not limit itself, accepts doing nothing, accepts being there, and is then absent, is dispersed. In describing the uncommon character of this "people" who refuse to endure, to persevere, who ignore the structures that could give them stability, in this mixture of presence and absence, he writes: "That is what makes them formidable for the holders of power that does not acknowledge them: not letting themselves be grasped, being as much the dissolution of the social fact as the stubborn obstinacy to reinvent the latter in a sovereignty the law cannot circumscribe, as it challenges it...."[151] It is this powerless power, asocial society, association that is always ready to dissociate, "always imminent dispersal of a presence momentarily occupying the whole space and nevertheless without a place (utopia), a kind of messianism announcing nothing but its autonomy and its *unworking* [désoeuvrement]," the sneaky loosening of the social bond, but at the same time the inclination to that which is shown to be as much impossible as inevitable — community.

Blanchot, on this point, differentiates the traditional community — that of land, blood, and race — from the elective community. He cites Bataille: "If this world were not endlessly crisscrossed by the convulsive movements of beings in search of each other [...], it would appear like an object of derision offered to those it gives birth to."[152] But what is this convulsive movement of beings in search of one another? Would it be love, as in saying the community of lovers? Or desire, as Negri points out when he says: "The desire for community is the spirit and soul of constituent power — the desire for a community that is as thoroughly real as it is absent, the trajectory and motor of a movement whose essential determination is the demand of

151. Maurice Blanchot, *The Unavowable Community*, trans. Pierre Joris (New York: Station Hill Press, 1988), p. 33.

152. *Ibid,* p. 47.

being, repeated, pressing on an absence."[153] Or is it a movement that cannot bear any name, neither love nor desire, but that attracts the beings in order to throw them toward each other, according to their body or according to their heart and thought, by tearing them from ordinary society?[154] There is something unavowable in this strangeness, unable to be common, it is nevertheless what establishes a community, always provisional and always already deserted. Something between working and unworking....

* * *

In this zigzagging journey, we have traversed the community of the celibate, the community of those who do not have a community, the negative community, the unworking community, the impossible community, the gaming community, the coming community, the community of whatever singularity — several names for a figure of community that is non-fusional, non-unitary, non-totalizable, and non-filial. It remains to be known if this community can be thought, as Negri suggests, as an ontology of the common. The response is insinuated in the first part of this chapter: in Deleuze's terms, inspired by Spinoza, and above all in his work with Guattari, and in the current conditions of an universal machinism, the question is that of the already given plane of immanence, and at the same time, the one always to be built. On the opposite side of the kidnapping of the common, the expropriation of the common, the transcendentalization of the common, it becomes a question of thinking the common as immanent. That is, on the one hand, it is already given, for instance the biopolitical common, and on the other hand it has yet to be built, according to the new figures of community that the common thus conceived could engender.

Perhaps it has also become clear that this reflection on the common and community is likewise, indirectly, an effort to comprehend the logic of the multitude. The challenge is to avoid an excessively molar, heroic, or voluntaristic conception of the

153. Antonio Negri, *Insurgencies*, trans. Maurizia Boscagli, (Minneapolis: University of Minnesota Press, 1999), p. 23.

154. Maurice Blanchot, *The Unavowable Community*, p. 47.

multitude. Maybe, at some moments, a book that is admirable in so many aspects like *Empire*, fall for this temptation, when localizing the resistance of the multitude in names like Beijing, Los Angeles, Nablus, Paris, or Seoul. In fact, these names have to do with struggles that have made and still make noise, in a traditional sense, struggles that everyone recognizes as struggles, sometimes victories that everyone recognizes as victories, and we have every reason to gloat over them. A young philosopher asked himself many years ago if there were not however, even in the multitude, kinds of resistances that were more obscure, more hesitating, voiceless, many other types of resistance whose surroundings we still do not know. *A Thousand Plateaus*, for example, he recalls, would have contributed not so much to the remembrance of struggles that we have already recognized as struggles, but rather contributes to the possibility of the emergence of new struggles, new political problems, a challenge that Negri strives to confront in several passages from his most recent books.

This small itinerary can serve to discover community where community was not to be seen, and not necessarily to recognize community where everyone sees community. It's about detecting new emerging desires of community, new forms of associating and dissociating that are arising, in the most auspicious and desperate contexts.

EXHAUSTION, MADNESS, OUTSIDE

EXHAUSTION AND CREATION

Pathosophy is the name the German neurologist Viktor von Weizsäcker gave to his general clinical practice, which he also refers to as medical anthropology.[155] To quickly summarize his practice — it concerns a science of suffering rather than a science of illness. *Pathos* points less to a painful passivity and more to "that which is experienced." As with the ancient Greeks, a question such as "what happens to you" accents the active dimension of that which happens to us. This is about an experience which is carried out by someone inasmuch as it is followed by him or her. The pathic being, after all, is the being which is able to feel — be it pain or pleasure. To use philosophical terms: it is about a power of being affected, of changing states, of traversing a threshold. For what good is all this if it does not allow us to speak of illness as an event rather than a deficit, or as an inauguration that changes our state? If illness is a form of life, both active and passive at the same time, it calls for an entire rethinking of the living being as pathic, regardless of any objectifying nosography. To live is to suffer, to experiment, with all the singular modulations this implies: wanting, having the power to, having to, etc. But there is a point in the life of an individual where that pathic dimension is accentuated and raised to an exclusive power[156]: the moment of crisis. Paradoxically, it

155. Viktor von Weizsäcker, *Pathosophie,* trans. Joris de Bisschop, Marc Ledoux and others, (Grenoble: Millon, 2011).

156. Jacques Schotte, "Une pensée du clinique: L'oeuvre de Viktor von Weizsäcker,"

119

is precisely where all possibilities open up, even if to the sick person the present appears to be completely blocked. It is crisis that reveals to us the forces which have been at play — and redistributes them, by answering the question: are things going in the direction of life or of death? Crisis is not the result of a series; rather it is a beginning that creates its own time and space, without obeying the coordinates of a world called objective or ontic. Hence the opposition between the pathic and the ontic, which was so important to von Weizsäcker, and which would force the knowledge of suffering to move, away from the medical gaze toward the domain of subjectivity, focusing on the mutation of experience and the new possibilities this opens up.[157] If crisis inhabits such a privileged place, it is because crisis is the means of "putting one's life into form anew, in a different way, and globally," departing from a rupture with the continuity or identity of the subject. Illness thus appears as a work of reconstruction, a new way of relating to life. The very definition of subjectivity that von Weizsäcker proposed fits this principle: subjectivity is conceived as a "relation to what is on the ground." Illness is the moment when this ground erupts. Or to put it differently: at critical moments, when causal chains are interrupted and the continuity of world and self is broken, it is the ground that cracks and erupts — we reach the bottom, perishing.

It is impossible to automatically transpose all these considerations onto the domain of so-called mental illness, since this would mean ignoring the heterogeneity between the physiological and psychological domains — yet we can still trace the eruption of this ground. François Tosquelles, a Catalan psychiatrist who accurately noted the similarity between concentration camps and psychiatric hospitals of the Second World War era, wrote a book with a title that is hard to outdo in its suggestiveness concerning such subjective upheavals: *The Lived Experience of the End of the World in Madness*. The living-through of catastrophe appears like an existential commotion, with its procession of troubling images: earthquake, end of the world, death, and resurrection by way of a spiritual

notes from the lectures given at the Faculté de psychologie et des sciences de l'éducation at the Université catholique de Louvain, directed by Ph. Lakeuche and reviews by the author; mimeographed.

157. Viktor von Weizsäcker, op. cit.

life, etc. But there is a task that always imposes itself, despite the destruction that is in progress: creativity. "In paraphrenia or in delirium of a paranoid structure, the sick person often manages to edify a new world, he or she becomes like the Prajapati of whom Jung speaks: the egg engendering itself, the egg of the world within which he himself hatches himself...."[158] Thus with every sick person — beyond the process wherein the personality dissolves — there is an effort, a "vital need," a drive to arrive at a "new form of life, of unitary wholeness." The genius of Freud already opened such a path: "The paranoiac rejects the universe [...] through his work of delirium. What we take for a morbid production, the formation of delirium, is really an attempt at healing, a reconstruction." Tosquelles nevertheless insists that a lived experience of the end of the world is not exclusive to schizophrenia, and that this matrix of catastrophe/creation fulfills a broader function even if it most dramatically displays itself within the mad person. Like Goldstein, for whom the catastrophic reaction is not the end of a chain, but rather the condition for a new beginning: "That is why we should not conceive *Erlebnis* of the end of the world as an *image* that reflects *supposedly real phenomena* of a psyche that is about to destroy itself. On the contrary: this lived event is the pure and simple manifestation of the continuity and even surplus of human efforts." Hence Tosquelles' conclusion, which is uncommon for a psychiatrist: "Madness is a creation, not a passivity."[159] At the clinical level, the existential catastrophe which finds its most precise expression in the phantasm of the end of the world implies the task of saving one's existence, affirming one's originality, or simply being reborn, creating one's life. Guattari offered an expanded account of madness, but it was also an account that goes beyond madness, and which is situated in another context: "It's in passing through this chaotic "earthing," this perilous oscillation, that something else becomes possible, that ontological bifurcations and the emergence of coefficients of processual creativity can occur."[160]

158. François Tosquelles, *Le vécu de la fin du monde dans la folie*, (Toulouse: Ed. De L'Areppi, 1986), p. 75.

159. *Ibid*, p. 108.

160. Félix Guattari, *Chaosmosis*, trans. Paul Bains and Julian Pefanis, (Indianapolis: Indiana University Press, 1995), p. 82.

Exhaustion

Exhaustion may be the term that acutely defines, albeit enigmatically, the hesitant and unnecessary passage from catastrophe to creation. And in this context, it could also bring to mind the interchangeability of the "nothing is possible" and the "everything is possible." It may be necessary here to recall the difference Deleuze points out between tiredness and exhaustion. Tiredness is part of the dialectic of work and productivity: one rests in order to return to activity. Tiredness comes when we realize the possibles that inhabit us, choosing and obeying certain objectives more than others, realizing certain projects, following clear preferences. Exhaustion, on the other hand, is another matter entirely. Let us follow Deleuze's lead. The exhausted is he who, having exhausted his purpose, is himself exhausted, such that this dissolution of the subject corresponds to the abolition of the world. Where tiredness perceives its activity as temporarily compromised and is prepared to resume it, exhaustion, on the other hand, is pure inactivity, pure testimonial. Its typical posture is not the man lying down but of the insomniac, sitting up, his head between his hands, the amnesiac witness (*Nacht und Träume*, the sublime film for television).[161] Using a Beckettian gestuality, the tongue is the first to disappear — ("Beckett could endure words less and less")[162] — the last being language, for after all language is the realm of the possible. The tongue identifies goals, preferences, choices: this or that, this way or that way, now or later, exiting or entering. It is necessary to wear out, to exhaust this mechanical spring of sense. The exhausted may even combine or recombine the variables, mull them over to the point of exhaustion, and the disjointed terms may subsist, but they no longer serve any purpose. Total permutability, even when it obeys an extreme rigor, is inseparable from the evacuation of interest — it is "for nothing" and it is the death of the Ego.

In Beckett, the attempt is made to exhaust words, to incite their dissolution into atoms, to deplete them entirely. Afterwards, it is time to restore them to the voices that enunciate them, to the waves or flows that distribute the "corpuscles

---

161. Samuel Beckett, *Nacht und Träume* (1982). Television play broadcast in Germany. See <http://www.youtube.com/watch?v=yWtIatoBK4M>.

162. Gilles Deleuze, *L'épuisé*, Paris: Minuit (1992), p. 103.

of language." Next come the Others that emit them, evoking possible worlds. After that comes the space that incarnates potentialities, as in *Quad*.[163] Only after these spheres have been exhaustively explored, and therefore "accomplished" or "performed" (*accomplies*)[164] — that is to say, emptied out at the limit of silence and the void, do we arrive at the point at which it is discovered that "nothing more, not even history, has been possible for a long time now," that we are all part of a strange, dead language. The exhausted is that which has the power to "produce a void or create holes, to loosen the tourniquet of words, to mop up the transpiration of the voices, to extricate oneself from memory and reason." Only then can there arise "the small, illogical image, amnesiac, nearly aphasic, now sustaining itself in the void, now trembling out in the open."[165] And so, when nothing else remains, there arises the "pure image," an intensity that drives words away and dissolves stories and recollections, storing a fantastic amount of potential energy that it unleashes when it dissipates." Deleuze adds: "What counts in the image is not its impoverished content but rather the mad energy it captures, ready to explode, for which reason images never last long. Images are confused with detonation, combustion, the dissipation of their condensed energy. [...] The image [...] captures all that makes it possible to explode." The works of Beckett would therefore be viewed as an exploration of pure intensities, in which it is necessary to create holes in language, given that words lack this "punctuation of dehiscence," this "disconnection" that arises like a "wave from the depths that is proper to art."[166]

Images

This is a theme that Deleuze dealt with in *Essays Critical and Clinical*. Literature, as it "splits" words, liberates Visions and Auditions that exist *outside* language but that can only emerge through language. The Sea, in Melville, The Desert, in

---

163. Samuel Beckett, *Quad* [*Quadrat 1+2*] (1981). Television play broadcast in Germany. See: <http://www.ubu.com/film/beckett_quad.html>.

164. Gilles Deleuze, *L'épuisé*, (Paris: Minuit, 1992), p. 103.

165. *Ibid*, p. 72.

166. *Ibid*, p. 105.

Lawrence. In Beckett's *The Exhausted*, Deleuze discovers a Language I (the language of names), a Language II (the language of voices) and a Language III (the language of images). The latter has nothing to do with things, words, or voices, but with immanent limits, hiatuses, holes and tears through which the pure image conforms to "the indefinite as the celestial state." An image, then, dislocated from words, voice, stories, memories, and space, breaks up "the combination of words and the flow of voices," and forces words "to become images, movements, songs, or poems." Thus, the image defies the language that imprisons and suffocates us, a language full of calculation, memories, stories, meanings, intentions, habits. Words in themselves, given their adherences, are incapable of this "disconnection," unless it is they themselves who are forced aside and turned upside down, exhibiting their outsides, as in the bloody Beckettian struggle against the "old style" that, with the help of Beethoven, Schubert, Rembrandt or van Velde, brings to light the *visible in itself* or the *audible in itself*, which are tangential to the invisible and inaudible. In Deleuze, and in his aesthetics as a whole, there exists a challenge to achieve this "external determination of the undefined as pure intensity." This does not entail, however, abandoning words, since it deals precisely with the effort to force them aside, in a dislocated transmutation.

In another context, while discussing the redundancy between "order words" and the images transmitted by the circuits of information, David Lapoujade reminds us that it is not a matter of opposing the slogans, whether by silence or screaming or music, but rather of "passing through the other side of the slogan, the exterior that is its nonlinguistic material, but which never ceases to work through the slogan and by extension, the entirety of language. [...] This other side constitutes the intensive aspect of language, the aspect through which language is ceaselessly operated on by continual variations, almost musical in nature, chromatic variations that do not tend toward silence, music, or outcry, but which serve as a tensor."[167] Hence the challenge of untying the relation of reciprocal correspondence between language and the visible, of separating seeing and speaking, as Blanchot would suggest. ("To see is not to speak"). It is not to place oneself outside language, for

167. David Lapoujade, "Deleuze: política e informação," *Cadernos de Subjetividade*, op. cit., p. 165.

"language has no exterior," and there is nothing outside of it, but to pass through the outside of language in an operation that consists in turning it upside down. Let us insist on this point: not "inverting" it — which would imply positing a closed system that could be made to collapse, but "turning it upside down" in all its parts. The political background for such a differentiation is found in what is called assemblage. Every assemblage tends to contain its own outside, and this "irreducible" outside is constantly reborn, as part of the system: "It has to do, above all, with noting that which, from within, bears witness to this outside; it has to do with establishing a diagnostic, a survey of the forces to which this outside bears witness."[168]

Refusal and Intensity

We can now amplify the spectrum of these notes. Exhaustion may be understood in the primary sense that Deleuze gave it: the exhaustion of the possible, in which the exhausted exhausts himself as a reservoir of possibles and has exhausted the possibles of language, as well as the potentialities of space and the very possibility of action. This exhausted figure appears passive, but we cannot fail to acknowledge the range of Beckett's project, which resonates with characters dealt with in the literary studies of Deleuze, such as Bartleby, or Billy Budd, in Melville; Dostoyevsky's *The Idiot*[169]; the Hunger Artist in Kafka, and so on. In all of these cases a certain stubbornness is manifest, together with an inexpressible refusal of the world and its dialectic: a vital, unavoidable affirmativity, an "obstinate Spinozism" whose political implications have yet to be explored, in a key much different than that proposed by Theodor Adorno, for example, in his lovely commentary on *Endgame*.[170] In this text, Adorno undoes the false relationship of Beckett with existentialism, a common misunderstanding during the late 1950s. As Adorno says, in Beckett, the absurd does not preserve the individual, his identity, his freedom, his sense, such that "the

168. *Ibid*, p. 166.

169. Philippe Mengue makes use of this figure in *Faire l'idiot: la politique de Deleuze*, (Paris: Germina, 2013).

170. Theodor Adorno, "Intento de entender fin de partida", Notas sobre Literatura, *Obra completa*, p. 11. (Akal, Básica de Bolsillo, 2003). Written in 1958.

situation loses its ontologico-existential components." Thus, the dissociation of the unity of consciousness does not reveal "the human condition" in its purportedly universal essence, but reveals instead its historical contingency, which the post-war period reduced to the obstinate survival of the biological body. "The *dramatis personae* seem to be dreaming of their own death, in a 'refuge' in which 'it is time for this to end.' The end of the world is viewed as certain, as though it were self-evident. [...] In Beckett, the characters behave in a primitive fashion corresponding to their circumstances after the catastrophe, which has mutilated them in such a way that they cannot respond in any other way: They are flies struggling after being hit by the fly swatter."[171] Adorno sees Beckett as a "realist," whose universe, reduced to the "sordid and useless," is a copy and photonegative of the managed world.

This is certainly quite different from the reading that Deleuze provides, taking into consideration the impersonal, insomniac, phantasmic dimension of Beckettian characters and texts, without any judgment of value. The "diluted self" is not a victim, but passes through our time like an operator that disarticulates it schizophrenically. Note the numerous references to this operation of dissolution in *Anti-Oedipus*, through the use of disjunctive synthesis: "The schizophrenic is dead or alive, not at the same time, but one or the other in terms of a distance that he overflies, that he glides over. He is the son or the father, not one or the other, but one in the extremity of the other like the two extremities of a stick in a space that cannot be decomposed. This is the significance of the disjunctions in which Beckett inscribes his characters and the events that spring from them. [...] They are 'trans-living-dead, trans-father-son.' [...] The contradictions do not cancel one another out. On the contrary, like a sack of spores, it releases them along with various other singularities that it improperly contains. [...] Molloy and Moran do not refer to persons, but to singularities that arrive from every direction, agents of evanescent production. This is the free disjunction: the differential positions subsist and even acquire a freely determined value, but all are occupied by a subject without a face and 'trans-positional.'"[172] Or, more

171. Theodor Adorno, *Teoria Estética*. (São Paulo: Livraria Martins Fontes, 1988), p. 44.

172. Gilles Deleuze and Félix Guattari, *Anti-Oedipus*, trans. Robert Hurley, Mark Seem and Helen R. Lane. (London and New York: Continuum, 2004). Written in 1972. pp. 85-86.

radically, these singularities yearn to penetrate the "cosmic and spiritual agitation" like a singular atom. There is no lamenting the condition of a subject shattered in this way. There is rather a rare joy, as if through him a new adventure has opened. In *The Exhausted*, Deleuze refers to the "fantastic dissolution of the I." The influence of Blanchot is explicit: "What Blanchot said about Musil applies perfectly to Beckett: the heightened degree of exactitude and the most extreme degree of dissolution; the indefinite exchange of mathematical formulae and the search for the formless or the unformulated. These are the meanings of exhaustion, and both together are necessary for the abolition of the real. Many authors are too polished. They content themselves with declaring the work complete and with it, the death of the Ego. And yet we remain in the realm of the abstract so long as "how things are" is not shown, or how an "inventory" is made, including its errors, and how the Ego decomposes, including the stink and the agony of it."[173] Joyce is probably the object of this reticent evaluation, and the contrast between Joyce and Beckett may find their equivalent in the pair Carroll-Artaud, as it is presented in *Logic of Sense* ("We would not trade all of Carroll for a single page of Antonin Artaud"). In any event, in invoking the exhausted, we are no longer dealing with the contrast between surface and depth, or with the play of meaning and the lived body, on one hand, or with infra-significance, on the other, but rather with something that Blanchot observed with great acuity in the course of Beckett's career: Narrative increasingly gives way to struggle, and figures give way to remains, such that "neutral" speech allows the impersonal, the incessant, the interminable, the nameless, the unnamable, to rise to the surface, an "empty speech that for better or worse recovers the porous and agonizing self" of one condemned to "exhaust the infinite."[174] In the same Blanchotian vein, Deleuze reassumes the singular status of the night, following Beckett: The night does not consist of the interval between two days, a mere interruption separating two daytimes. For this reason, it imposes a state that is other than the waking state (of the day) or the sleeping state (which covers it). Only insomnia is up to this task: We see here what Blanchot seeks to reclaim, a dream of insomnia, "which is a matter of

---

173. Gilles Deleuze, *L'epuisé*, (Paris: Ed. Minuit, 1992), p. 62.

174. Maurice Blanchot, *Le livre à venir*, op. cit., p. 313.

127

exhaustion," Deleuze adds.[175] For it is in insomnia, in dissolution, in the shapeless, by means of the porous subject, where the surface of words open out upon their outside, shaking off their senses, that a "determination of the undefined" is attained.

Political Chords

It is useful to refer here to the interpretation of François Zourabichvili, who brought to light the political dimension of this text. "The Exhausted," he recalls, was written not long after the fall of the Berlin Wall.[176] In a certain sense, an entire mode of thinking the possible in the political domain fell with the Wall. The *a priori* possibilities — the utopias, the ideologies, the projects for another world — were swept away. It is well known how the left deplored this development, how the right rejoiced in it, and to what extent a certain postmodernist strain subsequently clung to a skepticism that it wore as a badge of virtue. In Deleuze, however, there is not a drop of pity or lamentation in the description of the character of the Exhausted. It is as if the exhaustion of the possible (previously determined) was a precondition for reaching some other mode of the possible (the not yet determined) — in other words, not the eventual realization of a preordained possible but the necessary creation of a possible against a background of impossibility. The possible is no longer confined to the realm of the imagination, or the dream, or some ideality, but becomes coextensive with reality by virtue of its own productivity. The possible expands in the direction of a field — the field of the possibles. How is a field of possibles opened? Are moments of insurrection and revolution not precisely those that allow us to glimpse the distant gleaming of a field of possibles? In this way, the relationship between what happens and what is possible is inverted. It is no longer the possible that gives way to the actual, but the actual which creates a possible — as much as the crisis was not the result of a process but the event based on which the process was unleashed. "The event creates a new existence, produces a new subjectivity (new relationships with the body, time,

175. Gilles Deleuze, op. cit.

176. François Zourabichvili, "Deleuze e o possível (sobre o involuntarismo na política)", in É. Alliez (org.), *Gilles Deleuze: uma vida filosófica.* (São Paulo: Ed. 34, 2000.)

sexuality, environment, culture, work…).[177] Such moments, whether individual or collective (such as May 1968) correspond to a subjective and collective mutation, in the sense that what was once routine now becomes intolerable, just as the unimaginable becomes thinkable, desirable, visible. This is when the figure of the Seer emerges, a figure that Deleuze continually evokes in his work on cinema, and which, as a concept, has garnered the praise of Zourabichvili. The Seer perceives something in a given situation that surpasses it, that overflows it, and that has nothing to do with fantasy. The Seer takes reality as its object within a dimension that extrapolates its empirical surroundings, in order to capture its virtualities, which are entirely real but have not yet unfolded. What the Seer sees, as in the case of Beckett and his insomniac, is the pure image, in its brilliance and its extinction, its rise and its fall, in its consummation. The Seer perceives intensity, potential, virtuality. It is not the future the Seer sees, nor the dream, nor the idea, nor the perfect project, but rather forces that are on their way to redesigning the real.

Deleuze's text is traversed by this alternative: to realize a possible previously given or to effect a possible that remains undefined, that is, to actualize what is virtual, to affirm a new sensibility. He who realizes a possible may just as well not realize it, in which case it remains in a state of mere possibility. In Deleuze, however, there is the postulation of a necessity. What bores or paralyzes us, Zourabichvili recalls, is precisely the fact that today anything is possible, in the sense that alternatives are given, presented to us as though they were a multiple choice question, but also in the sense that everything appears consigned to the state of possibility. From this point of view, "everything is possible" is equivalent to "nothing is possible." The author insists: whenever we orbit a mere possibility, we are in the realm of a pseudo-experience that distracts us from effectivity and necessity.[178] For this reason, an attempt is made to drag the possible into the realm of actualization wherever it emerges.[179] The conclusion is clear: We create by exhausting the

177. Gilles Deleuze and Félix Guattari, "Mai '68 n'a pas eu lieu," in *Deux régimes de fous*, org. David Lapoujade. (Paris: Minuit, 1968).

178. There is, for this reason, an abyssal distance from Agamben's thinking on the subject, with its reflections on "the power of the no" — with political implications yet to be defined.

179. François Zourabichvili, op. cit., p. 354.

possible. It is necessary to learn to "breathe without oxygen" in order to profit from an "an energy more elementary and an air more rarefied (Sky-Necessity)"[180] — this is Deleuze's perversion.

Untying the Connections

We can now return to the question from a broader point of view. Exhaustion is not mere tiredness, nor a renunciation of the body and mind but rather, more radically, it is the fruit of a disbelief, an operation of disconnection. It consists of unleashing the possibilities that are presented to us relative to the alternatives that surround us as well as the clichés that mediate and dampen our relation with the world in order to make it tolerable. While these clichés make the world tolerable, because they are unreal, they conversely end up making the world intolerable and unworthy of belief.

Exhaustion undoes that which "binds" us to the world, that "imprisons" us in it and others, that "captures" us with its words and images, that "comforts" us with an allusion of entirety (of I, of We, of meaning, of freedom, of the future) in which we have long ceased to believe, even as we have remained attached to them. There is, no doubt, in this act of separation, a certain cruelty, which is in no way absent from the works of Beckett, but this cruelty carries within itself a certain pity of another kind.[181] Only through such a negation of adherence, such an unfastening, such an emptying, together with the impossibility that is established in this way, which Deleuze calls "rarefaction" (as much as he called for "vacuoles" of silence in order to be able, at least, to have something to say) does the necessity of something else arise, something which with excessive pomp, we call "the creation of the possible." We should not merely abandon this formula to the publicity experts, however; we should also avoid overloading it with an excessively imperative or

180. Gilles Deleuze, *Lógica do Sentido*, trad. Luiz Salinas Fortes. (São Paulo, Perspectiva, 1974), p. 329.

181. It is similar to the warrior-god Indra: "Witness to another justice, capable at times of an incomprehensible cruelty but at others an unknown mercy (inasmuch as it cuts the ties...)." Gilles Deleuze and Félix Guattari, "1227: Treatise on Nomadology — The War Machine." *A Thousand Plateaus: Capitalism and Schizophrenia* (1987), pp. 351-423.

capricious incumbency, replete with "will." Perhaps we should preserve, as Beckett does, the trembling dimension which, amidst the most calculated precision, in his visual poetry, point to that "indefinite state" to which beings are elevated and whose correlative, even in the most concrete contexts, is the vagueness of becomings, at the point where they achieve their effect of deterritorialization. If Zourabichvili is correct in detecting "political chords" in *The Exhausted*, this is because Deleuze himself never ceased to extract such chords from the authors he analyzed, from Melville to Kafka, from Lawrence to Ghérasim Luca. In the clinic, in art or in politics, there is a circuit that runs from the extenuation of the possible to the impossible, and from there to the creation of the possible, without linearity, circularity or determinism. It consists of a complex and reversible game between "nothing is possible" and "everything is possible."

INHUMAN POLYPHONY IN
THE THEATER OF MADNESS

We are the Ueinzz Theater Company, established in São Paulo, Brazil seventeen years ago. Lunatics, therapists, performers, maids, philosophers, "normopaths"– once on stage no
one can tell the difference. It's a sort of Ship of Fools, adrift
inside — and outside — the artistic circuit. We rehearse every
week, we have produced five theater pieces, we've given over
300 performances, we travel a lot throughout Brazil, and also
abroad, and all of this is part of our magnificent repertoire. But
this concreteness does not guarantee anything. Sometimes we
spend months in the stagnation of insipid weekly rehearsals.
Sometimes we ask ourselves if we have actually ever performed,
or whether we will go back to performing. Some actors disappear, sponsorships dwindle, scripts are forgotten, and the theater company itself seems like some intangible virtuality. And
then, suddenly, a date for a performance appears, some theater
becomes available, a patron or sponsor shows up, and there is
just the glimpse of a season, with an invitation to perform in
the Cariri or in Finland. The costume designer spruces up the
dusty rags, actors who had disappeared months ago reappear,
sometimes even running away from internment.... But even
when it all "happens," it is in straddling that fine line that separates construction from collapse. We move alongside Blanchot's
acute intuition that the basis of a work is unworking (*desoeuvrement*). And we follow Foucault's hypothesis that with the

historical decline of madness' aura and its subsequent transformation into a mental illness, madness reappears as unreason. That is, as redress, the absence of work, as "absolute rupture of the work." I would place the trajectory of our performances on that moving limit, between madness and unreason, like a steep experiment over the abyss, where chance, ruination, passivity, and the neutral speak: the outside.

First example: we were going to perform "Daedalus" at a major Brazilian theater festival. The cast was about to go on stage. Each actor was getting prepared to utter in Greek the combative clash that begins this piece; one "cannot make heads or tails of it" — according to the complimentary review of one critic from the São Paulo press. I wait, tense; in my head I run over the words we are supposed to shout at each other in menacing tones and frenetic rush. I am scanning the audience when I notice that our narrator is standing a few meters away from the microphone — he appears to be disorientated. I go up to him, and he tells me that he has lost his script. I slip my hand into his trousers' pocket, where I find the complete bundle of papers. The actor stares at the papers, which I hold up to his face. He seems not to recognize them. He puts on and takes off his glasses. And he murmurs that this time he will not take part in the play — that this was the night of his death. We exchange a few words and a few minutes later I am relieved to see him back at the microphone. But his voice, which was normally tremulous and stirring, was now slurred and washed out. In the middle of a scene in which he plays Charon, he suddenly walks right across the stage and heads for the theater exit. I find him sitting in the street, deathly still, murmuring the demand for an ambulance — his time had come. I kneel down beside him and he tells me: "I'm going to the swamp." The situation lightens up after this and we negotiate: he would accept a cheeseburger from McDonald's instead of the ambulance. I hear the final applause coming from inside the theater, and the public starts to exit through the small door that leads to the street, where both he and I are. What they see as they exit is Hades, king of the underworld (my character), kneeling at the feet of the living-dead Charon. And for this we receive the respect of each member of the audience who passes by us, because, for them, this intimate scene of collapse seems to be part of the performance. The whole thing by a razor's edge. It is by a razor's edge that we perform, it is by a razor's edge that we don't die. Work, unworking, absence of work.

Let's go back a few years. It is the Company's very first rehearsal, at the *A Casa* day clinic, where our group began, before it became autonomous. In a theatrical exercise on the different methods of communication between human beings, all the members of the group were asked in turn to state the other languages they spoke, apart from Portuguese. One patient, who never speaks and who only produces a sort of nasal sound, like some discordant mantra, replied immediately, with a clarity and assurance quite uncommon for him: German! Everyone is surprised, as no one knew that he spoke German. And what word do you know in German? Ueinzz. And what does Ueinzz mean in German? Ueinzz. Everyone laughed — this is the language that signifies for itself, that folds within itself, an esoteric, mysterious, glossolalic language. Inspired by material collected from the laboratories, the directors at the time, Renato Cohen and Sérgio Penna, brought their proposed script to the company: a group of nomads, lost in the desert, goes out in search of a shining tower, and on their way they come across obstacles, entities, and storms. When they come across an oracle, he must indicate to them, in his sibylline tongue, the most adequate course for the pilgrims to take. The actor is promptly chosen to play the part of the oracle: the one who speaks German. When asked where the tower of Babel is, he must reply: Ueinzz. The patient quickly gets into the role, and everything goes well together: the black hair and mustache, the small, solid body of a Turkish Buddha, his mannerisms, both aloof and schizoid, his gaze, both vague and scrutinizing, of someone who is constantly in conversation with the invisible. It is true that he is capricious, for when they ask him: Oh Great Oracle of Delphi, where is the Tower of Babel? he sometimes replies with a silence, sometimes with a grunt, and at other times he says Germany or Bauru [in the state of São Paulo] until they ask him more specifically: Oh Great Oracle, what is the magic word in German, and then, without fail, comes the Ueinzz that everyone has been waiting for. The most inaudible of patients, the one who urinates in his trousers and vomits in the director's plate, is charged with the crucial responsibility of telling the nomadic people the way out of Darkness and Chaos. After being uttered, the sound of his answer must proliferate through

135

the loud-speakers scattered about the theater in concentric circles, amplifying in dizzying echoes Ueinzz, Ueinzz, Ueinzz! The inhuman voice we could not hear finds in the scenic and ritual space a magical and poetic effectiveness. When the play was given this sound as its name, we had difficulty in imagining how it should be spelled. The invitation went with "weeinz," the folder had "ueinzz," the poster played with transcribing the word in a wide variety of possibilities, of Babel-like proportions. Today we are the Ueinzz Theater Company. We were born out of an a-signifying rupture, as Guattari would say.

Our third play was inspired by Batman and Ítalo Calvino. It was called Gotham-SP (São Paulo), an invisible or mythological city, taken from comic strips, movie screens, and the most persistent deliriums of one of our actors. Every night in Gotham-SP, from his tower, the mayor yells indiscriminately at tycoons, prostitutes, and psychiatrists. He promises worlds and wealth, control and anarchy, bread and cloning. The emperor Kublai Khan, nearly deaf and nearly blind, is the receiver of lost voices. A single resident repeats in her cubicle: "It's cold here." A passenger requests the company of a taxi-driver on a rainy night and recites fragments from Nietzsche or Pessoa. The decadent diva searches for that impossible note, Ophelia comes out of a water barrel seeking her beloved, the angels try to understand where they have just landed, Joshua, revived, demands a new order in the world. Singular speeches that clash in inhuman polyphony, sonorous, visual, scenic, metaphysical. Dissonant voices and sounds that no emperor or mayor manages to orchestrate, much less suppress. Each of those beings who appear on stage carry their icy or torrid world on their fragile bodies.... One thing is certain: from the bottom of their pallid isolation, these beings seek or invoke another community of bodies and souls. A community of those who have no community (Bataille), a community to come (Blanchot), an inoperative community (Nancy), a community of celibates (Deleuze), the coming community (Agamben).

I would now like to propose a theoretical leap, which in my opinion brings all these episodes together. What is at stake in this theatrical, paratheatrical, or performative device is the singular, unreasonable subjectivity of the actors and nothing more. That is, what is being staged or acted out are manners of perceiving, feeling, dressing, positioning oneself, moving, speaking, thinking, asking questions, offering or removing oneself from the gaze of the other as well as from the others' enjoyment. It is also a way of representing without representing, associating while disassociating, of living and dying, of simultaneously being on stage and feeling at home, in that precarious presence, at once concrete and intangible which makes everything extremely serious, and at the same time "neither here nor there," as defined by the composer Livio Tragtenberg — leaving in the middle of a performance, crossing the stage, bag in hand, because your part has now come to an end; one moment, letting go of everything, because your time has come and soon you are going to die, the next entering and getting involved in every scene like a center midfielder in a game of football[182]; then conversing with your line-feeder who should be hidden, and revealing his presence, then turning into a toad.... Or then grunting or croaking, or like Kafka's nomads in *The Great Wall of China*, speaking like magpies, or just saying Ueinzz....

I can't stop thinking that it is this life on stage, "life by a razor's edge," that constitutes the peculiarities of this experience. Some in the audience are under the impression that they themselves are the living-dead and that real life is on the other side of the stage. In fact, in a context marked by the control of life (bioPower), the modes of vital resistance proliferate in the most unusual of ways. One of them consists literally of putting *life* on stage, not bare, brutal life, which, as Agamben says, is reduced by bioPower to the state of survival, but life in the state of variation: "minor" modes of living, which inhabit our major modes, and which, on stage or off, gain scenic or performative visibility, even when one is on the edge of death or collapse, on the edge of stuttering or grunting, of collective hallucination or limit-experiences. Within the restricted parameters which I referred to, here is a device — among others — for a hesitant and always indecisive, inconclusive, and without promises, experimentation for changing *Power over life* into *power of life*.

Permit me to put this in a broader, more contemporary, biopolitical context: On the one hand, life was assaulted by Power, that is, Power penetrated all spheres of existence, fully mobilized them, and put them to work. Everything from genes to the body, affects, psychism, even intelligence, imagination,

---

182. Soccer (association football).

and creativity, have all been violated, invaded, colonized, if not directly expropriated by the Powers. The various mechanisms through which they are exercised are anonymous, scattered, flexible, and rhizomatic. Power itself has become "postmodern," undulating, uncentered, net-like, molecular. Taking this into consideration, power has a more direct effect over our ways of perceiving, feeling, loving, thinking, and even creating. If before, we still imagined that we had spaces that were protected from the direct interference of the powers (the body, the unconscious, subjectivity), and we had the illusion of preserving in these areas some independence, today our life appears entirely subsumed within those mechanisms of modulating existence. Thus even sex, language, communication, oneiric life, even faith, none of these still preserve any exteriority in relation to the mechanisms of control and monitoring. To summarize it in a sentence: power is not exercised from outside, nor from above, but more as if it were from within, steering our social vitality from head to toe. We are no longer struggling with a transcendent or even repressive power; rather we are forced to reconcile with a more inherent, productive power. This biopower does not seek to arrest life, but to take control of it, to intensify it, to make the most of it. Therein lies our extreme difficulty in resisting: we hardly even know where power is, or where we are, what power dictates to us, what we want from it; it is we ourselves who take on the task of administrating our own control. Power never got so far or so deep into the kernel of subjectivity and of life itself as in this contemporary biopower.

But when it appears that "everything has been dominated," as the lyrics of a Brazilian funk song say, at the end of the line there is a suggestion of a u-turn: that which appeared to be subdued, controlled, and dominated, that is, "life," which reveals in the process of expropriation its indomitable power, no matter how erratic it may be. That which appeared to be entirely subsumed by capital, or reduced to mere passivity — "life," "intelligence," "affection," "sociability" — now appears like an inexhaustible reservoir of meaning, a source of forms of existence, an embryo of directions that extrapolate the command structures, the calculations of the established powers and formatted subjectivity.

What would be required would be to tread these two major routes, bioPower and biopower, as a Moebius strip. Thus, if today capital and the governmentality that corresponds to it enters life on a scale never seen before, and saps its creative strength, the opposite is also true: life itself fights back, revived. And if the ways of seeing, feeling, thinking, perceiving, dwelling, dressing, of situating oneself, no matter how singular these may be, become an object of interest and capital investment and molecular monitoring, they also become a source of value that can, by themselves, become a vector for valorization or self-valorization or even of deviation. For example, when a group of prisoners composes and records their own music, what they show and sell is not only their music, nor their harsh life stories, but their style, their perceptions, their disgust, their caustic sarcasm, their way of dressing, of "living" in prison, of gesticulating, of protesting — their life, in short. Their only capital being their life, in their extreme state of survival and resistance, that's what they capitalize, self-valorize and what produces value. Taken from this point of view, if it is clear that capital increasingly appropriates subjectivity and forms of life, subjectivity is itself biopolitical capital, which virtually everyone increasingly has the use of, whether they are those so-called marginals, so-called lunatics, prisoners, or indigenous peoples, but also anyone and everyone with a singular lifestyle that belongs to them or which is given to them to invent — with the political consequences yet to be determined.

It's clear that bioPower and the new mechanisms of governmentality make individual and collective life an object of domination, of calculation, of manipulation, of intervention, if not of fetishization or aestheticization — and that there is a corresponding capitalization in this process. But it is necessary to add, at least in the case of so-called "minorities," that life resists such control mechanisms, and reinvents its coordinates of enunciation and self-enunciation.

In the case of madness — and perhaps that is the meaning of "unreason-subject-of-itself," as evoked once by Foucault — this happens in two simultaneous movements. On one hand, madness de-subjectifies itself according to unexpected lines of force, undoing familiar, professional, social, national, and religious identities — blurring borders, dismantling limits. On the other, it tries singular, plural, collective and inhuman ways of subjectivation. In this paradoxical movement, madness escapes the double straight jacket that imprisoned it, cutting through the limits which the subjectifying objectification would have imposed. If madness, as we know from Foucault, was expelled from the social collective, locked away and silenced in the 17th century, and then, with the advent of psychiatric medicine in the 19th century, it became mental illness, and consequently the object of moral, later medical, and finally psychological treatment, a schizoid flow never ceased to cut through the limits which scientific rationality reserved for it. The flow slides through the entire social body, schizophrenizing the surroundings and disseminating itself through the most varied domains, even through collective, political, and poetic practices, according to the sharp intuition of Deleuze and Guattari.

Therefore, it would be necessary to insert our experience in that fluctuating lineage which goes from the history of madness to the schizoid flow, and which runs into the realm of the performing arts.[183] This is how it was intuited, since the beginning of our trajectory, by Renato Cohen, a well known theorist and proponent of performance art in Brazil. Commenting on his experiences with our company, whose activities he occasionally defined as a *work in progress*, Cohen wrote: "The actors of the Company have a rare ally on their side who destroys representation in its most artificial sense: time. The time of the uncommon actor is mediated by all his dialogues; it is traversed by subtexts which become the actual text itself. In dialogues, the reply does not come immediately, nor is it rational; rather it goes through other mental circuits. There is a delay, a scenic slowing down, that puts the whole audience in production. The actor, in an intuitive manner, moves between Stanislavskian identification and Brechtian distancing. And he becomes excited by the applause of the audience; he performs his dramatic "bullfight" by measuring forces with the audience and with his own inner shadows." This is not the fictional time of representation, but the time of the actor or performer, who enters and exits his character, thus allowing other dimensions of his acting to be seen: "It is in that narrow passage from representation to a less deliberate acting, with its space for improvisation and spontaneity, that live art treads, along with the terms 'happening' and 'performance.' It is also that tenuous limit

183. See for example, John Rajchman's formula on extra-disciplinary spaces and de-disciplinizing moments.

where life and art approach one another. As one breaks away from representation, from fiction, a space opens up for the unpredictable, and therefore for living, since life is synonymous with the unpredictable and risk,"[184] says Cohen, inadvertently getting close to Foucault's last formulation, in a text on Canguilhem, where he defined life as an error. In the group's experimentation, several movements confirm this insight. "Actors who abandon their positions in order to attend the others' scenes, and then resume the dramatic sequence again. Actors who give lengthy monologues, and who also abandon them without finishing their sentences. Such strident distribution of errors, of discoveries, of script reinvention, is built in front of the audience. The performance then becomes a ritual, where everyone witnesses the impossible going on, the curved bodies dancing, the inaudible voices that gain amplified strength thanks to the electronics installed for the performance."[185] The microphones are visible, since the "sound that remains in the sub-conscious is the sound of the media — the sound of television, of radio, of electronic music, of the computer." Others, even with a microphone, do not impose their voice and are barely even heard, whether because they do not possess the vocal technique or because they have difficulties in speaking or due to problems with their diction. Speech loses a little of its weight with all the different elements that make up the scene, thus giving space for other speeches (corporal, for example),[186] in a disjunction between "bodies without voices and voices without a body."[187] Of course there are resonances here with the works of Bob Wilson, as the various elements on stage acquire the same weight, with no hierarchy, as they also do with Cunningham, by the way. Each one with a life of its own: the music, the dance, the speaking, the light, without any one being subordinate to the other; but all juxtaposed, even if together they form a fantastic whole with pictorial scenes and emotions that are derived more

184. Renato Cohen, *Performance como linguagem* (Performance as Language). (São Paulo: Perspectiva, 2002), 58. I follow Ana Goldenstein Carvalhaes, an actress in the company who studied its process in light of Cohen's perspective, in "Performance and Madness: accompaniment to the creative process of the Ueinzz Theater Group", and later in *Persona Performática* (São Paulo: Perspectiva, 2012).

185. Renato Cohen, release, *Gotham SP*.

186. Ana Goldenstein, op. cit.

187. Flora Sussekind, "*A imaginação Monológica*," *Revista USP*, July, 1992. Renato Cohen *Work in Progress na cena contemporânea*, (São Paulo: Perspectiva, 1998).

from the unconscious, than from intelligence.[188] Paraphrasing Jacob Guinsburg, the heterogeneous elements that make up that "de-totalized" *Gesamtkunstwerk* are submitted one by one to a process of "neutralization," which silences the utilitarian character of these same elements and modifies them into new material — ready to be reintegrated into the whole in a less conventional way.[189] More than creating a formal and organized poetic structure, this is about transcribing gestures and words that are spoken and thought in contemporaneous contexts, thus using a type of unconscious reservoir of our culture. The fact that an incoherent text is produced is not in itself a problem, because there is no narrative development here, as all the activity on stage is maintained in a state of permanent "absolute present" by the continuous stimulation of the performer's energy.[190] All that energy, together with the free manipulation of the scenic codes, reinvents the relationship and boderline of the tension between art and life — in contrast with the symbolic time of the theater. "Visual landscapes, textualities, performers and luminescences in a scene of intensities in which several creative procedures circulate without the classical hierarchies of text-actor-narrative."[191] By recovering the ambivalence between reason and unreason, says Cohen, the field of drives — of unconscious irruptions, of sinister places, of transverse narratives — is legitimized within atmospheres of abstract intensity, critical attacks, mental landscapes, derivative processes, resonant indices and abrasions.

A Plan of Evasion

In a slightly different key than the theatrical scene, it's worth mentioning a partnership that influenced the Company's course and in a certain way put it in suspension. It's about a project with Alejandra Riera, which is not presented under any definitive status, be it that of an artist, a filmmaker or a writer. Born in Buenos Aires and settling in Paris, although a nomad, she calls herself "status-less," despite documenting in texts and images "how to deal with

188. Jacó Guinsburg, *Os processos criativos de Bob Wilson* (São Paulo: Perspectiva, 1996).

189. *Ibid.*

190. Jacó Guinsburg, *Da cena em cena*, (São Paulo: Perspectiva, 1986), p. 23.

191. Renato Cohen, *Work in Progress na cena contemporânea*, p. 24.

others and with the stories that pass through us." Since 1995, she has been dedicating herself to stockpiling an imaginary archive: what she has called Maquettes-sans-qualité (*Mockups-without-quality*).[192]

In this unprecedented form of archive, photographs, subtitles, writings, accounts, and filmed documents are all mixed together like a "book in movement," with no regular format. They are like the outline, "the plan of evasion," and for all those that participated in her adventure, it's about a place "where you can narrate, think about the world and ourselves," where one can deal with "unresolved issues." Light or precarious, the mockup can be made or unmade, and has no intention for posterity. It can adapt itself to the present, and it's the present that's important. Each one of the mockups-without-quality opens up a place in which many voices make themselves heard, where multiple complicities are interwoven and question the status of the work, of author, and of the artist. "More than proper names, they are places that are needed in order to liberate the word, to share responsibilities, shames, hopes, resistances."[193] This is how the mockups-without-qualities became true "refuge-spaces," where a work in progress unfolds, always collectively.

The publication of one of the moments from this project begins with the words of a shepherd from the French region of Lozère: "Certainly we will better understand the true nature of current desolation ('in what type of world we live') if we exclusively return to our own senses, instead of to systems of interpretation that are all misguided and which carry with them nothing but solace: the false illusion of mastery, at least intellectual. In any case, for whoever wants to reconstruct his or her

---

192. Between the accomplices that populate her maquettes, she mentions the pseudonym "a woman-photographer.": "A photographer then could have also been a nurse or a sweeper and her looks on this world (or also this *café waiter* on whom it was written that at the same time he is and is not that which is fit to him to represent and whose voice would probably have been heard if, in the face of the philosopher, he would cease to represent). "Photographer-nurse-sweeper" mentioned not as socio-professional categories, but as an overcoming of such. What remains to be done is always in a state of becoming and puts in check any assumptions. A *woman-photographer* is several at the same time and in this plurality the gestures rest, the acts performed alongside any other women or men. Also there rest the senses opened by the *anarchitecture* of the mockups-without-quality." *Maquetas-sin-cualidad*, Autonomous production, (Barcelona: Fundació Antoni Tàpies, 2005), p. 13, to be published by n-1publications.

193. *Idem*.

intelligence in practices, without the filter of representations, the obligatory route one must take is to attach oneself as such to sensory perception, without limiting oneself to it: this is the inevitable individual beginning of all excarceration, awakening your atrophied sensibility at the bottom of yourself. At first it's painful, like all detoxification, and simply shows the personal suffering upon which everyone's apparent adaptation rests."[194]

Indeed, there is no way to mortgage perception to competent discourse. Thus, the place of the author in this anonymous, unsigned book, where citations also do not refer to their authors, where we are deprived of the authority that their celebrity could confer to what they say: "Abandon the author as evidence to rescue it as a problem." Therefore, this way of erasing the mark of names, this operation of cunning is not a game of hide-and-seek, but a way of highlighting that which they say or make seen, erasing themselves, in a certain way, so that their names don't blur the questions. Furthermore, the risk of transforming the unknown into the known through the erasure of names, pushes this operation toward its inverse. "If one could see the 'author as someone who runs the risk of transforming the already known — or supposedly known — into something unknown, for whom all the known necessarily entrenches a part of the unknown'; ... 'if the author is whoever accepts becoming the other who everyone carries inside themselves, whose manifestations are precisely impeded by society's efforts,' in this case, this 'author,' 'throughout his/her work, would discover in him/herself another, different than what he/she had believed to be.'"[195]

And Riera adds, in her unique modesty: "When the hostility in which we live impedes us, for a number of reasons, from carrying out our projects and indefinitely delays our plenitude, it is probable that we can only live by opening very small interstices here and there...."

It's possible to inscribe part of Riera's work in Jacques Rancière's description of some strategies of "artists who propose to modify the benchmarks of what is visible and utterable, of making us see what was not seen, of making us see differently that which was seen all too comfortably, of placing in relation things which weren't initially in relation, with the objective of

---

194. *Ibid*, p. 9.

195. *Ibid*, p. 13.

producing ruptures within the sensitive fabric of perceptions and the dynamic of affects. This is the labor of fiction. Fiction is not the creation of an imaginary world opposed to the real world. It is the labor that works with dissensus, that modifies the modes of sensorial presentation and the forms of enunciation when modifying the frames, the scales or the rhythms, by building new relationships between appearance and reality, the singular and the common, the visible and its signification. This labor changes the coordinates of the representable; it changes our perception of sensorial events, our way of referring to them as subjects, the way by which our world is populated by events and figures."[196]

Of course, as Rancière says, no reality, outside of fiction, exists as such since all reality is already the configuration of what is given to us as reality, space constructed wherein the visible, the utterable, and the feasible are connected. In this sense, both fiction and political action scratch the surface of this reality, "they fracture it and multiply it in a controversial manner."[197] Thus, the challenge would reside in building spatial-temporal *devices*, "different communities of words and things, of forms and significations." And he concludes, regarding the function of art, if this expression still fits: "The images of art do not provide weapons for battles. They contribute to designing new configurations of the visible, of the utterable, and of the thinkable, and thus, a new landscape of the possible."[198] For now we can accept these formulations, leaving aside, provisionally, all of Rancière's controversy with Deleuze, derived, nonetheless, from an unconfessable proximity.

Politics of Perception

In 2005, Alejandra Riera came to São Paulo and got to know the Ueinzz Theater Company's work. Shortly after she arrived, she proposed a collaboration with the theater company involving a project she called *Enquête sur le/notre dehors*, along the

196. Jacques Rancière, *Le spectateur émancipé*, (Paris: La fabrique, 2008), p. 72. This chapter is not found in the English translation *The Emancipated Spectator*, but rather a revised version was published in *Dissensus*. Due to the differences in wording, the translator opted to translate from the original French.

197. *Ibid*, p. 113.

198. *Ibid*, p. 113.

lines of her previous research. Out of this, a *device* was activated with the actors from the company for very a specific, though open, inquiry and recording. It consisted of a group outing every day for several days to some place in the city suggested by the actors, where the group would approach someone of their choice — a pedestrian, street vendor, a student, a police officer, a stranger, a homeless person — and directly fire at them any questions that came to mind. In an unusual situation where the interviewee knows nothing about the interviewer — but sometimes perceives a certain strangeness — the rules of a journalistic interview are reversed and everything starts to go wrong, without anyone managing to detect the reason for the derailing. Postures begin to become undone, the personal, professional or institutional masks which everyone dearly holds onto fall to the ground, allowing a glimpse of the unusual dimensions of the disturbing "normality" which surrounds us every day, as the artist used to say. With a displaced camera that questions the anchoring point of discourse, a hiatus is created between image and speech, and thus a suspension in the automatism of comprehension.

Let us take one minuscule example. We were in front of the Legislative Assembly in São Paulo talking with a peanut vendor. One of our actors asks him what the magic of this place is. The street vendor does not understand, and asks if the interviewer wants to know how much he earns. "No, I wanted to know what is your happiness here?" "I don't understand", says the peanut vendor. The actor, a little agitated by his interlocutor's deafness, asks him point blank: "I want to know what is your desire, what is the meaning of your life." Then everything stops, there is a suspension in the dialogue, a silence, and we see the man sinking into a dimension that was totally other, far from any journalistic context. And he replied, quietly, with a certain difficulty: "suffering...." This is the basis without a basis of the entire conversation, the disaster which already occurred, the exhaustion which cannot be spoken of; it is the bitter isolation of a man cornered in front of a monumental building which represents an unshakeable, but nonetheless empty power; everything which only appears by means of a sudden interruption, triggered by a sort of vital irritation. An interruption provoked by the one who is supposed to be drowned in his own abyss — the crazy actor. And here everything shifts, and the spectator suddenly wonders what side life is on, and if that question still has any meaning, since it is nothing but a whole context of misery which emerges from this unusual dialogue. What causes an eruption is the psycho-social instability upon which everything else rests; and also, for fleeting moments, the germs of something else. In making the situation schizophrenic, for a time there is the impression that everything may become derailed: functions, places, obeisance, discourses, representations. Everything may fall, including the device itself. Even if we encounter what was there from the very beginning — suffering, resignation, impotence — we witness disconnections that make so-called normality flee, along with its linked automatic reactions; and also the evocation of other possible bonds with the world. As Riera says, this is not social reporting or a survey with humanist ends, but the recording of an experiment. It has no make-up, no claims to denounce a situation, and no inclination toward aesthetics. At the end, we do not really have a proper documentary, or a film, but an unusual object, a trace of an event that when seen may trigger other events — as was the case when some fragments were shown in the La Borde clinic, where Guattari once lived, in the presence of dozens of patients and psychiatrists, including the founder of the clinic, Jean Oury. In the enormous central hall of this decaying castle, one late Friday afternoon in September 2008, the people were waiting for the "Brazilian film" made by a theater group, according to the rumor that was going around. But there will be no "Brazilian film," nor any "documentary," nor any "film," nor any "theatrical piece." Absence of work. How to explain this without disappointing such high expectations? The weekly meeting ends, the hundred people seated in the auditorium turn toward the screen already stretched, the windows are closed in order to allow for the showing of the "Brazilian film," and Alejandra Riera compliments those present and straightaway points out that she does not intend to show a film. She explains that this is only an experiment, that it is very difficult to talk about this … and instead of giving a talk on the project, on her intentions and its logic, as one would expect, she confesses that she has experienced great difficulty working lately … that in the end she could not manage it any more … to work or to build … imagine the effect of this talk on people who long ago had abandoned the circuit of "work," "projects" and "results."

147

She then adds that lately all she could manage was to take things apart. She does not even stop from taking apart the tools with which she once worked, such as the computer.... And she takes from her handbag two plastic bags with fragments of the disassembled keyboard: one of them contains the alphabet keys, the other the functions (Delete, Ctrl, Alt, etc.). She then passes around the transparent plastic bags containing the pile of pieces so that they can be circulated among those present. The spectacular expectation of a film gives way to an extraordinary complicity with an artist who does not call herself an artist, who does not bring her work, who confesses that she is not able to work, who shows the remains of her computer, pieces that have been dismantled, evoking a project whose impossibility is immediately made known, leaving only the impasse, the fiasco, the paralysis, the exhaustion that is common to us all, whether we are lunatics or philosophers, artists or psychiatrists.... Only once the link between "art" and "audience" is short-circuited, once the glamor, entertainment, culture, work, or object which could be expected from that "presentation" of images is undone, and the central protagonist who leaves the stage is "de-individualized": only in this way can something else occur — an event as the effect of a suspension. A projection of fragments can even take place, or a controversial discussion, at times accusatory or visceral, that drags into the night, into the twilight of the auditorium which no one has taken the trouble to light up and which ends with the hilarious question from a patient: "Do you all have a project?" As if reconnecting to Alejandra's initial speech, in which she confessed about her difficulty in working, in constructing a project, in doing work, it evokes Blanchot's intuition on the common ground existing between art and unworking, or Foucault's idea about the relationship between madness and the rupture of work. Perhaps this is where we can find a performative exhaustion of the project or of the work, so that inaudible voices and improbable events can emerge.

Regarding the projected images, they are far from what you would expect. As Deleuze says: "Civilization of the image? In fact, it is a civilization of the cliché. [...] There is no knowing how far a real image may lead: the importance of becoming visionary or seer. A change of conscience or of heart is not enough. [...] Sometimes, it is necessary to make holes to introduce voids and white spaces, to rarefy the image. [...] Not enough, for victory, to parody the cliché, to make holes in it and empty it. [...] It is necessary to combine the optical-sound image with the enormous forces that are not those of a simply intellectual consciousness, nor of the social one, but of a profound, vital intuition."[199]

It's true that the projection of the fragment with a street prophet (called by Riera: *De la Modernité*) evoked an irate explosion from one of the residents at La Borde. "Why are you showing us this, what right do you have to intensify the mystical delirium of a paranoid person on the street? This is not a film, it's a provocation, an insult!" An inaugural, necessary explanation, which perhaps a more sane public wouldn't dare to recriminate in such a harsh, beautiful, exotic, and unbearable scene. Indeed, there is pain everywhere, and the film is not about exotically exploring it, but it is also not about covering it up. It's not about avoiding the insanity there is on the streets, nor the loose word that rarely finds a place to land. The actors gave themselves the liberty to grab fragments of what runs loosely around them and that no one notices, or can't stand to see, or is forbidden to notice — and yet makes noise. It's about a buzzing that cannot read the threshold of affectability, given the sensory and media shield that cushions the harshness and the friction. Indeed, in the filmed fragments one notices and recognizes "types," somewhat like caricatures, but precisely, when they appear, they end up being divested from their parameters and uniforms in an involuntary corrosion. As is the case with Kafka's father in *Letter to His Father*, according to Deleuze and Guattari, in the chapter "An Exaggerated Oedipus": the father is inflated to such a point, he becomes so fat, he grows disproportionately, and explodes, leaving something else to be seen, a whole other movement underneath, molecular, which was previously hidden. That's what happens in the inquiry: the recognizable identity of the interviewees or the interviewers crumbles throughout the conversation. As critic Jean-Pierre Rehm has observed, in an article about Riera's work:

"Those who seek the movement of expertise or of research will be disappointed. Or the odious gallery of portraits and their simple exhaustivity. For it is the logic of roles that one

---

199. Gilles Deleuze, *Cinema 2: The Time Image,* trans. Hugh Tomlinson and Robert Galeta, (London: Continuum, 1989), pp. 20-21.

finds reversed here. The interlocutors express themselves in the mixed space of conversation, to take the title of one of the film's chapters. And if none of them is here freed from their eventual recognition (when this is helped by the uniform, commercial counter, or in the reinforced signs of psychological disorder), no one is found, however, stuck, mortgaged to an identity that would behoove one to exemplify, according to the sinister logic of the documentary that lingers within the particular in order to better immerse itself in the typology. For no one exactly knows who asks the questions, who responds to them, or above all, what the precise aims are. It's the experience of an insufficiency of this type of transmission that is, primarily, transmitted,"[200] he concludes, Benjaminianly.

It's because there is, precisely, an effect of suspension in the very exhibition of the fragments or of the experience, or what Rehm called a "defensive logic." Even in the titles of Riera's works, as he lists them: "*Maquettes-sans-qualité*," "*unresolved problem*," "*work in progress*," "*work on strike*," "*fragments*," "*partial views*," "*unrealizable film*" are some among countless descriptions, hence prescriptive, given according to a rule of one *by fault (par défaut)*. "It would be mistaken, however, to read here the topos, or even the pathos, let's call it Beckettian or Blanchotian, of an essential misery of art. Even if the motive of the 'scandal' of art, as Bataille said, of its placement in crisis, or even worse, of its condemnation, remains an inherited debt of the avant-garde, we shouldn't deceive ourselves. Negation, attenuation, exhibition of the deviation or the retreat are weapons bristled in a jealous way. This depreciating logic, submitted to the power of pretermission, represents more than a strategy dictated by the circumstances; the very *form* of one's work. Or better yet, the mark of one's precious and unique *formalism*. Exposition, catalog, projection, Alejandra Riera is dedicated to dressing them up in scare quotes and laying out a very effective obstacle course for any attempt at their apprehension. What does she organize as such: a mode of resistance to the work itself. There is no fragility, nor deficit, here, despite objections to the contrary. It is a fortress whose edification was calculated by the fatigue of its siege."[201]

200. Jean-Pierre Rehm, "Enquête sur le/notre dehors de Alejandra Riera na Documenta 12," in *Vacarme* n. 41, Paris, Autumn, 2007.

201. *Ibid*.

In this strategy of reserve and retreat, of obstinate opacity, it's not about a mystification of the unspeakable or elitist hermeticism. As Rehm continues to say, "this trap does not signal any kind of paralysis, it doesn't make a motor out of powerlessness, nor the helpless conclusion of the work. It underscores, on the contrary, the inordinacy of ambition. For, contrary to the retreat, stingily lyrical in vogue, of which we know how much politics offers alibis or allegedly objective protections, here it is an epic regime that is aimed for. Epic, and we admit, in part wrecked. Better yet, frenzied. That is: traversed by a lyricism that doesn't merely find its place inside *by excess*. Without a doubt it is because of this reason that her work often takes on the aspect of an epidemic unfolding in space, a propagation without borders perpetually pointing toward a utopia of an 'outside.'"[202]

(Dis)occupation

The collective occupation of one floor of the cultural center Sesc Paulista, in 2009, suggested by Ricardo Muniz Fernandes, intensified this coexistence between interruption and event, excess and the outside, opacity and the endeavor to "make visible." The group performed their play inspired by Joyce's *Finnegans Wake* — called *Finnegans Ueinzz* — interspersed with the presence of several guests, among them psychiatrist Jean Oury, philosopher David Lapoujade, sociologist and critic Laymert Garcia dos Santos, author and critic Celso Favaretto, psychoanalyst and cinematographer Miriam Chnaiderman, as well as the projection of several films about the La Borde clinic, interviews with Guattari, Tosquelles, a short film by François Pain of a dance by Min Tanaka in front of the residents at La Borde, etc. At the same time, Alejandra Riera proposed a *place of studies* (*lieu[x]d'etudes*) where actors, building security guards, cleaners were invited to situations of common reflection, with the intention that each one leaves aside his/her place of origin, and questions competencies, places of enunciation, instruments of perception that are available to be heard and seen. A dismantled computer on a table, the technique of the body without organs, a surgery in which one reinvents the body, inspired by Artaud,

---

202. *Ibid.*

an anagram by Maya Deren drawn on the floor.... In this context, Godardian scenes were proposed, for example the reading of a very dense theoretical paper by the actors or cleaners, while they moved machines of perception and recording, shifting recognized competencies, and stirring the distribution among those who speak and those who work, those who represent and those who are represented, those who go crazy and those who theorize about the unconscious. This occupation lasted twelve days and created a time-space of large density and movement, with migrations of meaning and non-meaning in several directions, roaming the most heterogeneous registries: psychoanalytic, philosophical, or aesthetic discourse, theatrical play, conversations, filming, questioning the objective of the occupation, of the possibilities open to it, of the aesthetic and political intentions implied in the proposition and others which came up throughout the twelve days. "Do you think we were about to constitute an independent state?" Asks one of the actors, while the group took down one of the bleachers that the institution considered to be irremovable.

Evidently, very important questions remained unanswered, in the wake of such an experience. For example, regarding the coefficients of freedom conquered at the micro level, and their disproportion in relation to the mechanisms of domination in the macropolitical sphere, which specifically operate through the molecular dimension, by the capture of desire's microprocesses. As Lazzarato says, the artistic act becomes resistance as soon as there is transversality between the molecular action of rupture and the composition in a specific domain and the external domains, with every problem of scale, of translation, of skipping about in affective logic. However urgent it may be to think this relation, it remains entirely undetermined. As Guattari exclaims in a different context: "Who knows if the revolution that awaits us will not have its principle enunciations stated by Lautréamont, Kafka or Joyce?" We would add: also something enunciated by the common man, the singular whatever, the anonymous devices, with their power of interruption or of invention, however minuscule it may be, under the conditions of a contemporary contagion. Yet it is necessary to adduce: these conditions become increasingly dim. The Argentinian collective *Situaciones* speaks of cloning, when referring to this context where signs circulate encapsulated, sterile, like specters separated from the forces that engender them. It's as if the word had ceased producing embodied meanings, linking their luck to the destiny of the general equivalent, money.[203] As Deleuze noted it: "Maybe speech and communication have been corrupted. They're thoroughly permeated by money — and not by accident but by their very nature. We've got to hijack speech. Creating has always been something different from communicating. The key thing may be to create vacuoles of noncommunication, circuit breakers, so we can elude control."[204] This diagnostic is entirely current, so much so that not only is it the power of speech that vanishes into this *separate* state, but the connection of the word to the body, of meaning to desire, and the ability of the organism itself to perform when facing this saturation that placed it in parentheses. "We've quite lost the world, it's been taken from us," Deleuze said, in order to subsequently evoke the necessity of returning to believe in the world: "If you believe in the world you engender new space-times, however small their surface or volume."[205] Believing in the world is believing in the possibilities of the world, it is being in conditions to connect your strength with the strengths of the world, it is being able to believe in that which is seen and heard. Sympathizing with the becoming of the world and the becoming of the others in this world, and the becoming other of the others in this world.

Performative Wedding

At the invitation of the Théâtre du Radeau in 2005, part of our troupe traveled to spend a week with the actors from that company in La Fonderie, in the middle of France, in a project of "reciprocal affectation." Director François Tanguy and his group met us at a level of empathy, body-to-body, with hardly imaginable shamanic communication, in spite of the undeniable language barrier. He went around with a wooden pole that had teeth on one end, an object that we would use to scratch our backs, which was gifted to him by our common friend

203. Colectivo Situaciones, *Conversaciones en el impasse: dilemas políticos del presente*, (Buenos Aires: Tinta Limón, 2009).

204. Gilles Deleuze, *Negotiations*, trans. Martin Joughin, (New York: Columbia University Press, 1995), p. 175.

205. *Ibid*, p. 176.

Laymert Garcia dos Santos, who had received it from a Xingu chief. For the indigenous people, this instrument serves to scarify the interlocutor's back during a conversation, and leaves a mark of the encounter on the person's body. Tanguy used this same principle with our actors.

Throughout the next several days, we ate together listening to Tanguy read aloud from *The Man Suicided by Society*, while I sat next to an elderly anthropologist, a personal friend and publisher of Artaud, Alain Gheerbrant. After Artaud's death, Gheerbrant said that he needed to look for new "unknown languages" which led him to the Amazon where he met the Yanomami. In this atmosphere of intersecting artists and writers coming from such diverse places — including the essayist and translator of Carmelo Bene, Jean-Paul Manganaro, as well as Walter Gomes, an exceptional young singer (and a Brazilian connoisseur of indigenous plumage) — one of our actors, asks Tanguy if we were invited because we were fallen angels. On the last day, before our presentation, François placed an enormous pair of wings made of rags on this actor's back, which he wore during the presentation. Right before this, the most unusual thing happened. On our second day in France, this same actor proposed marriage to Laurence, one of the actresses from the French company. Being extremely talented and sensitive, once she understood the tenor and the performativity of the proposal, she embraced it immediately. After the theatrical presentation of our final day, in a fairy-like ambiance, a wedding took place, she with her flashy bride's dress, he with a lavish cape of green velvet, and on his head was placed a gigantic deer mask, lacy and transparent. The guests wore exotic wigs, and that's how the wedding of the fallen angel and the seasoned actress took place; officiated by François Tanguy. With a festive reception on that night, something was shifted between reality and fiction, art and life, unreason and the everyday. Afterward, the bride and groom went their separate ways. The next day, bidding farewell, the actress thanked the former groom for the celebration, and with humor suggested that he was the only person in the world capable of giving her such an experience.

You Don't Need Solidarity, You Need a Cell Phone

On a trip to Finland, in 2009, at the invitation to the International Baltic Circle Festival, after having experienced such a detachment from our typical theatrical format, as described above, I feared a return to the logic of the politically correct spectacle, to the representation of a group of outcasts, to the insipid glamor of festivals. Well, at the airport in São Paulo, from the outset, one of our actresses, in a state of great agitation, after having passed through immigration control, with great commotion threw her bag to the floor and started speaking to her belongings in English. I understood immediately that I was mistaken; we would travel without any glory or serenity, but rather in a state of absolute tension and uncertainty, not toward international acclaim, but rather toward our own unknown. This young lady managed to get through every barrier of the airplane's crew so as to go sit next to the pilot and contemplate from the sky, and with such happiness, an island next to Africa that we had just flown over. Throughout the journey and stay, with irritation and joy, she denounced the micro-fascism that surrounds us at every corner, at all ends of the planet, she lent us her gaze, she impregnated our perception, she disseminated her sensibility and inflected ours, detecting the intolerable that has become our everyday banality, from the magazines in airports to the details of urban discipline — in an act of poetic guerrilla warfare that recalls Godard's character who threatens to blow up his backpack (of books) in a cinema in Jerusalem, in *Notre musique*.

On the ferry that took us to our lodgings on the island of Suomenlinna, in Helsinki, in an emergency we had to turn to a stranger to ask to borrow a cell phone. In response to our request, outlandish in his eyes, he submitted us to a police-like interrogation about the reasons for our stay on the island where he had lived for years, so as to eventually refuse the use of his cell phone, rubbing his black leather gloves together with contempt. I couldn't contain myself and retorted that some day he would need solidarity and would remember this moment — to which he responded: you don't need solidarity, what you folks need is a cell phone. One could not better sum up an era. We found out later that he is the director of a Finnish national museum, brother of a known artist, in short, a small fascist of the local aristocracy.... Getting off of the ferry he wanted to beat me up for my impertinence, but I grabbed onto an actor whose size would intimidate even a fascist.

Perhaps this group is at times like Kafka's nomads. Despite the emperor's efforts to avoid the invasion of the nomads coming from the North, there are reports that they are already camped in the main square of the capital, out in the open, speaking their strange language, eating horse meat, with their bulging eyes and their strange laws.... It's not them who are always moving, but in their way of being there and having brought the outside with them makes it so that something around them moves or flees.... Now, all of this is not given, neither for Kafka nor us, be it in our presence, or in our travels, be it in our presentations, be it in our articulations … it is important to weave it every day, this plane of consistency, stitch by stitch, as the *Situaciones* group says so well, it is a work of great delicacy, a kind of craftwork, which retreats when faced with thundering expectations, but which resumes effectiveness when tackling micro-mutations, in concrete surroundings which are necessary to sustain and to incessantly broaden. But such a wager can only sustain itself if it finds allies in unconsciouses that protest, to take up a beautiful formula from the 1960s. It is a movement that only breathes if it refuses the standard recognition, made of social inclusion or of glamorous incorporation, but also constantly overflows from its basic group framework and looks for its resonances with other collective affects that nourish it or prolong it. Thus, it is important to go beyond the aesthetic *device*, theatrical in this case, necessary, no doubt, since it opens to a wind from outside that sweeps away clichés of madness or of art or simply of relations, raising different vectors, still unknown. It is important to dig deep down in order to get to this exceedance, even if it is submitted to the reigning opacification and redundancy, even if one still doesn't find the expressiveness or narrativity that befits the vitality that is one's own. In any case this is the only point of departure, within our scale, for a type of counter-performativity, against the grain of what Negri has called Capital performativity and its global incidence.

The Shipwreck

In 2011, the Finnish collective *mollecular.org* invited us along with the French group *presque ruines* to conjointly make a film and put together a play inspired by Kafka's book *Amerika, or the Man Who Disappeared*. The extravagant aspect of this proposition, hailing from the bold mind of Virtanen Akseli consisted of carrying out this endeavor on a transatlantic voyage, during the two-week crossing between Lisbon and Santos, as a remote evocation of Ship of Fools, but also as in a possible "rediscovery" of Brazil. When Akseli asked us if we could confirm the reservation of the ship for the 25th of November, he added humorously: does the project seem sufficiently impossible to be desirable? Indeed, some years before he had made a trip between Finland and China, through the Trans-Siberian railway, with 40 people from different collectives, in a daring artistic/political Project called *Capturing the moving mind*. This innovative experiment and the texts published by him were an inspiring precedent.[206] In our case, the film's project was inspired by a small paper by Félix Guattari entitled *Project for a film by Kafka*, where he tries to imagine what a film made *by* Kafka would be like.[207] Having flown into Lisbon, we embarked on the 25th of November, 2011, the three collectives from different parts of the globe, on *The Splendour of the Seas*. Here is, quite summarily, the context of this micro-political experiment.

In order to understand it, however, it's necessary to minimally describe what a cruise consists of — something that I had ignored entirely before we threw ourselves into this adventure. About two thousand people confined to the pseudo-luxury of a floating hotel ten stories high, velvet hallways, enormous chandeliers hanging everywhere, gilded handrails, panoramic elevators, swimming pools in the open air surrounded by gigantic television screens, huge saunas, bars, casinos, and restaurants everywhere, music and shows, slot machines and dance halls, theme parties next to the pool, dinner with the captain,

---

206. The beautiful article of Virtanen Akseli and Jussi Vähämäki *Structure of Change*, and the dialogue between Virtanen Akseli and Bracha Ettinger, "Art, Memory, Resistance", in Framework, Issue 4 December 2005, The Finnish Art Review, 2006.

207. This work by Félix Guattari was published by Stéphane Nadaud as *Les 65 rêves de Franz Kafka*, Paris, Nouvelles Editions Lignes, 2006 — and its translations into Portuguese and English were put out by n-1 publications, São Paulo, 2011, as *Máquina Kafka/ Kafkamachine*.

commemoration when crossing the Equator with glowing champagne glasses. The hallucinating overdose of entertainment stimuli, gastronomic stuffing, an imperative for pleasure, produces an absolute saturation of the physical, mental, and psychological space of the passengers. A true semiotic bombardment from which no one can escape anywhere, not even in the cabin where the loudspeaker announces the next bingo competition or the internal television irradiates the news from the ship itself. However, there is nothing extraordinary about the floating entertainment machine — it condenses our daily life, propelled contemporary capitalism. If it wouldn't offend historical victims, I would say that it is a type of concentration camp in reverse, postmodern, organized thoroughly according to the logic of consumption, of the spectacle, of the interminable intensification of pleasure, of the imperative for enjoyment, of the "your smile is my smile," that one of our actors translated as "your card is my card." Of course, all of this works thanks to an army of 700 underpaid employees who live in the basement and circulate smiling at the disposal of the clientele 24 hours a day, and whose living quarters are blocked from passenger visitations.

Personally, I experienced our time on the ship as an individual and collective shipwreck. Of course we were stunned by everything: the dimensions, the enormity, the abundance, the solicitude, and the actors were increasingly shocked at being treated with such solicitude — if someone asked for ten desserts, the waiter brought ten desserts — after all, the final objective is to satisfy the client, however absurd their caprices seemed to be. This type of inclusion through consumption, with its grotesque side, however, merely highlighted the contrast at stake. There couldn't be anything more discrepant than our group, with its unique fragility, on the one hand, and the ostentatious and glaring luxury present everywhere. Two poles, two worlds, in an asymmetric confrontation, in an inevitable friction, in which we set out as losers and scorched. We had no chance of "winning," we barely knew if we would be able to "survive." It recalls the beautiful observation by Didi-Huberman about the fight between the fireflies, that need the dark in order to appear, and the light of the projectors that entirely sweep away the social space, concealing the glow of the fireflies. It's the triumphant fascist industry of political exposition, as Pasolini said.[208]

Of course, we also had a project — we weren't mere tourist passengers. If the unfavorable context for our project led those of us invested in the objective to double our efforts, what ended up emerging within this task was an irritation produced by the anxiety to achieve it, to finish it, to complete the anticipated goal. As for me, I was overcome not so much by a laziness, but by a type of passive, Bartleby-esque refusal, an "I would prefer not to" make a film, make a play, make a work, make something nice, to finish.... An anarchist desire, or rather, the desire to dive into a different dynamic, non-productive, a desire for unproduction, where quitting, unwillingness, withdrawal, the plunge, the surf, heading out to sea, all became interlaced in an intensive logic, of interpenetrated sensations, much more than constructive and displayable articulation. It's hard to describe to what extent the set of tiny gestures, miniscule movements, and humorous or hilarious deviations appeared more effective in their parodic contrast to what from the outset some experienced as confinement, with its dose of violence and coercion.

Little by little we noticed that everything that we had planned went wrong, or worked poorly, or barely worked, or simply revealed its laughable or absurd dimension, where we re-encountered the disturbing, inevitable, and necessary question: but what the hell are we doing here anyway? What an idea to put ourselves in such a maze of coercion and strangulation, in the midst of two thousand tourists, which one of our actors named the "contemplastic world!" And so now, from within this situation of saturation, how does one leave, if there is no exit, surrounded by a sea that is definitely lived as decoration, and doesn't remotely evoke an exterior, an outside? It's important to say it: everything on the ship is made for you to turn your back to the ocean. It's the absolute inside, of pleasure, of consumption, impermeable to any exteriority, the hypnosis of the casino, of the giant screen above the outside pool that displays precisely what is next to it: the ocean. It's incontestable that, at a certain moment, even inside of this protective bubble in which we had taken refuge, in a room on the fourth floor, in order to resist the athletic or flaccid normopathy that surrounded us,

---

208. Georges Didi-Huberman, *Survivance des lucioles*, p. 32.

there was something that dissolved in us, among us. Everything slid: roles, functions, references, objectives, meanings, reasons. A kind of viscous collapse, which derailed the "what," the "what for," the "how," the "where," the "when," despite the fact we occupied an enclosed space and followed our own routine: rehearsal in the morning, filming in the afternoon, conversations at night. Despite this agreed-upon plan, some of us went through an involuntary chaotization, a subtle catastrophe, with its terrors, angst, nausea, claustrophobia, the "nothing is possible" that would make outbursts, the "it could have been so much better…" from this type of collective de-subjectivation, this vacuity, where everything seemed to go to pieces, or drown, including the planned and programmed projects.… Chaosmosis.

While the ship worked perfectly, we were shipwrecked. It was necessary to part from this complex and confusing material, from this body without organs that was being proclaimed, and to follow the lines that arose from it. If the functions seemed disturbed, the actors, with their presence, affectivity, body relation, contaminated the surroundings and created a magnetic field that surprised and attracted the other collectives, who had trouble decoding the nature of this connection to which they couldn't resist, which held onto different things, much smaller or larger than the completion of a project.

And did it really make sense to oppose such an invasive surrounding with a theatrical play, even one inspired by Kafka (what better author than he to expose such claustrophobia, such an army of workers, such a maze of meaning)? Was it really a question of making a film that rivaled the cinema-becoming of this "contemplastic" world? In this context of extreme capture, an option would be, in fact, "to compete." Placing oneself in a situation of rivaling, of "defeating" this background bombardment, to try to do "more" than it, or be "better." Another option was to constitute, by withdrawing and shrinking, a space where flows circulated differently. It's always about ways for circulating desire, flows, drainage, overflows, leaks, escapes. Singularities could appear as long as they were not linked to places, functions, roles, or accomplishments, but rather along different lines, were susceptible to appear and be "exposed," perhaps even in the photographic sense, as long as a different surface were offered, detached from the organizational framework, thus, supported in small deviations, interruptions, even the growl of a peevish actor.

Of course, countless situations of collective joy alternated with moments like these, in a dizzying oscillation of what was offered by the ship at high sea. It was necessary to learn to "navigate," in its most diverse meanings. When Deligny defines his attempts with individuals with autism by using the metaphor of a raft, he explains to what point it is important that, as in this rudimentary structure, the logs are connected in such a way as to allow them a certain flexibility, so that amidst the torrent they let water pass through them so they don't break upon the impact with the water. As he says: "When the issues abate, we don't straighten out the lines — we don't tighten the logs … on the contrary. We merely maintain from the project that which connects us. You perceive the importance of the knots and the way they are tied, and the distance that the logs can have between them. It's important that the knot be loose enough so that it doesn't let go."[209] Perhaps, the question is this — how to accompany this flow that was constituted there, amidst the nuisances that unsettled the articulation of signs, of signifiers, of functions, undoing the "functioning," leading to an "unproduction," a "slipping," that actually constitutes a different collective corporeity? Simone Mina, our costume and set designer, with her sewing machine, clothes hanging on lines, and threads and ribbons, came up with a "corner" in our rehearsal refuge — a cozy and rich space where one and all could try out fabrics, come up with their own costumes or characters, sew, or just lie down sheltered by hanging clothes, like a protective cabana.

Atmosphere

All this is a matter of atmosphere. But one of the hardest things to do is to sustain an atmosphere, not heroically holding on to a framework, but rather a simultaneous state of lightness, presence, alertness, humor, and openness.… In a different context, Jean Oury and Danielle Sivadon discussed what could be called a "constellation": an opening, a grafting of fantasy, a delimitation, the feet, (coming and going, walking), humor, emerging,

209. Fernand Deligny, *Oeuvres*, ed. Sandra Alvarez de Toledo, (Paris: L'Arachnéen, 2007), p. 1128.

the possibility of inscribing oneself [210] … now, for Oury, (or for Deligny in his own way) these can be considered as the conditions for something to happen precisely because nothing needs to happen — when, on the contrary, it's exactly when something needs to happen that the most impalpable events run the risk of being aborted. This is where you see what's important. But what is it exactly that is important? What is seen? What is produced? What happens in the cracks? What is in a state of almost-being? What escapes? What lives in a state of exhaustion? What is composed together? What is it that, inside of this, lives together, alone, in the between, and questions, in a skewed manner, the thing that the factory-ship requires? What community is this, that doesn't need to show any work, which doesn't necessarily base itself on the work it creates?

At a certain moment, Erika Inforsato, one of the coordinators, wanted to read for the group some passages from her doctoral thesis in which she explained, among other things, what it meant for her to travel with this group. Written long beforehand, but resounding perfectly with the situation, since it made explicit the risks that accompanied us on the trips, even death. Indeed, there was an omnipresent risk on the ship — with the low railing on the decks and the individual cabin terraces with even lower railings. At any instant someone could, abruptly or in anger, go overboard and disappear. And one of the unwritten "rules" that we bring with us on our trips, obviously, is this: it is forbidden to disappear, even if Kafka's book which inspired us was *Amerika: The Man Who Disappeared*!!! In one of the most beautiful passages from her thesis, entitled, *Unworking: Clinical and Political Constellations of the Common,*[211] she exposed, in the context of her work, the Blanchotian idea of *unworking,* or inoperativeness, which designated, with great precision, something that many were going through at that moment: a type of resistance to "create a work," precisely amidst the filthy production offered by the ship. Nevertheless, a set of impossibilities opened up for a common event: we had to run the risk of concluding that nothing happened, nothing, that there was

210. Jean Oury and Danielle Sivadon — *Constellations*, a conversation promoted, recorded and transcribed by Olivier Apprill, published in Portuguese in *Cadernos de Subjetividade,* São Paulo, PUC-SP, 2012.

211. Erika Alvarez Inforsato, *Desobramento: constelações clínicas e políticas do comum/ Unwork (Desoeuvrement): clinical and political constellations of the common* (São Paulo/ Helsinki: n-1 publications, soon to be published).

no work, but that in this absence of work something could happen in the nature of the common. "Community for the art of not creating work," says Erika Inforsato. Sustaining the unsustainable, an encounter with the gravity of life, above all facing populations in processes of disaffiliation and vulnerability, the author states, requires a readiness, a distance that doesn't break the affect, this ascesis, she adds, of never presuming what someone else's life is like, or never investing in obligatory bonds, freeing oneself of the *telos*, resisting spectacular, overly visible, or prescriptive interventions: resisting not by reinventing the wheel, but by making it spin in a different direction, even if it comes to a point of crushing the encounter. At times it is necessary to leave the situation, the author observes, to stop wanting to save and be saved, give up on the charade so that something may be possible. Sustaining the suspension, adrift instead of in opposition, infiltration instead of intervention, leaving the field open, instead of betting on the constructions.

The ambiguity of the notion of "absence of work," inspired by Blanchot, is known by every reader of the *History of Madness*. On the one hand, Foucault shows that in the relationship between art and madness, work collapses and is abolished. On the other hand, according to Foucault, this work on madness is triumphant, to the extent that it forces the world to measure itself up to its inordinacy. In this sense, instead of measuring ourselves based on the size and scale of the ship, we could evaluate this surrounding based on this "inordinacy" that was ours. In fact, throughout the voyage we had lost several things — meanings, hierarchies, projects, certainties, securities. Perhaps these are the best moments, to be able to "think." Not thinking an "object," but asking oneself: why make a group, why sustain a group like this, what is this Ueinzz. A group that experiments something on the order of the unlivable, perhaps of the useless. But through which one attempts to breathe life into something, especially in unbreathable surroundings.

When debarking onto solid ground, for a long time everywhere I looked I saw, with an indescribable sickness, *The Splendour of the Seas*. The ship caricaturely explicated something of the contemporary world, as well as the distance to which they are thrown, these fragile, precarious, unique existences, and the means by which they can sew among themselves invisible threads that give support to an existential territory where they insist upon living, not just surviving. After all, what is the crossing of an Atlantic Ocean alongside this other challenge, a chaosmotic crossing?

In a radiophonic conference aired in 1967, Foucault referred to the ship, especially those from the 19th century, as a "floating space, a place without a place, living on its own, closed off to itself, free in its own way, but fatally at the hands of the sea's infinity" and that, from port to port, it goes to the colonies to seek out what they hold most precious. One can understand, therefore, since the 16th century, the ship has been our largest "instrument of economic development [...] but simultaneously the greatest reserve of imagination. The ship is the heterotopia par excellence. In civilizations without boats, dreams dry up, espionage takes the place of adventure, and the police take the place of pirates."[212] Certainly, today's ship is the mere prolonging of the world and has ceased to be what Foucault described. Perhaps it is needed, in light of this, to look back to the image of the raft as Deligny described it.

Years after this conference, Foucault referred to the infamous men and their insignificant, inglorious lives, men who by a game of chance were illuminated for a brief moment in the floodlights of power, which they came face to face with, and whose words then appeared to have been traversed by an unexpected intensity. Perhaps we no longer find those resplendent, although inessential, lives; those poem-lives, "particles endowed with more energy the smaller and more difficult to detect they are." Diluted between the multiple mechanisms of anonymous and arbitrary power, the words do not enjoy that theatrical resplendence and fleeting vibration which Foucault savored in the archives — it is banality which takes center stage. But from within, signs of singularity appear to confirm the desire for something else. As Deleuze used to say, even before the term biopolitical was coined, we are all in search of a "vitality." Singular, collective, anonymous, plural, suspensive, intensive, unworking — within an undefined boundary, each time reinvented, between exhaustion and a fleeting vision.

---

212. Michel Foucault, *Le corps utopique - Les Héterotopies*, (Paris: Lignes, 2009), p. 36, published in portuguese by n-1 publications as *O corpo utópico, As heterotopias*.

THE UEINZZ THEATER COMPANY

Ueinzz is a scenic territory for whoever feels the world staggering. As in Kafka, by way of a seasickness on land it creates material for poetic and political transmutation. On the whole, they are masters in the art of soothsaying, with notorious knowledge in improvisation and neologisms; specialists in maritime encyclopedias, frustrated trapeze artists, dream hunters, interpretive actresses. There are also inventors of pigeon-slang, musical unknowns, brew masters. The theater company lives by a razor's edge experimenting by way of aesthetic practices and transatlantic collaborations. The community of those without community, for a community to come.

The Voyage mentioned in the preceding chapter was made possible thanks to the generous collaboration of a vast network of the company's friends, whose list can be found at: **ueinzz.org**

The group currently consists of the following people: Adélia Faustino, Alexandre Bernardes, Amélia Monteiro de Melo, Ana Goldenstein Carvalhaes, Ana Carmen del Collado, Artur Amador, Eduardo Lettiere, Erika Alvarez Inforsato, Fabrício de Lima Pedroni, José Petronio Fantasia, Leonardo Lui Cavalcanti, Luis Guilherme Ribeiro Cunha, Luiz Augusto Collazzi Loureiro, Maria Yoshiko Nagahashi, Oness Antonio Cervelin, Paula Patricia Francisquetti, Pedro França, Peter Pál Pelbart, Simone Mina, Valéria Felippe Manzalli.

THE DETERRITORIALIZED UNCONSCIOUS*

It is well-known that the expression "Refoundation of the Unconscious on Deterritorialization" comes from Guattari's work found in *Schizoanalytic Cartographies*. It has the advantage of condensing, if not his larger theoretical project, at least an incontrovertible guiding thread of Guattari's thought throughout his life — whether through his individual work, his partnership with Deleuze, or even in his diverse practices — as much in the clinical field as in his political militancy or other intersections. Therefore I consider this thread not as a legacy to be revered, but as a problematic line to be unfolded, prolonged, and varied. It's part of this Guattari-Effect that our encounter brings to light, as well as by way of the dislocations it implies. I can't help but mention a supplementary circumstance without which this communication would lose its meaning. More than two decades ago, parallel to my academic activities in the University in São Paulo as a professor of Philosophy, I started a clinical activity in a Psychiatric Day-Hospital. The first time that I stepped foot in that institution, by chance, was in the company of Guattari himself, whose institutional supervision I had the task of translating. So began my daily contact with so-called psychotic patients, which has since inflected my personal and professional life, and which has inevitbaly nourished my philosophical research. I cannot deny that Guattari's theorizations regarding schizophrenia, the machinic unconscious, transversality in the institution, his experience at La Borde, the way he smuggled fragments of his practice into the philosophical and micropolitical domains has inspired me enormously over all these years. One of the fruits of this proximity was the constitution of the aforementioned theatrical troupe with so-called psychiatric patients. But this experience soon extended beyond the walls of the institution and poured into the theatrical circuit of the city, intriguing critics and irrigating art collectives. A few years later, we had already become disconnected from the hospital circuit and had begun to show our work throughout Brazil, France, and Finland. One of the montages we did was based on *Finnegans Wake*. As soon as we decided to set up *Finnegans Wake*, I was compelled to read Joyce frenetically, including a few critics of his work. In passing, I could not ignore the ambiguous place Joyce occupies in the Deleuze-Guattari trajectory. There appears a certain reticence as to Joyce's desire for a total work of art, despite the fragmentary nature of his writing. The contrast with Beckett is obvious: in a similar personal situation (foreign, Irish, unearthed) Beckett does the inverse of Joyce: a minor literature, made of stuttering, subtraction, without totalizing pretensions, almost without "work."

Curiously, as Dosse says, when he died, Guattari had two books on his bedside table: *Les Chiens D'Éros*, by D. H. Lawrence, and *Ulysses*, by Joyce, in English. In the same biography, Marie Depussé gives us a strange testimony about Guattari's literary ambitions: "He wasn't a true writer and I think he suffered for it. He had the desire to create. I believe he was too obsessed with Joyce." Guattari's last book carries in the title the distorted mark of Joyce, *Chaosmosis*. Fate decided to intersect my reading of Guattari with that of Joyce, and I doubt that this coincidence has helped me understand one or the other. *Schizoanalytic Cartographies* and *Finnegans Wake* — truly an anomalous junction. In their genre, style and purpose, it would be difficult to imagine two writings more distant from each other. A text by Beckett regarding his friend in exile, however, allowed me to situate myself in the distance that separates both and make each of these very extravagant and diverging projects resonate. Beckett says, addressing himself to the critics of *Work in Progress*: "And if you don't understand it, Ladies and Gentlemen, it is because you are too decadent to receive it. [...] You complain that this stuff is not written in English. It is not written at all. It is not to be read — or rather it is not only to be read. It is to be looked at and listened to. His writing is not *about* something; *it is that something itself.…* When the sense is sleep, the words go to sleep. When the sense is dancing, the words dance. […] The language is drunk. The very words are tilted and effervescent.… Mr. Joyce has desophisticated language. And it is worthwhile to note that no language is as sophisticated as English. It is abstracted to death. Take the word 'doubt': it gives us hardly any sensuous suggestion of hesitancy, of the necessity for choice, of static irresolution. Whereas the German 'Zweifel' does, and, to a lesser degree, the Italian 'dubitare.' Mr. Joyce recognizes how inadequate 'doubt' is to express a state of extreme uncertainty, and replaces it with 'in twosome twominds.' […] This writing that you find so obscure is a quintessential extraction of language and painting and gesture, with all the inevitable clarity of the old inarticulation. Here is the savage economy of hieroglyphics. Here, words are not the polite contortions of 20th century printer's ink. They are alive. […] This inner elemental vitality and corruption of expression imparts a furious restlessness to the form, which is admirably suited to the purgatorial aspect of the work. There is an endless verbal germination, maturation, putrefaction. […] In what sense, then, is Mr. Joyce's work purgatorial? In the absolute absence of the Absolute. Hell is the static lifelessness of unrelieved viciousness. Paradise the static lifelessness of unrelieved immaculation. Purgatory a flood of movement and vitality.…"[213]

Joyce, Lacan, Guattari

Might there be a relation between Guattari's passion for Joyce and his reading of Lacan? In the 1975-6 Seminar XXIII, Lacan asks: "Why is Joyce unreadable? […] Maybe because he doesn't invoke in us any sympathy." [214] But in noticing that he is in fact read, even without an understanding of what is read, Lacan suggests that maybe it relates to the readers feeling that what is present is "the enjoyment of the one who wrote it." The essential is the relation to language as enjoyment. The pure game with language, the *pun*, even when it fails, proves in any case, Lacan

---

213. Samuel Beckett, in *Our Exagmination Round His Factification for Incamination of Work in Progress*, (Paris: Shakespeare & Co., 1929).

214. Jacques Lacan, *Séminaire XXIII, Le Sinthome*, (Paris: Seuil, 2005), p. 151.

says, that Joyce is exonerated (*desabonné*) of the unconscious. In it, language "is the only thing of his text we can hold on to," even if it leaves us bewildered. "Where it speaks, it enjoys, and it knows nothing."[215] But the sinthome which Joyce would carry, according to Lacan, differs from the classical symptom (message directed at the other). Given the weakening of the paternal metaphor, he would be nothing other than a prosthesis which offers him a replaced ego upon which he "makes his name." The necessary relation with the Name-of-the-Father is noticeable. The sinthome is equivalent, in fact, with the Oedipal complex. Unlike the symptom, which one can be relieved of by way of a cure, the sinthome is that which cannot be abandoned in its prosthetic function of maintaining the conjugation of the three spheres of the Real, the Symbolic, and the Imaginary. For certain artists the sinthome's residue can fuse with their art. For certain mathmaticians the sinthome can even fuse with their work in mathematics, it can fuse with God for believers, with the psychoanalyst itself for certain analysands, and with the loved one for the lover. In sum, it would be a part of the "structure."

Now, nothing of this is present, not even from afar, in Guattari, and from his very first texts he joyfully gets rid of the very notion of Name-of-the-Father. When he invokes Joyce, it is in an entirely different sense, one which goes against all structuring or unifying functions. In *Psychoanalysis and Transversality*, for instance, Joyce is summoned as a machinic opening: "the unconscious is nothing more than the real to come, the transfinite field of potentialities hidden by an open chain of signifiers that await to be opened and articulated by a real agency of enunciation and effectuation. [...] It is the same as saying that the links in this chain, including the more 'intimate,' and (why not as well the intended 'private life') could be revealed as decisive nudes of historic causality. Who knows if the revolution that awaits us will not have its principles of enunciation bent by Lautréamont, Kafka or Joyce?"[216] Lacan's theorization of sinthome as a function of prosthesis or of the "individual's" psychic destiny and Guattari's poetico-political opening, the

---

215. Jacques Lacan, *Le Séminaire, Livre XX, Encore,* (Paris: Seuil, 2005), p. 95 : *Là où ça parle, ça jouit, et ça sait rien.*

216. Félix Guattari, *Psychoanalysis and Transversality: Texts and Interviews 1955-1971*, trans. Ames Hodges, (Cambridge: Semiotext(e) 2015).

prefiguration of the collective assemblage of enunciation, couldn't be any more different.

To continue this unwise comparison, it isn't at all certain that Guattari experienced the same enjoyment that Joyce did in his writing, even if Guattari's word games express at times a great freedom, intermediated with fragments of "jargon" and hardenings which testify above all else to a true suffering in writing. "Writing so that I won't die. Or so that I die otherwise.... Deleuze is concerned that I'm not producing anymore.... I'm home, kind of fucking around.... It's the first time I write Deleuze here instead of Gilles. No more Fanny. Epiphany. A cavity of lack. Gilles writing a big article.... He works a lot. We're really not of the same dimension. I'm a sort of inveterate autodidact, a do-it-yourself guy, a sort of Jules Verne — *Voyage to the Center of the Earth*. In my own way I don't stop.... But you can't tell. It's the work of never-ending reverie. Lots of ambitious plans. Everything in my head, nothing in the pocket. Epiphany.... I will keep giving these texts to Fanny and, at the end of the chain, Gilles. I can tell they don't mean anything to him. The ideas, sure. But the trace, the continuous-discontinuous text flow that guarantees my continuance, obviously he doesn't see it like that. Or he does, but he's not interested. He always has the *oeuvre* in mind."[217] The reader finds himself faced with a true *malaise*: "Have to be accountable. Yield to arguments. What I feel like is just fucking around. Publish this diary for example. Say stupid shit. Barf out the fucking-around-o-maniacal schizo flow. Barter whatever for whoever wants to read it ... write right onto the real. But not just the professional readers' real, '*Quinzaine* polemical' style. The close, hostile real. People around. Fuck shit up. The stakes greater than the oeuvre or they don't attain it.... Writing to Gilles is good when it enters into the finality of the common project. But for me, what matters, really, is not that. The energy source is in the whatever, the mess."[218] His appeal to a right to derail finds added to it an almost Kafkian formulation: "I still have no control over this other world of systematic academic work, secret programming over dozens of years. I lack too much. Too much lag has accumulated.... I need to stop running

217. Félix Guattari, *The Anti-Oedipus Papers*, (New York: Semiotext(e), 2006), ed. by S. Nadaud, p. 399.

218. *Idem*, p. 400.

behind the image of Gilles and the polish, the perfection that he brought to the most unlikely book.... Dare to be an asshole. It's so hard, being strapped onto Gilles! Be stupid in my own way."[219]

Psychosis and Chaosmosis

Let us skip then directly to the heart of this book whose title was inspired by Joyce, *Chaosmosis'* greatest wager is to reconcile chaos and complexity on a same plane of immanence. Guattari refuses a simple and static idea of chaos: "especially those which would try to illustrate it in the form of a mixture, of holes, caverns, dust, even of fractal objects."[220] He insists mainly on the following points: 1) chaos "chaotizes," 2) it is "virtual," 3) it carries with it "hypercomplexity." An infinite velocity, bypassing discursive logics, and "generates as much disorder as it does complex virtual compositions."[221] "Chaos thus becomes the primary matter of virtuality, the inexhaustible reserve of an infinite determinability. This implies that in returning to it, it will always be possible to rediscover in it matter for the complexification of the state of things."[222] In a surprising parenthesis in *Chaosmosis*, he adds: "It is to Freud's credit that he showed the way in the *Traumdeutung*."[223] Guattari's Chaosmosis, however, does not coincide with the primary process. Unlike Freud, he privileges access to chaosmosis, what he calls a "chaotic umbilical zone," which passes primarily through psychosis and its pathic apprehension rather than neurosis, dreams or their interpretation. The chaosmic dimension, prior to discursivity, which the psychotic incarnates, literally "leaps at your neck," as Guattari puts it. What characterizes it is a singular combination of homogenesis and heterogenesis, of frozen repetition and incessant deterritorialization, where we pass from the "feeling of catastrophe about the end of the world" to the "overwhelming feeling of imminent redemption of every possibility," as we

---

219. *Idem*, p. 404.

220. Guattari, *Schizoanalytic Cartographies*, trans. Andrew Goffey, New York: Bloomsbury, p. 103.

221. *Idem*, p. 103.

222. *Idem*, pp. 103-104.

223. Félix Guattari, *Chaosmosis*, (Indianapolis: Indiana University Press, 1995), p. 80.

have seen before.[224] The existential ecstasy alternates between vacuity and complexity. This coexistence exceeds the figure of the mentally ill, with both poles finally rejoining everywhere, under diverse modalities. "We are confronted by it (chaosmosis) in group life, in economic relations, machinism (for example, informatics) and even in the incorporeal Universes of art or religion."[225] It is up to the schizoanalyst to dive into the homogenetic immanence and liberating heterogenetic coefficients where they can be found, beyond any oral performance, conception of the family or the idealized figure of the analyst.

According to this context, we would have to suppose two kinds of homogenesis converging within the primary heterogenesis of the depths. That of the neurotic, with his everyday "distraction and avoidance" of the chaosmosis, and that of the pathic-pathological, the loss of colors, flavors, tones, where we also find emerge an "alterification relieved of the mimetic barriers of the self."[226] Guattari's formula is twofold: on the one hand, as with Nietzsche, we "have to move quickly, we mustn't linger on something that might bog us down: madness, pain, death, drugs, the vertigo of the body without organs, extreme passion."[227] On the other hand, we must fight the reactive approach to chaosmosis, which secretes "an imaginary of eternity, particularly through the mass media, which misses its essential dimension of finitude: the facticity of being-there, without qualities, without past, without future, in absolute dereliction and yet still a virtual nucleus of complexity without bounds."[228] Everywhere it falls on us to detect the chaosmotic "congealings," which Guattari calls "Z or Zen points of Chaosmosis."[229]

If psychosis overwhelmingly reveals an essential source of being-in-the-world,[230] it is followed by a nuanced warning. "It is not therefore Being in general which irrupts in the chaosmotic experience of psychosis, or in the pathic relationship one can enter into with it, but a signed and dated event," with its ontological homogenesis, the sentiment of catastrophe, of the end

---

224. *Idem*, p. 81. Cf. the chapter of the present work "Exhaustion and Creation".

225. *Idem*, p. 85.

226. *Idem*, p. 84.

227. *Idem*, p. 84.

228. *Idem*, p. 84.

229. *Idem*, p. 84.

230. *Idem*, p. 77.

of the world, its peculiar texture, after which nothing will be as before, except for the "alarming oscillation between a proliferating complexity of sense and total vacuity, a hopeless dereliction of existential chaosmosis."[231] If Guattari compares this ontological petrifaction, so notable in psychosis, with a freeze-frame, he adds the following: it reveals its basic (or base) position in the polyphony of chaosmotic components. It is not, therefore, a degree zero of subjectivation, but an "extreme degree of intensification. It is in passing through this chaotic "earthing," this perilous oscillation, that something else becomes possible, that ontological bifurcations and the emergence of coefficients of processual creativity can occur."[232] One could object that the congealing to which pathology attests is contrary to the processuality that Guattari defends, and the status of schizophrenia in his work carries this paradox from the beginning. But the terms in which the question is put clarify the anchoring point of Guattari's approach. The fact that the sick psychotic patient is at times incapable of a heterogenetic reestablishment does not contradict the richness of the ontological experimentation with which he, in spite of himself, is confronted. He isn't the postmodern hero or normative model, and the chaosmotic ecstasies aren't the privilege of psychopathology; in the psychotic there appear, with less mediation, simultaneous strident combinations of speeds and slownesses, births and wreckings of worlds. As he recalls it: "A world is only constituted on the condition of being inhabited by an umbilical point — deconstructive, detotalizing and deterritorializing — from which a subjective positionality embodies itself. [...] At the same time, this vacuole of decompression is an autopoietic node on which existential Territories and Incorporeal Universes of reference constantly reaffirm and entangle themselves, demanding and developing consistency."[233] The fact is that the collapse of sense, in general, promotes a-signifying discursivities, causing ontological mutations. "So chaosmosis does not oscillate mechanically between zero and infinity, being and nothingness, order and disorder: it rebounds and irrupts on states of things, bodies and the autopoietic nuclei it uses as a support for deterritorialization.[...] Here we are dealing with an infinity of virtual entities infinitely

231. *Idem*, p. 81.

232. *Idem*, p. 82.

233. *Idem*, p. 80.

rich in possibles, infinitely enrichable through creative processes. […] Infinite speeds are loaded with finite speeds, with a conversion of the virtual into the possible, of the reversible into the irreversible, of the deferred into difference."[234] One last formula, a Nietzschean one, calls upon the "incorporeal eternal return of infinitude."[235]

Modulations of Existence

The entire question rests on how the "becoming consistent" of these autopoietic foci come into effect, how these "choices of finitude" occur, in which manner the inscription in a "memory of being" is given, and how to produce such an intensive ordering, what we could subsequently call proto-subjectivation or subjectivation *tout court*. This second fold, of active and creative autopoietic ordering which unleashes from the passivity inherent in the first chaosmotic fold, constitutes Guattari's fundamental interest.[236] "To produce new infinities from a submersion in sensible finitude, infinities not only charged with virtuality but with potentialities actualizable in given situations, circumventing or dissociating oneself from the Universals itemized by traditional arts, philosophy and psychoanalysis: intensive and processual becomings, a new love for the unknown."[237] The event is simultaneously actualization and intensive deterritorialization, "instantaneous and eternal, although already crystallized in spatial coordinates, temporal causalities, and energetic intervals." But there is an "existentifying" clause, which is reiterated innumerable times. The proto-subjective or even subjective finitization, supported on a prominent component of the infinite chaosmotic and deterritorialized velocity doesn't abolish the infinitization and the deterritorialization that it promotes, a little like a throw of the dice wouldn't abolish chance. Guattari's writing continually traverses these themes, and by means of instances which put complexity into discourse, wherein he is especially interested in manners of auto-referencing that coincide with the very process of subjectivation.

234. *Idem*, p. 112-3.

235. *Idem*, p. 113.

236. *Idem*, p. 112-3.

237. *Idem*, p. 117.

Hence, a self-founding subjectivity, consisting of itself, and processing its own coordinates. Referring to the neurologist Viktor von Weizsäcker, Guattari alludes to the idea of a subjectivity in relation to the depths (*Grundverhältnis*) — which proposes that the living (*vivants*), following different modulations, have an originary relation with life as depth. As Schotte explains: "As paradoxical as it may appear, the living phenomena cannot be represented through the natural forms of space and time. To take the example of causality, the living is an undergoing and a self-moving, it presents itself as being its own cause. The objectivity of the clinician consists, then, in substituting the ontic for the pathic. While physics presupposes that a conscious I be put face to face with a known object, biology [… assumes] that the living finds itself in a determination whose depth cannot itself become an object. The living, in its 'relation with the depth' (*Grundverhältnis*) discloses the ground: a non-objectifiable 'zoè'. [...] In its critical moments, life plunges into 'the depths,' from where it eventually resurges. The decision [which corresponds to the crisis] is '*Grundlegung*,' attestation and positioning of deepenings through the originary moment of a 'relation with the depth,' the obscure ground, indefinite life."[238]

As Maldiney says: the *depth* is the indeterminable, Anaximander's *apeiron,* from which emerges all finitude as its own abyss.[239] This is perhaps what Guattari, in the countercurrent of Heidegger's lineage and even of phenomenology, will call Chaosmosis. The consistency and subjective inflection thereby arising, in their turn, shall depend more on the categories which von Weizsäcker called pathic, more on the modalities of "existentifying" than ontic determinations. What interests a patient, for example, is not what he is in the eyes of the doctor (ontic category), but what he is capable of, what he wants, what he should become, what he does or doesn't desire and so on. Such verbs modulate the pathic subject, and as Schotte — to whom Guattari refers in his *Schizoanalytic Cartographies* — puts it in any human or clinical situation, what is at stake is always the will, action, power, that pass through sieves provisionally

---

238. Jacques Schotte, *Une pensée du clinique. L'oeuvre de Viktor von Weizsäcker*, Université Catholique de Louvain, Faculté de psychologie et des sciences de l'éducation, May 1985. Notes by Ph. Lekeuche and reviewed by the author.

239. Henri Maldiney, *Penser l'homme et la folie*, (Grenoble: Millon, 1991).

halting the flux of becoming, modulating it. In this way, the pathic dimension is less of the order of suffering than that of experimentation, neither passive nor active, close to Blanchot's "neuter" or Deleuze's 'impersonal,' an a-subjectivity.

At stake is the abandoning of the logic of the all or nothing: "Here, existence is won, lost, intensified, traverses qualitative thresholds due to its adherence to this or that incorporeal Universe of endo-reference." In a philosophical amplification, he affirms: "an open range of existential intensities is substituted for the brutal caesura Being/Nothingness" since "Being is the modulation of consistency, the rhythm of putting together and dismantling [*montage et démontage*]. Its cohesion, if not its coherence, arises neither from an internal principle of eternity nor from an extrinsic causalist framing that would hold existents together at the heart of the same world. Rather, it results from the conjugation of processualities of intrinsic consistency, themselves engaging in generalized relations of existential transversality."[240]

Psychoanalysis and Post-Psychoanalysis

The ethical wager is to multiply the "existential shifters" to infinity, joining creative mutant Universes. The ontological pragmatic corresponds to this function of existentialization, detecting intensive indices, diagrammatic operators in any point or domain whatsoever, without any ambition to universalize them, so that what is required are not instruments of interpretation, but cartographic tools. Even the little "a" of Lacan, with its admirable deterritorializing character, or the partial objects of Melanie Klein, can be considered as "crystals of singularization," "points of bifurcation outside the dominant coordinates, on the basis of which mutant universes of reference can spring up."[241] However, it is not fitting to make universals of desire out of them within a cartography that is itself mutant. If we approach Guattari in this manner, little by little the psychoanalytic notions that he invokes, in an entirely redesigned landscape, will more clearly indicate the direction of his schizoanalytic project. He defends a post-mediatic age,

---

240. Félix Guattari, *Schizoanalytic Cartographies*, op. cit., p. 107-08.

241. *Idem*, p. 36.

indicating with this not so much the surpassing of media but rather its miniaturization, its personalization, multicentering, decentralization, fractalization, proliferation, its propagation as well as the diversification of its modalities of enunciation, the molecularization and dissemination of its apparatus, in sum, the generalized appropriation of its enunciative potential. This implies and at the same time results in a sociotechnical, semiotic and above all subjective reinvention. In the same way, we could say that his schizoanalytic elaboration points to a post-psychoanalytic age whose theoretical and cartographic operators he intends, without any universalizing ambition, to establish. The first pages of *Schizoanalytic Cartographies* are very clear regarding the status of this theorization. No monotheism, no scientificity, but a liberty to take or abandon whatever is wanted from this open collection that he does not stop completing, remaking, amassing, redesigning, in order to rearrange cartographic criteria in face of the urgencies of the present, the evoked situations, always singular, whether clinical, institutional or scientific. As we read in his eighth rule for analysis of the machinic unconscious: "any principle idea must be held suspect."[242] The theoretical elaboration is even more necessary and more audacious to the extent that a schizoanalytic assemblage admits its precarious nature. Or, as it was already stated in the preparatory texts for *Anti-Oedipus*: "Theory is, or needs to be, instrumentalist, functionalist.... Break with the theory-oeuvre, and arrive at: 'to each his own theory.' Collective assemblages of enunciation *produce* their own theories by articulating themselves on planes of consistency.... Theory is artifice. Its foundation is what, historically, is most deterritorialized, it works with machinic indices," this movement being, by definition, unending. [243] It is as if Guattari suspected an end to oeuvres and canonical redundancies, academics included, that could weaken what for him was in play, in this vanishing, maddening, derailing construction. So then, the ethics that guide the project are clear: to make "the pragmatic of incorporeal events that will recompose the world flourish."

All efforts move in the direction of rethinking that which has conventionally been called the Unconscious: this time

242. Félix Guattari, *The Machinic Unconscious: Essays in Schizoanalysis*, trans. Taylor Adkins, Cambridge: Semiotext(e), 2011, p. 198.

243. Félix Guattari, *The Anti-Oedipus Papers*, op. cit., p. 366.

thinking of it *as a function* of the assemblages. What Freud may, in the end, have accomplished, is a mutation of the Assemblage of Enunciation. In this sense, the very problematization of the unconscious should be refounded in the direction of a partial subjectivity, pre-personal, polyphonic, collective and machinic — under the sign of a logic of non-discursive intensities on the one hand, and the pathic incorporation-agglomeration of these vectors of partial subjectivity within deterritorializations on the other, all of which are to be adequately mapped. "Everything leads me to think that [...] it would be preferable for psychoanalysis to multiply and to differentiate the expressive components that it puts into play, as much as possible. And for its own Assemblages of enunciation not to be arranged next to the couch, such that the dialectic of the gaze is radically foreclosed. Analysis has everything to gain from enlarging its means of intervention; it can work with speech, but equally with modeling clay (like Gisela Pankow), or with video, cinema, theater, institutional structures, family interactions, etc. In short, everything that allows the a-signifying facets of the refrains that it encounters to be stimulated, in such a way that it is better able to set off their catalytic functions of crystallizing new Universes of reference [...] and to explore their pragmatic virtualities."[244]

We do not think that this task of amplification, initially attributed to transversality, and then to institutional analysis, and finally, schizoanalysis, has suffered decisive inflections throughout Guattari's trajectory, ever since its first, still stammering formulations, but also in the midst of terminological or even conceptual changes. In a chapter of his *Machinic Unconscious*, Guattari shoots at close range: "First of all, what is this unconscious really? Is it a magical world hidden in who knows which fold of the brain? An internal mini-cinema specialized in child pornography or the projection of fixed archetypal plans?"[245] And he answers: "I would see the unconscious instead as something that we drag around with ourselves both in our gestures and daily objects, as well as on TV, that is part of the zeitgeist, and even, and perhaps especially, in our day-to-day problems. [...] Thus, the unconscious works inside individuals in their manner of perceiving the world and living their

244. Félix Guattari, *Schizoanalytic Cartographies*, op. cit., pp. 213-14.

245. Félix Guattari, *The Machinic Unconscious: Essays in Schizoanalysis*, trans. Taylor Adkins, Cambridge: Semiotext(e), 2011, pp. 9-10.

body, territory, and sex, as well as inside the couple, the family, school, neighborhood, factories, stadiums, and universities... In other words, not simply an unconscious of the specialists of the unconscious, not simply an unconscious crystallized in the past, congealed in an institutionalized discourse, but, on the contrary, an unconscious turned toward the future whose screen would be none other than the possible itself, the possible as hypersensitive to language, but also the possible hypersensitive to touch, hypersensitive to the socius, hypersensitive to the cosmos...."[246]

In relation to these processes, the challenge is "to semiotically and machinically assist them."[247] Hence, no order-words, only words of passage. Everything is passage, from one consistency to another, from a complex of possibilities to another, from one assemblage to another.[248] Well, in the end, we should not speak of reality. Social, mental objects, the intrapsychic entities should be translated in the terms of an assemblage. An assemblage, contrary to a structure, always depends on the heterogeneous components that contribute to its specific consistency. "An assemblage is inconsistent when it is emptied of its quanta of possibles, when the signs-particles desert it to emigrate towards other assemblages, when the abstract machinisms that specify them become sclerotic, degenerate into abstraction, and become encysted in stratifications and structures, when finally it subsides in a black hole of resonance or falls to the threat of pure and simple disintegration (catastrophe of consistency). On the contrary, it takes on consistency when a deterritorialized machinic metabolism opens it up to new connections, differentiates and complexifies...."[249]

Status of the Infinite

When Guattari defines the unconscious as being productive and not representational, when he places it back within the Assemblages of Enunciation, or when — mostly at the end of his life — he thinks it in terms of Chaosmosis, it is clear that he

---

246. Félix Guattari, *The Machinic Unconscious*, op. cit. p. 9-10.

247. op. cit., p. 186.

248. *Idem*, pp. 187-88.

249. *Idem*. p.220.

carries out an increasing radicalization in the relation of the unconscious with the Outside, an incessant effort to proliferate, molecularize and infinitize it which redesigns the unconscious entirely.

It is worth recalling the passage in *What is Philosophy?* on chaos and the brain: "We require just a little order to protect us from chaos. Nothing is more distressing than a thought that escapes itself, than ideas that fly off, that disappear hardly formed, already eroded by forgetfulness or precipitated into others that we no longer master. These are infinite *variabilities*, the appearing and disappearing of which coincide. They are infinite speeds that blend into the immobility of the colorless and silent nothingness they traverse, without nature or thought…. We constantly lose our ideas. That is why we want to hang on to fixed opinions so much. We ask only that our ideas are linked together according to a minimum of constant rules. All that the association of ideas has ever meant is providing us with these protective rules — resemblance, contiguity, causality — which enable us to put some order into ideas, preventing our "fantasy" (delirium, madness) from crossing the universe in an instant, producing winged horses and dragons breathing fire."[250] For Guattari, thinking in light of schizophrenia intensifies the relations between form and its dissolution, unlivable velocity and its interruption, heterogenesis and homogenesis. The pathic relation with the mentally ill, that is, the complex and immediate body-to-body relation with the intensive and infinite movements, put at risk a plurality of temporalities, fragments, disjunctive syntheses, transversal schizo connections, collapses, paralyses, slips and destructions of sense…. That a delimited and precise frame such as the one proposed by Freud should have difficulty coping with such a proliferation isn't surprising.

From there, I can understand perfectly the final observation of an article published by Monique David-Ménard in the journal *Rue Descartes* on the subject of transference, counterposing the contributions of Deleuze-Guattari to those of Foucault. By exposing accurately the notion of Deleuzian assemblage, she writes: "But there is a difficulty in simultaneously postulating the positive and precise character of the assemblages and how

---

250. Gilles Deleuze and Félix Guattari, *What is Philosophy?* (New York: Columbia University Press, 1994), p. 201

they are 'sucked in' by the infinite. The infinite is not only in-finitesimal in Deleuze, but also the near exhaustion of a figure, a character, when it connects itself to another thing through a relation of intensity."[251] And she asks: "How can we think the consistency of an event and its affinity to chaos conjointly, de-fined as the circulation within infinite speed and in all direc-tions, of the microelements of matter? The chaotic being ex-actly the indetermination of apparitions and vanishings, when the particles composing a body circulate at such a speed that no factual connection can either form or enunciate itself. It is this third meaning of the infinite, an affinity with chaos, that makes a metaphysics out of the thought of transformations, to the extent that every individual, body and expression defined, is considered by the way he or she 'surfs' the chaos. If the term 'metaphysics' is no longer appropriate for a philosophy that can conjure transformations without submerging itself into cate-gories, one might, however, as Foucault himself did, speak of a metaphysics of an 'extra-being': all the transformations in-tertwine within a rhizome on the plane of immanence whose characteristics the philosopher enunciates."[252] By valorizing the contribution of the questions Deleuze raised to psycho-analysis, which had already been done in spades in her book titled *Deleuze et la psychanalyse,* especially regarding the sta-tus of repetition, negativity, transformations and assemblages, within the clinic and within philosophy, David-Ménard points out: "Nothing awakens psychoanalysis as much as the ques-tions raised by Deleuze. But it's not certain that the concept of imperceptible-becomings, the thought of unqualified affects versus that of the destiny of drive, helps comprehend the limit of transfer. For this we need to look toward Foucault and his *dispositifs.* [...] To speak of the 'Unconscious' has no meaning outside of the discreet elements and connections that manage, borrowing contingent details of the space or figure of the ana-lyst, to draw themselves there."[253] I believe that the author's ef-fort is entirely pertinent to the psychoanalytic field and within the healthy intersection that this field proposed to philosophy and in the healthy provocation that the philosophies, Deleuze's

251. Monique David-Ménard, "Agencements deleuziens, dispositifs foucaldiens" *Rue Descartes*, n. 59, Collège International de Philosophie, (Paris: Puf, 2008), pp. 44-5.

252. *Idem*, p. 5.

253. *Idem*, p. 55.

among them, proposed to psychoanalytic practice and theorization. And yet, what we have been describing with Guattari moves in direct opposition to the author's conclusion, which in turn does not discredit her observations, on the contrary — it only indicates the point of view that is prominent in the work of Guattari: that of overflowing the "discreet and connected elements" that draw themselves based on the contingent details of space and on the "figure of the analyst." If I privilege Guattari's texts from the very beginning within the present context, it is to indicate how his thought (starting from the point-sign and its own potency, including his transversality and his "transcursivity," as he would point out during the initial period of his reflections, or later on by way of his explication of the machine and its indefinite opening to an infinite exteriority, either from the status of the group or institutional phantasm overflowing the individual) extrapolates the classic clinical "dispositif," initially developed by Freud. Furthermore, when Guattari introduces the theme of chaos, even before the "systematization" jointly proposed in *What is Philosophy?* (even though in order to define chaos, chaosmos or chaosmosis, he reintroduces characteristics previously attributed to the body without organs in *Anti-Oedipus* or *A Thousand Plateaus*), it must be stated that the assemblages, in their contingency and consistency, inevitably imply the infinite, despite how polysemic this term's acceptance is. "Polyvalent doctrine of the infinite,"[254] as David-Ménard says: as an infinite speed, as the verb's infinitive in the event, its impersonality, or even as the Leibnizian infinitesimal.[255] None of this means an incompatibility, and even less so the disqualification of the relevance of this fertile discussion that the author, among many others, face with superior courage. We must recognize that there is, in this program that Guattari sustains with

---

254. Monique David-Ménard, *Deleuze et la psychanalyse*, (Paris: Puf, 2005), p. 109.

255. *Idem*, p. 118. And David-Ménard's question: "The true question to be put forward to Deleuze, the one I do in any case, is to know […] whether if in order to know the contingency of the assemblages that sustain themselves, it is necessary to conceive the infinite […] We have difficulty in comprehending why, in the field of analysis, would we speak of the infinite to characterize that which threatens to undo poorly-constructed assemblages of desire. The symptoms that make life unbearable have a finite configuration, and the transferences that allow, in the favorable cases, to engage those analyzed in other transformations have, them as well, a finite configuration. It's even in fact to this limit of transference that the destructivity of desires can be repeated, extracted from chaos, so to speak, and transformed into a new assemblage whose key does not predate the cure" (*Idem*, p. 126).

a peculiar stubbornness, his taste for Jules Verne, his militancy, and his effort for placing on the same plane (as formulated by Deleuze) philosophical concepts, scientific functions, lived experiences, artistic creations as necessary for "surfing" around the infinite, or the infinitization, or the slide in the infinitive.

It's not about an ontology of the infinite, nor of a dialectic between the finite and the infinite. I tend to think, strangely, that part of this ambition comes from his experience with psychosis and from a political gamble. To launch a formula that is equivalent in worth to the categoric formulae: on one side, a post-psychoanalytic direction of his thought, on the other, a post-nihilistic stance.[256] In any case, thinking in light of schizophrenia compels one to install a multiplicity that calls into question the dichotomies inside and out, the interior and exterior, corporeal and incorporeal, individual and social, psychism and history, internal space and geography, human and inhuman, anthropological and ethological, the sphere of man and machine (several machines, both technical and social), the form and its dissolution, the unlivable speed and its interruption. That a delimited and precise frame, such as the one proposed since Freud, would have difficulty in containing such blurriness and proliferation is not surprising, and the very experience of La Borde itself, ever since its birth, already constitutes an experiment toward that amplification, to which Guattari had referred to since his first writings in *Psychanalysis and Transversality*, relating his clinic with the sociohistorical exteriority (note the example of the patient similar to Kafka, and the use of the tape recorder or of writing). The reiterated reclaiming of the opening to alterity does not make reference to an alterity of another subject (such as in the phenomenological conceptions on intersubjectivity), but rather to a more complete alterity, that of the situation itself — in some instances, the name of "transversality" was given to this. However, this described situation is precarious and mutant. Hence the theme of the recognition of finitude, of death, of the without-meaning, in the midst of a group or institution, the complete refusal of eternization, that an institutional, group, social-phantasmic structure could spawn, and what will later be called Assemblage, should

---

256. I realize, however, the opposite of that stance, formulated with such grace by João Perci Schiavon: schizoanalysis is still psychoanalysis, just as quantum physics is still physics, in *The drive pragmatism*, n-1 publications, forthcoming.

include. "Will the day ever come when President Schreber's and Artaud's definitions of God are studied with the same attention and same rigor as those of Descartes or Malebrache? [...] Philosophical research would therefore have to concern itself not only with a constant conceptual reordering, but also with developing, in the "field," conditions for establishing and maintaining a logic of nonsense as it emerges in every domain, updating the register of the possibilities of signification of human existence, here, elsewhere and now."[257]

Let Us Return to the Problem of Writing

A reader already familiar with the books and the independent texts of Guattari, in perusing the sketches laid out in *The Anti-Oedipus Papers*, recently published by Nadeau, will be initially struck by a paradoxical impression. On the one hand, there is the spewing, the associative velocity, the whimsical nature of his articulations, the freedom of the leap, the heterodoxical language, the colloquial examples of the most elementary quotidian form, the insults, alternating with the denser constructions, neologisms, the still so remarkable presence of Lacan, the fundamental formulae, all this matter that drips everywhere, and that will make up for the conceptual center of *The Anti-Oedipus Papers*; at the same time, when confronted with this logbook, this reluctance to "do the work," the reader may be surprised and admire how Deleuze took a chance and took it upon himself to do this task, connecting himself with the general direction of Guattarian constructivist and cartographic explosivity, even if the logic of this machination has not been completely unraveled. We would have to return, here, to Deleuze-s observation written for the occasion of Guattari's death, where he recommends the reading of his texts: "Félix's work is waiting to be discovered. That is one of the best ways to keep Félix alive."[258] Now, Guattari's autonomous books are not directly comparable to the notes found in *The Anti-Oedipus Papers*, and the effort of his friends, notably Danielle Sivadon, to assist him by providing them with some sort of contour, gives us a clear indication that

257. Félix Guattari, *Psychoanalysis and Transversality,* op. cit., p. 135

258. Gilles Deleuze, "Pour Félix", in *Deux Régimes de Fous*, (Paris: Minuit, 2003), pp. 357-8.

this is the case. But there seems to be a rare impression that falls over each of Guattari's readers to do something similar to what Sivadon did to his physical papers, or at least mentally, in the manner of Deleuze: that is, to take something from his machinations, to extend them and connect them with different domains — to make them work. To grant them the freedom to evolve on their own, reaching out to them for matter's sake, in lieu of reducing them to some polemic formulae, even though they do not lack formulae of their own, even less so polemic *enjeux*, in the most diverse of fields.

* This chapter was translated with help by Filipe Ferreira and generous revision supervision by Andrew Goffey

THE THOUGHT OF THE OUTSIDE,
THE OUTSIDE OF THOUGHT

We should evoke the name of Maurice Blanchot in order to remind ourselves of the barely audible voice that uniquely marked the thought of an entire generation — which includes Deleuze, Foucault and Derrida. Blanchot became a sort incarnation of Kafka'a "Josephine the singer" during the postwar French philosophy. In Kafka's story, even though the nation of rats greatly admires the voice of the singer, which they need in order to come together, they do not understand what makes it so special or whether it really is special. In fact, her song resembles a gentle hissing or even silence. It is possible, in the last analysis, that her glory is the result of this gracious and undecipherable mystery: perhaps, she has never sung anything at all, but, in her own way, in her "insufficiency" (*rien de rendement*) she has nevertheless delivered people from "the chains of everyday existence."

This existence is always paradoxical in Kafka, as Blanchot makes clear: "we do not know if we are excluded from it (which is why we search vainly in it for something solid to hold onto) or whether we are forever imprisoned in it (and so we turn desperately outside)."[259] There is an invisible and always displaced boundary between life and death, between exiting and entering, and between an ardent desire for community or the distancing of ourselves from it in solitude. Kafka has often described this solitude as an exile: "Now I am already a citizen in

---

259. Maurice Blanchot, *The Work of Fire*, trans. Charlotte Mandell (Stanford: Stanford University Press, 1995).

this other world which compares with the usual world just as the desert compares to the cultivated land."[260] But, says Blanchot, the meaning of this banishment that we would be wrong to characterize as flight is this: this other world inhabited by the author from Prague is not just any old "beyond," not even another world, but rather the other of all worlds. For the artist or the poet, perhaps there are no two worlds, not even a single world, but only the outside in its eternal flow.

Wandering, desert, exile, the outside. How can we conquer the loss of ourselves and go to the heart of the anonymous dispersion, indefinite, albeit never negligent? How can we enter into a space without place, in a time without begetting, in "the proximity of that which flees unity," in an "experience of that which is without harmony and without accord?" At any rate, we are at the opposite end of a metaphorics of proximity, of shelter, of security, and of harmony — the kind that Heidegger established for an entire generation. Underlining this contrast with Heidegger, Françoise Collin has found the right words: in Blanchot's case, poetic language "directs us not toward what gathers together but rather toward what disperses, not toward what connects but rather toward what disjoins, not toward work but rather toward the absence of work [...] so that the central point toward which we seem to be pulled as we write is nothing but the absence of center, the lack of origin."[261] Not Being, but the Other, the Outside, the Neutral. This passion for/ of the Outside which runs through the febrile writing of Kafka, also runs through the impalpable work of Blanchot and resonates in Foucault's obsession with the themes of boundaries and limits, of alterity and exteriority, or in Deleuze and Guattari, in their relation to the outside and to the entire nomadic machinery which derives from it.

260. Franz Kafka, *Journal*, quoted by Maurice Blanchot, *The Space of Literature*, trans. and with an introduction by Ann Smock (Lincoln: University of Nebraska Press, 1982), p. 68.

261. Françoise Collin, *Maurice Blanchot et la question de l'écriture* (Paris: Gallimard, 1971).

The Passion for/of the Outside

Deleuze used to say that, as a rule, two thinkers encounter each other at a blind spot. And indeed, Deleuze and Foucault cross each other's path at this eccentric point *par excellence*, which is the thought of the outside. I will try to show how this passion for/of the outside traversed their philosophy as a frenzied wind, inflecting the relations between thought and its borders, whether we call these borders outside, unreason, madness, or schizo-flux. For that purpose we must be situated between philosophy and madness, reason and unreason, thought and the outside of thought. Allow me to briefly justify the choice of this theme of madness and unreason, as we settle into this new millennium. I think that the interface between philosophy and madness in Foucault and Deleuze could help us rethink today's status of exteriority at a moment in which exteriority is the object of a frightful overturning; the most immediate consequence of which is the suffocating impression that the field of the possible has been exhausted. Allow me to explain: for a long time, the promise of an absolute outside has been linked to the domain of madness, to the domain of literature, or to that of the revolution. This has changed completely. As far as I can see, the contemporary claustrophobia — whose consequences of political and psychic strangulation are not, I suppose, Brazil's prerogative — is nothing but an index, among many others, of a situation in front of which we feel entirely disarmed; that is, an index of a thought without an outside in a world without exteriority. Before getting into the details of this hypothesis that I intend to develop, I should perhaps indicate the parallel questions that motivate my intervention. Indeed, what is left today of this passion for/of the outside that our authors have explored and given us? From the point of view of this inspiration or even in spite of it, how can we rethink the very concept of the outside? What about the exteriority of madness? How do we evaluate whether or not the outsides, to the extent that they are still accessible to us today, are still capable of grounding our resistances to the intolerable, or to incite the creation of new possibles?

Foucault and Blanchot

Let us return to the seminal study of Michel Foucault on madness, from which these questions arise. We should first of all remember Blanchot's brief, yet penetrating and sober commentary concerning this issue: the existence of madness, he said, responds to the historical demand to fence in the outside.[262] This is an enigmatic formula, the meaning of which appears only in the light of the secret dialogue linking Blanchot and Foucault, through the distance that an excessive admiration imposed. In an interview, following the publication of his book in 1961, Foucault spoke of the influences that inspired him: "Above all works of literature," he immediately states, placing Blanchot's name above all the rest.... "What interested and guided me was a certain form of the presence of madness within literature."[263] How can we understand this alleged "influence" of Blanchot on the *History of Madness*? Rather than taking up his novels, we must perhaps look to the seductive readings that Blanchot proposed of the works of Hölderlin, Sade, Lautréamont, Nietzsche, Artaud — in short, we must look to the entire lineage evoked in the last pages of Foucault's own book. Indeed, ever since his first critical essays, and in his very own way, Blanchot worked on issues that many of his contemporaries have taken up after him: the necessary proximity between speech and silence, writing and death, work and erosion, literature and demolition, language and the anonymous, poetic experience and the breakdown of the author. According to *Le Livre à venir*, "what is first is not the plenitude of being, it is the crack and the fissure, the erosion and the tear, intermittence and the gnawing privation."[264] In literature, Blanchot discovers the rarified space from which every subject is absent. What speaks within the writer is that "he is no longer himself, he is already no one": not the universal, but the anonymous, the neutral, the outside. When one is releasing herself to that which is incessant and interminable in language, "the day is nothing more than the loss of a dwelling place. It is intimacy with the outside, which has no location

---

262. Maurice Blanchot, *The Infinite Conversation*, trans. Susan Hanson (Minneapolis: University of Minnesota Press, 1992), pp. 196–201.

263. Michel Foucault, *Dits et Écrits 1954–1988*, vol. 1, 1954–1969, ed. Daniel Defert and François Ewald (Paris: Gallimard, 1994), p. 168.

264. Maurice Blanchot, *Le Livre à venir* (Paris: Gallimard, 1959), pp. 49–50.

and affords no rest."[265] He who inhabits this literary space "belong(s) to dispersal [...] where the exterior is the intrusion that stifles [...] where the only space is its vertiginous separation."[266] This is the work as an experience which ruins all experiences and places itself underneath the work, "a region [...] where nothing is made of being, and in which nothing is accomplished. It is the depth of being's unworking (*désoeuvrement*)."[267] It is an uncanny experience that dispossesses the subject of self and world, of being and presence, of consciousness and truth, of unity and totality — experience of limits, experience-limit, as Bataille would have said.

This whole thematic spread is present in the original preface to the *History of Madness*.[268] In it, Foucault makes references to an originary language, "very crude," in which reason and unreason still speak of each other, through "imperfect words, without fixed syntax, stammering a bit." Through these means, the limits of a culture are put to question against all triumphant dialectics. Beneath history, one finds the absence of history, a murmur of the deep, the void, the vain, nothingness, residue, ripples. Beneath the work, one finds the absence of work, below sense, nonsense. Beneath reason, one finds unreason. In sum, a tragic experience is concealed by the birth of madness as a social fact, object of exclusion, confinement and intervention. What can possibly be done for unreason? To preserve unreason in its irreducible alterity, in its "tragic structure" to investigate the birth itself of psychiatric rationality that reduced unreason to silence while at the same time turning it into madness?

At any rate, we should keep in mind the first two words of the original title of the 1961 edition which was later suppressed — *Madness and Unreason: The History of Madness in the Classical Age*. Setting aside the lyrical misunderstandings to which they gave rise, this binomial continues to intrigue us. Blanchot made this point when he asked whether, in the space which opens up between madness and unreason, literature and art could gather their own liminal experiences and thus,

---

265. Maurice Blanchot, *The Space of Literature*, p. 31.

266. *Ibid*.

267. Maurice Blanchot, *The Space of Literature*, 46.

268. Michel Foucault, "Préface" in *Folie et déraison. Histoire de la folie à l'âge classique* (Paris: Plon,1961) I–IX; reprinted in *Dits et Écrits* vol. 1, pp. 159–67.

"prepare beyond culture, a relation with that which rejects culture: speech of the border, the outside of speech."[269] Foucault responded to this, according to the dialogue that my imagination reconstructs and imposes, with the example of Blanchot. He explained that, in Blanchot, the erosion of time speaks louder than time's links. The erosion of time speaks of the non-dialectical forgetting, which opens up the anticipation of the radically new, the sliding toward a naked exteriority — language as an endless whisper that deposes the subjective source of enunciation as much as it deposes the truth of the statement, letting the anonymous emerge, free from every center and fatherland, capable of echoing the death of God and the death of man alike. In the place where "it [ça] speaks, man no longer exists." Against the humanist dialectics that, from alienation to reconciliation, promises man the authentic man, Blanchot expresses the outline of another original choice emerging in our culture. At any rate, if language is not "truth or time, eternity or man, but rather the form of the outside always coming undone,"[270] then we can understand why Foucault is able, echoing Kafka, to advance his splendid formula that writing is not of this world — it is its "antimatter."[271]

Literature and Madness

We are already in the position to put forward a more general hypothesis. If Foucault *believes* so strongly in literature, perhaps it is because at this moment along his trajectory he believes in its *exteriority*. And if the language of madness interests him, it is because what is at stake in the language of madness is again its exteriority. From this point of view, writing and madness would be on the same plane, taking into account their noncirculatory character, the uselessness of their function, and the self-referential aspect which characterizes them.[272] But we should take

269. Maurice Blanchot, *The Infinite Conversation*, p. 290.

270. Michel Foucault, "The Thought of the Outside" in *Michel Foucault: Ethics, Subjectivity and Truth: Essential Works of Foucault* vol. 1, ed. Paul Rabinow (New York: The New Press, 1997) p. 168.

271. Michel Foucault, "A Swimmer Between Two Words: Interview With C. Bonnefoy" in *Michel Foucault: Ethics, Subjectivity and Truth* p.172.

272. Michel Foucault, "Madness Only Exists In Society" in *Foucault Live: Collected Interviews 1961–1984. Michel Foucault*, ed. Sylvère Lotringer (New York: Semiotext(e),

into account their subversive and transgressive dimension, "the absolutely anarchic speech, the speech without institution, the deeply marginal speech that traverses and erodes all other discourses."[273] Literature and madness, therefore, would belong to what Blanchot called the part of fire," namely, that which culture destines for destruction and reduces to cinders, that with which it cannot live, and that with which it makes an eternal conflagration.

And yet, in the very moment that Foucault makes explicit this site of literature, he asks himself whether the times when "writing was enough to express a protest against modern society" have not already gone by.[274] In catching up with the space of social circulation and consumption, perhaps writing has been, as they used to say at that time, recuperated by the system, in fact vanquished by the bourgeoisie and the capitalist society. It is no longer in "the outside," it no longer maintains that exteriority. Hence the question: in order to cross to the other side, in order to set oneself on fire and be consumed by it, in order to enter into a space irreducible to our own and into a space that would not be a part of society, shouldn't we do something other than literature? If we discover today that we must exit literature and abandon it to its "meager historical destiny" Foucault said, it is Blanchot, always he, who taught us. The one who has been the most impregnated with literature, but always in a key of exteriority, the anti-Hegel of literature, the one who showed us that works always stay external to us and we to them, obliges us to abandon literature at the very moment that literature deserts the outside in order to become this inside where we communicate and recognize one another very comfortably.

The same logic would apply to madness, whose dimension of exteriority would also be on the path of disappearance. Very early on in his trajectory, as early as 1964, Foucault prophesied the imminent effacement of madness in favor of mental illness.[275] If madness was for man this enigmatic exteriority

1989) pp. 7–9.

273. Michel Foucault, "La Folie et la société" in Michel Foucault and Moriaki Watanabe, *Telsugaku no Butai* (Tokyo: Asahi-Shupansa, 1978); reprinted in *Michel Foucault, Dits et Écrits* vol. 3, 1976–1979 (Paris: Gallimard, 1994) p. 490.

274. Michel Foucault, "Folie, littérature, société" in *Dits et Écrits* vol. 2, 1970–1975 (Paris: Gallimard, 1994) p. 115.

275. Michel Foucault, "La Folie, l'absence d'oeuvre" in *La Table Ronde* (*Situation de la Psychiatrie*) no. 196 (May 1964): pp. 11–21; reprinted in *Dits et Écrits* vol. 1, pp. 412–20.

that he excluded, but in which he also recognized himself, and which reflected everything that he found abominable, but was also integral to his most intimate constitution, his Other but at the same time his Same, now that the future is approaching, madness will be incorporated in the human as its ownmost originary. This is a process to which we gave the name, perhaps ironically: the "humanization" of madness. With the help of this diabolical dialectics, we will have achieved the unthinkable: we will have robbed ourselves of our own exteriority.

Let us dare raise the burning question: has not Foucault, through the case of "literature" and "madness" outlined a more general diagnostic of the status of exteriority in our culture? And, if this is the case, is this diagnostic of any use to us today? Michael Hardt and Toni Negri have shown that the world's integrated capitalism has assumed the form of Empire[276]; in order to do this, it had to abolish all exteriority, devouring its most distant frontiers, encompassing not only the totality of the planet, but also the enclaves which were until recently inviolate — like the Unconscious or Nature, as Jameson would have added. Is it possible then that Foucault's diagnosis, no less cruel than precocious, together with its imperial planetary realization, has the capacity to shed light on our contemporary claustrophobia? We are now inhabiting a world without outside, a capitalism without outside, a thought without outside — in view of which our fascination with the alleged exteriority of madness, predominant only a few decades ago, sounds completely obsolete today. Foucault himself caustically criticizes all those "lyric anti-psychiatric discourses" and especially the illusions that madness, delinquency, or crime speak to us from the vantage point of an absolute exteriority. "Nothing is more interior to our society (says he), nothing is more within the effects of its power, than the affliction of a crazy person or the violence of a criminal." In other words, we are always on the inside. The margin is a myth. The word from beyond is a dream that we keep renewing. The "crazies" are in an outside space of creativity or monstrosity. And nonetheless, they are caught in

276. Michael Hardt, "La Société mondiale de contrôle" in *Gilles Deleuze. Une Vie Philosophique*, ed. Eric Alliez (Paris: Synthélabo, 1998) 359–75; Michael Hardt and Toni Negri, *Empire*, (Cambridge: Harvard University Press, 2000).

the network, they are shaped and function within the mechanisms of power.[277]

Now, this radical reversal of perspective in Foucault should not surprise us, if we consider his work on prisons, and the new problematization of power that his genealogical inflection has elicited. In this sense, it is understandable that he writes "madness is no less the effect of power than non-madness."[278] It is, "according to an indefinite spiral, a tactical response to the tactic that invests it," and we should not go so far as to "overvalue the asylum and its infamous walls," since it must be understood "from the outside,"[279] as a pawn in a broader positive strategy that gave birth to an entire psychology of the psyche.

Let us stop here and suspend the burning question — if we are always inside, what is left of the outside? I will no longer follow the detours of this theme throughout the work of Foucault, especially from his third theoretical period. Instead, I will only focus on one, all-too-illuminating example: when, in 1980, he evokes the limit experience by means of which the subject tears itself from itself, and is led to its own annihilation and dissolution (a theme which was dear to the 1960s), the question is no longer for him the experimentation with an outside of culture, but rather a personal and theoretical experiment by means of which it would be possible *to think otherwise*. If literature and madness no longer send us over to an absolute outside, since all is inside, the experience-limit keeps its own value to the extent that it is an operation on one's own self. Not a lived experience, but the unlivable for the sake of which we must produce ourselves. No more a transgression of a frontier or a prohibition, even if Bataille's name is invoked once more, but a demolition and refabrication of the self. This way, the outside attains an altogether surprising subjective immanence. Perhaps a reading of Deleuze will better elucidate the immanent status of this exteriority, which sprung up again in a subject within a world already without outside.

277. Michel Foucault, "The Social Extension of the Norm" in *Foucault Live*, p. 198.

278. Michel Foucault, "Sorcery and Madness" in *Foucault Live*, p. 201.

279. Michel Foucault, "L'Asile illimité," *Le Nouvel Observateur* no. 646 (March 28th–April 3rd, 1977): pp. 66–67; reprinted in *Dits et Écrits* vol. 3, p. 273.

Deleuze and the Outside

With Deleuze, we must say it from the beginning, everything takes place in a different way right from the start, whether it is a question of madness or of the outside. For him, madness has never been an object of study as such. And yet it frequently reappears in the vicinity of thought, as if this vicinity was intrinsic to it, as if the act of thinking necessarily reaches this volcanic region where that which madness reveals, in a crude and very Oedipalized way, is being realized. What is being realized is the dissolution of the subject, of the object, of the Self, the world and God, in favor of a generalized nomadization where the psychosocial figure of the schizophrenic is nothing more than a caricatural interruption, crystallized and institutionalized. In fact, nomadism and the relation to the outside are not exclusive attributes of the schizo, but they belong to thought as such. Deleuze increasingly insists upon this: to think comes always from the outside, and is directed toward the outside, belongs to the outside, is an absolute relation to the outside.[280] As Zourabichvili remarks, thought is not an innate faculty; it is always the effect of an encounter and an encounter is always an encounter with the outside, despite the fact that this outside is not the reality of the external world, in its empirical configuration, but rather the heterogeneous forces affecting thought, those that force thought to think, those that force thought toward that which thought does not yet think, urging thought to think otherwise.[281] He adds that the forces of the outside are not such because they come from the outside, from the exterior, but rather because they place thought into a state of exteriority, throwing it into a formless field where the heterogeneous points of view, corresponding to the heterogeneity of the forces at play, enter into a relation with one another. We can easily see that, although he inherited it from Blanchot, and accepted the extended sense that Foucault attributed to it, Deleuze gave the outside a characterization which is much more clearly Nietzschean: much less in relation to the being of language as in Foucault, and much less in relation to literature as in Blanchot, the

---

280. Gilles Deleuze, *Foucault*, trans. Seán Hand (Minneapolis: University of Minnesota Press, 1988).

281. François Zourabichvili, *Deleuze, une philosophie de l'événement* (Paris: Presses Universitaires de France, 1994) p. 45.

strategic dimension of the outside carried for him a great interest — hence the absolute privilege of force, the "discovery" of which nevertheless Deleuze generously attributed to Foucault. The consequences of this perspective are many: (1) the task of thought is to liberate the forces that come from the outside; (2) the outside is always openness unto a future; (3) the thought of the outside is a thought of resistance (to a state of affairs); and (4) the force of the outside is Life.[282] The major challenge has therefore been present from the very beginning: to seize life as a power of the outside.

Subjectivity and Madness

Now we must call forth a second movement of the sequence: how this outside, when folded, becomes subjectivity. How is an inside created which includes in itself this very outside, with its decelerated particles ("these slow beings that we are"), where we become masters of our speeds, and to a certain degree masters of our molecules and of their singularities? According to Deleuze, "as long as the outside is folded, an inside is coextensive with it," as memory, as life, as duration.[283] We carry with us an absolute memory of the outside. This is the outside-in-us; an unlimited reservoir that nourishes our field of possibles, to which Simondon gave the Greek name of *apeiron* — the Unlimited.[284] Subjectivity is this fold of the outside, the folding of nomad forces, the pocket of the *apeiron*.

If we now look at the strange diagram that Deleuze outlined in regard to Foucault, we find between the subjective fold and the outside, a kind of floating line, and above it a half-blocked bottleneck that filters and slows down the forces of the outside at the same time that it serves them as a passageway. Hence the question: how can we unblock this passage to the maximum degree possible in order for the Other, the outside, and that which is the farthest to become most intimate to the thinker? Jacques Derrida made use of a suggestive metaphor in this context — thought as a tympan, as a stretched screen ready to

282. Gilles Deleuze, *Foucault* p. 89, 90, 95.

283. op. cit. p.108.

284. Gilbert Simondon, *L'Individu et sa génèse physico-biologique* (Paris: Presses Universitaires de France, 1964) and *L'Individuation psychique et collective* (Paris: Aubier, 1989).

balance the pressures between the inside and the outside. To tympanize philosophy would then mean to make this membrane more oblique so that, as we increase its surface of vibration and its permeability to the outside, philosophy can leave behind its autism.[285] To plot the line of the outside otherwise in order to think otherwise. Inflect this relation to the outside in order to remodel subjectivity and at the same time open up thought (these two aspects always go together).

And yet behold, this extreme point to which every thought of the outside aspires, is also the point where we become exposed to the risk of discovering that the subjective fold opens wide, being led astray into madness or being dissolved in death. Hence the proximity of thought and madness — thought as openness to the outside, madness as prison in the outside, and its collapse in an absolute inside. This is what happens when the tympan is broken, when all borders between the outside and the inside, between surface and depth, are abolished. *The Logic of Sense*, as it compares Artaud and Lewis Carroll, is a variation on this theme: what happens when the surface is torn, when the line of the outside crumbles into a groundless depth and the subject is imprisoned in it? Deleuze underlines the imperious desire which tempts every thinker: to will the event, not only upon the incorporeal surface of sense, but in the mixture of bodies, in a kind of "schizophrenic depth." This is the major — almost the demented — temptation: to embrace the becoming-mad of the stuff of the world. Deleuze is then correct in asking whether it is possible to think without becoming insane. How can one aspire to the outside, without being swallowed up? How do we separate the ambition of thought from the risk which is intrinsic in it? Aren't they necessarily neighbors — thought and the collapse of the thinker, the thought of the outside and the closure of it within an absolute inside?[286] The boundary between the one and the other is so very thin, as Nietzsche and Artaud attest. It is only by a thread that the one with the most open relation to the outside is not swept up in it as an "exceptional interiority," according to the beautiful expression of Blanchot.

285. Jacques Derrida, "Tympan" in *Margins of Philosophy*, trans. Alan Bass (Chicago: University of Chicago Press, 1982).

286. All these themes have been developed in a book published in Brazilian: Peter Pál Pelbart, *Da clausura do fora ao fora da clausura: Loucura e Desrazão* (São Paulo: Brasilense, 1989, 2009).

A few decades ago, Foucault raised the question: what is it that condemns to madness those who have once experienced unreason? Or, in our own terms: how is the relation to the outside possible without its collapse in an absolute inside? If, in some moments of its history, our society was able to confine access to madness to the outside (forcing poets and artists, if not to become mad, at least to imitate madness), in other times and elsewhere different spaces of "the outside" were capable of opening up (shamanistic, prophetic, mystical, and political spaces). Nowadays, madness is no longer this privileged voice, as Foucault saw it early on, when he underlined how madness (having crushed unreason) was in the process of being extinguished in favor of mental illness. Nevertheless, from a certain time onwards Foucault no longer asks where exteriority would have migrated after it deserted the space of the asylum and of literature. Perhaps, as we argued, because he considered it abolished. But was it really abolished for him?

The Immanent Outside

In Deleuze, on the other hand, a more explicitly immanent conception renders the outside less dependent upon the sites of exteriority which are visible and localized, even if all sorts of minorities are present in *Anti-Oedipus* (and how noisily!). But Deleuze insists many times: it is not a question of a cult of minorities, but rather of the becoming-minority of all and each one. In this sense, the question is not to idealize the schizophrenics, but to call for a generalized "schizophrenization." In other words, there is no praise of madness, but of the process with respect to which the psychosocial fact of madness is a sad fixation. The unfortunate thing with madness is that it was called upon to be the lone witness to deterritorialization as a universal process, and therefore caved in under the weight of this untenable assignment. Hence the order to liberate the schizoid movement in every flow, so that this characterization could no longer qualify one particular residue alone as a flow of madness. Deleuze and Guattari repeat Foucault's prophecy about the imminent disappearance of madness qua outside, but turn it completely upside down, giving it an almost jubilant sense! The progressive abolition of the binary frontiers between madness and nonmadness is no longer read as a loss of exteriority, but rather as a gain of exteriority. The outside is no longer snatched up but liberated from its closure in confined or privileged spaces. If it is no longer confined, it is because, at last, it is able to extend everywhere. Alterity is not beyond the frontier, and not necessarily in the defeated margins. It is a virtuality of the lines that make us up and of the becomings which result from them.

In this sense, this geography without borders, let's say, this fall of the Berlin Wall does not necessarily represent the victory of a so-called totality — Deleuze and Guattari have taught us how to laugh at that. This is what Deleuze was saying à propos of an alleged planetary and unidimensional thought in 1964: there is a point in which this nihilism turns back against itself, with the strangest of results: it renders forces elementary to themselves in the brute play of their dimensions. The outside, considered as abolished, keeps reappearing *as agnostic*. This is what we see clearly in Foucault, at a certain moment, and it matters little whether the term "outside" disappears from his vocabulary, whereas it subsists in Deleuze: the fact is that a basic conception becomes more and more common between the two of them the moment that it looked as if it were branching off definitively. Deleuze himself expressed this much later: Foucault would have been the one to discover the element that comes from the outside — the force. In other words, with his work on power, Foucault had given the outside its strategic immanence.

I would like to insist on a final encounter between these two thinkers, which is just as hidden as the previous one. To the extent that Deleuze conceives exteriority as groundless ground from within which subjectivity itself emerges, it is obvious that he cannot think of it as abolished; on the contrary, he discovers it in the very heart of subjectivity as fold, absolute memory of the outside, contraction of the outside, duration and life. It is not, therefore, surprising that Deleuze encountered it, as the most intimate texture of the process of subjectification, precisely during his writings on Foucault's late work, here where the reader thinks to be very far away from the thematics of the outside already presented during the genealogical period along with the domains of madness and literature. Deleuze rediscovers the "passion for/of the outside" in the later Foucault, when he recognizes the outside to be immanent in subjectivity and in the process of subjectification (the account of which was made by Foucault) or when he conceives of "thinking otherwise" as an invitation to otherwise fold the forces of the outside. To think otherwise: to be invited to fold otherwise the forces of the outside. The invitation to the outside or the passion for/of the outside finds here its strategic and political function, when it triggers a subjective mutation, that is, a redistribution of affects, of what attracts and what repels, according to the beautiful analysis that Zourabichvili made of it.[287]

I will add one last word about the displacement of the boundaries between the desirable and the intolerable. Our two authors thought seriously about madness and the possibility of dialoguing with it. If Foucault did it by taking it as a complex historical object, the genesis of which he read as the reverse and the non-necessary condition of our thought, then Deleuze, in turn, in close relation with Guattari, gave in to the temptation of this vicinity in the creation of his own concepts. Perhaps, the rhizome is the most extreme expression of it. We could, in fact, think of it as an X-raying of the thought of the outside, in its most intimate logic, that is, when it is the most turned toward the outside. We find in it the opening of a desert, the forgetting mobility, the errant connectivity, the multidirectional proliferation, the absence of center, of subject, of object — a topology and a chronology which are hallucinatory enough. In short, we find not the map of another world, but rather the other possible cartography of all worlds — that which precisely makes this world become another, delivering us from "the chains of everydayness," as Kafka had wanted it.

---

287. François Zourabichvili, "Deleuze et le possible (de l'involontarisme en politique)" in *Gilles Deleuze, une vie philosophique*, pp. 335–57.

TIME,
EXPERIENCE,
DESUBJECTIVATION

IMAGES OF TIME IN DELEUZE

Deleuze's major theses on time reappear in a dramatized manner in his books on cinema, where they conquer an aesthetic operationality that illuminates them as a whole. Take the most enigmatic idea that organizes these books, the emancipation of time. *Time is out of joint*, exclaims Hamlet. Time is off its hinges! What does it mean for time to have left its axes, returned to itself, as pure time? Deleuze alludes to a time freed from the tyranny of the present that it had previously bowed down to, and henceforth, became available to the most eccentric of adventures. Bruno Schulz says, in another context, that time is a disordered element kept in check solely thanks to an incessant cultivation, a care, a control, a correction of its excesses. "Free of this vigilance, it immediately begins to do tricks, run wild, play irresponsible practical jokes, and indulge in crazy clowning."[288] Schulz recalls that we carry a supernumerary load that neither fits on the train of events nor on the two-track time that supports it. For this precious contraband that he calls Event, there are those lateral tracks of time, blind detours, where they are "suspended in the air, errant, homeless," in a multilinear streak, no "before" or "after," neither "simultaneously" nor "consequently," the most remote murmur and the furthest future, all communicating at a virginal beginning. Thus, in the continuous time of linked presents (Chronos) the time of the

---

288. Bruno Schulz, *Sanatorium under the Sign of the Hourglass*, trans. Celina Wieniewska, (New York: Houghton Mifflin, 1977), p. 283.

Event (Aeon) is constantly insinuated, in its non-dialectical, impersonal, impassible, incorporeal logic: "the pure *reserve*," pure virtuality that never stops supervening.

In light of this, Deleuze stresses a cinematographic procedure that consists of unlinking the peaks of present from their very actuality, subordinating this present to a flow that crosses it and overflows, in which precisely there is no more past, present, or future, wherein they are all rolled up into a "simultaneous, inexplicable" event. In the Event, the peaks of de-actualized present coexist, or yet one single event is distributed within distinct worlds according to different times, in such a way that what for one is past, for another is present, for a third is future — but it is the same event (*Last Year at Marienbad*). Deleuze calls this Sidereal time, or a system of relativity, because it includes a pluralist cosmology, in which one single event is distributed as incompatible versions in a plurality of worlds. Not a god that chooses the best of possible worlds, but a Process that passes through all of them, "simultaneously" affirming them. It is a system of variation: given an event, not hitting it against a present that actualizes it, but making it vary in diverse presents that belong to distinct worlds, although in a certain, more generic sense, they belong to a single shattered world. Or, given a present, not exhausting it within itself, but rather finding the event in it through which it communicates with other presents in other worlds, swimming upstream in the common event in which all are implicated: the Virtual Tangle.

Suppose there is a gigantic ontological Memory, made up of sheets or deposits of the past, types of strata, that communicate among themselves in order to be funneled and exert pressure on a peak of present. Some of Resnais' characters, for instance, go from one stratum to another, stroll between levels, traverse ages of the world, transversalize Time, or they constantly re-create the distances and proximities between the diverse singular points of their lives. Sticking to a comfortable image, time as a handkerchief: each time we blow our nose, we slip it into our pocket, crumple it in a distinct way, so that two points of the handkerchief that were previously distant and did not touch (like two distant moments of life according to a time-line) have now become contiguous, or they even coincide, or contrarily, two points that were next to each other have now irremediably been separated. As if time were a big mass of clay, every time it is molded the distances between the points marked within it are rearranged. This is a curious topology in which we witness an incessant transformation, a modulation that reinvents and causes the relationships between the many sheets and their scintillating points to vary, each rearrangement creating something new, plastic memory, always remade, always to come. Moldable mass of time, or better, modulatable, and about which Deleuze comes to exclaim, like some kind of Christopher Columbus: Land, muddy vital means! When cinema is embroiled in this order of virtual coexistence it invents its paradoxical, hypnotic, hallucinatory, indecisive sheets. Along this Bergsonian line, the memory stops being a faculty inside of man, it is man that inhabits the inside of a vast Memory, a World-Memory, a gigantic inverted cone, a virtual multiplicity of which we are a determined degree of distension or contraction. Even the philosopher and the pig, as in a metempsychosis, take up the same cone, the same life at distinct levels, jokes Deleuze.

Time comes to be conceived no longer as a line, but rather as a tangle, not like a river, but like land, not flow, but mass, not succession, rather coexistence, not a circle, but a whirl, not order — but conceived as infinite variation. Instead of referring to a consciousness of time, it seems befitting to bring it closer to hallucination.

Time and Madness

Always speaking of time, Deleuze evokes a profligacy: time which is de-centered, aberrant, wild, paradoxical, floating, or even sunken. It does not seem abusive to consider that time's going mad, as Deleuze works with it, communicates directly with the temporality of so-called "clinical" madness. Meanwhile, a good part of the literature on psychoses is entirely unarmed when facing the multiple temporal figures that proliferate before one's very eyes in the clinic, and that "psychological" theories find it difficult to embrace, keeping in mind a temporal normalcy of which they are habitually prisoners. It is quite rare to think about the temporality of psychosis in any other way than in a privative mode. Even a phenomenological or existential approach to psychoses, from Minkowski to Maldiney, in Binswanger or Jaspers, despite the undeniable descriptive interest that is presented, in these approaches the confirmed multiplicity ends up being referred to a modality of time presupposed as an ideal, prioritizing, for example, certain structures of being-in-the-world, transcendence, anticipation, the project, out of an originating present, etc. But also within strictly psychoanalytic literature, with rare exceptions, the non-unity of the psychotic temporal experience is subsumed to its failed futuration in the form of timeless representations, in such a way that there is a chaotic immanence that is refused in the name of a significant elsewhere that is precisely not assumed by the psychotic. Ultimately, this amounts to an apology for historicizing, whose fulcrum is the I historian, as Piera Aulagnier would say. Thus, somehow temporality ends up being identified with historicizing. With everything that this perspective can present as interesting, or useful, and even as necessary in the clinic, it has the inconvenience of hindering the reception of becomings in psychosis. Deleuze and Guattari's reflection, in opposing becomings to history, could help rethink this temporal heterogeneity of psychosis that so defies the time of reason, even psychoanalytical reason.

Deleuze says it clearly: History is a temporal marker of Power.[289] People dream about starting or restarting from scratch, and also fear where they will arrive, or fall. We always seek the origin or outcome of a lifetime, as a cartographic addiction, but we scorn the middle, which is an anti-memory. That's when it hits the highest speed, where the most different times communicate and cross one another, where there is the movement, becoming, whirl, as Deleuze says literally.[290] And the question to be answered is simple: what temporal figure do we create in order to think such a turbulent medium, such a virtual multiplicity? Anyway, what should not fail to intrigue us is the fact that certain phenomena of psychic disturbance expose, more than any other, pure virtuality *as* virtuality, precisely detached from any centered or oriented actualization. The temporal incongruences that appear in determined subjective configurations, and that have also marked cinema since its inception, touch upon, as is seen, a very philosophical issue.

289. Gilles Deleuze, *Superpositions*, with Carmelo Bene, (Paris: Minuit, 1980), p. 103.

290. *Ibid*, pp. 95-6.

The Philosopher and the Schizophrenic

But what would it serve to converge Deleuze's times and the temporality of madness? Not, in fact, to suggest that Deleuze would be in possession of a theory of time that the psychological domain has had trouble elaborating — a pretension that would come to contradict the same idea that Deleuze has made of the relationship between philosophy and non-philosophy, since philosophy's role is not to legislate over other domains; nor for these other domains to apply philosophical concepts, insofar as each discipline constructs its instruments "with its own means."

It would be necessary to start at Deleuze's relationship with schizophrenia, or better, the intrinsic relationship that entertains him *and the schizophrenic that inhabits him*, this schizophrenic, "who lives intensely within the thinker and forces him to think," initiating an "event that is too intense," of a distinct nature, however, from "a lived condition that is too hard to bear" that strikes the clinical schizophrenic-entity, the psychosocial type.[291] What temporal disturbances does this produce, that is, *the schizophrenic on the inside of the philosopher*? Or rather, which kinds of time engender this conceptual persona in him? What thought of time is he impelled to forge, starting from there, and what "maddened" images of time is he tempted to liberate? And, lastly, how does he see his philosophy being harassed, from end to end, by these images?

To say it in the most simple way: several images of time collected above from a problematic of madness, although they contrast with the gathered images of time in Deleuze such as those that we briefly referred to, can go into free play with them, made of distance and proximity, contrasts and interferences, overlays, transvariations, remissions, abductions, and skills. The power for investigation that is inferred in this discordant accord, as much in the relation to the *times of philosophy* with its own rationalities as to the *times of madness* with its unreasonings, should not be underestimated.

---

291. Gilles Deleuze and Félix Guattari, *What is Philosophy?*, trans. Hugh Tomlinson and Graham Burchell, (New York: Columbia University Press, 1994), p. 70.

Time and Thought

Cinema revealed to Deleuze some of these conduits of time, emanating images that are diverse, evolutionary, circular, spiral, declining, broken, saving, fleeting, unlocalized, multi-vectorial. Time as bifurcation, discrepancy, gushing, oscillation, split, modulation, etc. It's plausible to assume that the interest that Deleuze dedicated to them comes from a more radical determination than he lets us glimpse, in stressing the ambition of cinema to penetrate, apprehend, and reproduce thought itself. Thought and time would thus be, immediately, in a relation of indissoluble co-be-longing. Indeed, what is inferred from Deleuze's writings on time is that the very act of thinking about time could not remain foreign to the project of freeing itself from a certain idea of time that formatted it, or from the axis that bends it. In this sense, Hamlet's enigmatic exclamation about time that leaves its axes is coupled with the exigency of a thought off its axes, that is, of a thought that has finally stopped spinning around the Same.

As well as criticizing the sameness of a so-called dogmatic image of thought, Deleuze fustigates a hegemonic image of time. In asserting a thought without image, so that other images may come toward thought, Deleuze also calls for a time with no image in order to liberate more or other images of time. The so-called dogmatic image of thought is well known: it is explored from *Nietzsche and Philosophy* to *What is Philosophy?* But what would it be, this image of hegemonic time that is refused by Deleuze? In short: it is time as a Circle. This is not exactly circular time, but the circle as a profound structure, in which time is reconciled with itself, in which beginning and end rhyme, as Hölderlin says. What characterizes the circle is its monocentering around the Present, its chained and oriented Movement, as well as its underlying totalization. The circle with its center, a metaphor of the Same. And even if the Present is situated in a remote and nostalgic past, or an eschatological future, this doesn't stop it from still functioning as an axis that bends time, around which it spins, redesigning the circle which we thought we had just escaped. It is there, ultimately, again and again, the time of Re-presentation.

In opposition to time as a Circle, Deleuze proposes time as Rhizome. No longer rediscovered Identity, but open

Multiplicity. The logic of multiplicity was exposed and worked on, among other texts, in the description of the rhizome in *A Thousand Plateaus*. A rhizome can be entered from any side, every point connects with any other, it is made of movable directions, without beginning or end, but just a means, through which it grows and overflows, without referring to a unity or derivation from one, neither subject nor object. What does time become, therefore, when it comes to be thought of as pure multiplicity or operating within a pure multiplicity? The rhizome has no temporal sense or direction (the direction of the arrow of time, good sense, the sense of common sense, ranging from less differentiated to more differentiated); nor does it rediscover a prior totality that it would be in charge of, abolishing itself, making it explicit in the concept. It possesses no sense or direction and is unrelated to any teleology.

But is this Deleuze's last word with regard to time? For this virtual multiplicity is as if it were plowed and stirred at every point, along its entire length, no longer by a circle, which he refuses, but by what might be called — and the expression is already in Plato's *Timaeus* — a Circle of the Other. A circle whose center is the Other, this other that can never be the center precisely because it is always other: a de-centered circle. It is the figure that best suits Deleuze's original reading of Nietzsche: in the repetition there returns only the non-Same, the Unequal, the Other — Being of Becoming, the Eternal Return of Difference.

You can call this Other the Future (the regal repetition is that of the future, says *Difference and Repetition*). But if there is in Deleuze, as in Heidegger, a privilege of the future, it is not deducible from a problematic of Finitude, but rather from the Work, which rejects its supports, Habit, Memory, and Agent. For man, the future is not an anticipation of his own end, his own death, the extreme possibility of his being; nothing presents it as a being-for-death, since it is not from the ipseity that it can be thought, but from a proto-ontic flow. If in Deleuze's elaboration of this future the Open is an important benchmark, it then refers to the Outside, more than to Being. Let's say that the Open for Deleuze is closer to Blanchot than it is to Heidegger. It is under the sign of an Exteriority, then, that thought can gain a determination of future.

Time of Creation

As already mentioned, Deleuze's criticism of a so-called dogmatic image of thought is made on behalf of a thought without image. Now, this means that thought, without a prior Model of how to think (for example: thinking is to seek the truth), opens up for other adventures (for example: thinking is creating). Everything changes from one to another. Deleuze says that there are two different planes of immanence, classic and modern, that of the will to truth, on the one hand, and that of creation, on the other. And each is inseparable from a certain concept of time that fills it. Should we not suppose that a philosophy of difference, like that of Deleuze, has given itself the task of filling this modern plane of immanence with a concept of time belonging to thought defined as creation, and no longer as the will to truth?[292]

The theorization of Deleuzian time, despite its many obscurities, would be to then think of a time in agreement to the force of the new. If there is a profound fidelity to the Bergsonian project, it can only be carried out successfully when, with Nietzsche, time is elevated to its ultimate power, making it return to ... difference. Only the selective eternal return, affecting the new, equaling the Unequal itself, only Time as Difference can inaugurate with the Future, discontinuous and disruptive, a relation of excess, such as the Work or the Overman, for which Zarathustra is not mature enough and yet he announces it. The future as the unconditioned that the instant affirms — is what Nietzsche would have called Untimely, the importance of which Deleuze never stops emphasizing.

If Michel Serres is correct in attributing to philosophy the function of "inventing the conditions for invention," we must add that, in the context which concerns us, this would mean reinventing the conditions for the invention of other times which are not those already consecrated by history. It deals with, ultimately, undoing the solidarity between Time and History, with all the ethical, political, and strategic implications of such an ambition. In thinking the substantive multiplicities and processes operating within it, driving out the most unusual temporalities, in the arc that goes from the Untimely to the Event,

292. This thesis was developed systematically in Peter Pál Pelbart, *O tempo não-reconciliado: Imagens do Tempo em Deleuze*, São Paulo, Iluminuras, 1998/2010.

will Deleuze not have given a voice to those who, as he says in a Benjaminian echo, "History does not take into account?" It is not, evidently, only the oppressed or minorities, though it always deals with them as well, but the becoming-minority of each and every one: not exactly the people, but the "missing people," the people to come.

EXPERIENCE AND
ABANDON OF THE SELF

In an interview from 1980, Foucault says that his books are for him *experiences* in the full sense of the word, since from them he himself came out transformed. An experience, therefore, could be defined based on this criterion: it regards a transformation of the subject. A book conceived as an experience is something that transforms the person who writes it and whatever the writer thinks, before even transforming whatever it addresses. Foucault confesses that the authors who most marked him were not great builders of systems, which upon completion their machinery could be applied to the most distinct domains, as if holding onto a truth, or progressively complementing it, but those others who actually allowed him to escape from that university education, that is, those for whom writing was an experience of self-transformation, such as Nietzsche, Bataille, and Blanchot. Not only does his trio often return in the articles and books from his first phase, but they also appear in interviews up until the end of his life. It is difficult not to see some sort of ritornello here. Now, what was it that was so essential that these authors gave Foucault, despite being marginal in what is usually understood as the history of philosophy? Precisely a conception of experience conceived as a metamorphosis, a transformation, in relation to things, with others, with oneself, with the truth. This transformation also happened with the objects and themes studied by Foucault, such as madness, delinquency, and sexuality. Every book written by Foucault concerning these themes resulted in a profound transformation not only in the relationship that the author and the reader had with the themes dealt with, but the books also had a profound effect on the fields themselves — whether it be through the contestation of psychiatric knowledge or the very definition of madness itself, the enclosure of the madman or the delinquent, or the investment of sexuality as the revelation of an unavoidable subjective truth. It is clear that Foucault's contribution to these diverse areas did not consist of reaffirming a progress of knowledge, an accumulation in constituted knowledge, but in the problematization of the truths produced by knowledge and powers, in their reciprocal overlapping, as well as in the subsequent effects resulting in, among other things, the production of the subjects implicated therein: the subject of madness, the subject of a sexuality, the sick subject, the delinquent subject. But let us return to his writings and interviews where he defines the notion of experience as well as the experience he and his work necessarily go through. How does the notion of experience evoked by Foucault differ from the experience of the phenomenologist? If the experience of the phenomenologist, he says, consists of putting a reflexive eye on any object of the lived, on everyday life in its transitory form, in order to extract significations from it, the experience to which Foucault refers, contrary to the phenomenologist, deals not with reaching an object of the lived, but a point of life that is closest to the unlivable. Not the lived life, but the unlivable of life. Not the possible experience, but the impossible experience. Not the trivial experience, but the one in which life reaches the maximum of intensity, doing away with itself. In short, not the everyday experience, but the limit-experience. Phenomenology tries to apprehend the meaning of the everyday experience to re-encounter, through it, the founding subject of this experience and of these meanings, in its transcendental function. The experience as Foucault understands it, along the lines of the above-mentioned authors, on the contrary, does not refer to a founding subject, but debunks the subject and its foundation, yanks it from itself, opens it to its dissolution. In short, the limit-experience is an undertaking of desubjectivation. Hence, that which will have been decisive for Foucault in his readings of Nietzsche, Bataille, and Blanchot: the experience that goes to its limit, experimentation which in its course separates from the subject, leaves it behind, and abolishes it. This is also what allows Foucault to say that his books, however erudite they may have been, were always conceived as direct experiences aimed at yanking him out of himself, preventing him from continuing to be himself. Clearly we have here a necessary perversion of the very concept of experience, since it generally is precisely remitted to a subject that lives it, passively or actively. But Foucault's question goes against the grain of this supposition: "Can't there be experiences in the course of which the subject is no longer posited, in its constitutive relations, as what makes it identical with itself? Might there not be experiences in which the subject might be able to dissociate from itself, sever the relation with itself, lose its identity?"[293] Thus, by way of these terms like dissociation, dissolution, dilution, loss of identity, Foucault contests the very status of the subject, be it the psychological subject, the subject of knowledge, or the transcendental subject.

(Im)personal Existence

In a very prosaic sense, Foucault adds, at a different moment, that each of his books was born out of a "personal experience," a "direct experience." In the case of madness, here is his observation: "I have a complex, personal relationship with madness and with the psychiatric institution." The reader may ask what he is referring to exactly, but one need only take a quick look at any of his biographies or even at the biographical notes published in *Dits et Écrits*, and all suspicions of sensationalist ambition are quickly cleared up. These remarks by Foucault speak of the crises that he went through at the École Normale, fits of rage, his attempts at suicide, even a visit to a psychiatrist, taken by his father. Furthermore, his interest in the topic was incessant, as his academic trajectory attests to. Look at his parallel training in psychology, his internship in the psychiatric hospital, his translation of *Dream and Existence* and his personal frequenting of Binswanger because of the translation, not to mention all of his academic positions in which he was the chair of psychology or psychopathology, or even his interest in psychoanalysis, his ambivalent relationship with Lacan, etc. If

293. Michel Foucault, "Interview with Michel Foucault," with Duccio Trombadori, in *The Essential Works of Foucault, 1954-1984, Volume 3: Power,* ed. James D. Faubion, (New York: New Press, 2001), p. 248.

his personal experience, in this trivial sense, was decisive, this doesn't even remotely mean that he had transposed personal experiences to the plane of writing in an autobiographical form — no self-complacency or narcissism — moreover, in none of his writings do we find any biographical reference of this order. Here we have a small paradox, which we could formulate as such: how a book is born from a personal experience, but results precisely in the abolition of the same author who lived it, as the postulate pointed out above, according to which there are experiences, and experiences of thought or writing, which precisely question the author regarding his identity and even his coherence? The whole challenge is in conciliating the fact that a book starts from a personal experience, but it doesn't constitute the account of this experience, since the book is in itself an experience in a sense more radical, that is, a transformation of the self, and not the reproduction of the lived experience "such as it occurred" and that would be in the origin of this writing, nor its direct transposition. Now, this dimension is inseparable from the fact, obviously, that a book is made for others, and thus, ultimately, a collective scope, concerning a collective practice, to a way of thinking that extrapolates the individual subject, and addresses itself to an experience of those that read or utilize it. That is, ultimately, what Foucault calls an experience-book, as opposed to a truth-book, or a demonstration-book. As he states: "An experience is something that one has alone, but which can be had only to the extent that it escapes pure subjectivity and that others can also — I won't say repeat it exactly, but at least encounter it — and go through it themselves."[294]

The Experience-Book

The destiny of *The History of Madness* has shown itself to be that of an experience-book — the frequent use made of it by anti-psychiatrists is due less to the fact that the book was written "against" psychiatrists than by the transformation that it lead to regarding the historical, theoretical, institutional, ethical, and even juridical relations — with respect to madness, madmen, and the psychiatric institution — that is, its relation to the truth of psychiatric discourse. It is "therefore a book that

---

294. *Ibid*, p. 245.

functions as an experience, for its writer as well as for its reader, much more so than as the establishment of a historical truth. For one to be able to have this experience by way of the book, what it says does need to be true in terms of academic, historically verifiable truth."[295] And in fact, Foucault works with historical material that essentially does not differ from that used by more classic historians, with demonstrations, proof, allusions to writings, references, relations between ideas and facts, schemes of intelligibility, types of explanation — in short, he says nothing original. Nevertheless, what is essential about it resides precisely within an "experience" that is worthwhile, based on this material, "an experience of our modernity in such a way that we might come out of it transformed. Which means that at the end of the book we would establish new relationships with the subject at issue: the I who wrote the book and those who have read it would have a different relationship with madness, with its contemporary status, and its history in the modern world."[296]

The essential, therefore, is not found in the series of true or historically verifiable ascertainments found in a book, but rather in the experience that such a book makes possible. Now, this experience, as any experience, is neither true nor false. "An experience is always a fiction: it's something that one fabricates oneself, that doesn't exist before and that won't exist afterward."[297] Hence one of the possible meanings *in jest* is of never having written anything besides fiction. It's not about lies, fabulations, or untruths, but rather the fabrication of an "experience," which, on the other hand, is the polar opposite of any return to a "lived," "authentic," "true," or "real." This is what a book is. It is precisely a production, a creation, a singularity, an event, with its effects of reality. Foucault came to define himself as a pyrotechnic, that is, someone who fabricates explosives. The intention of his books, he says, is to bring down walls. And when he refers to the *History of Madness*, he says in 1975: "I envisaged this book as a kind of truly material wind, and I continue to dream about it that way, a kind of wind that shatters doors and windows.... My dream is for it to be an explosive

295. *Ibid*, p. 243.

296. *Ibid*, p. 242.

297. *Ibid*, p. 243.

as effective as a bomb, and beautiful like fireworks."[298] We cannot deny that it worked on both registers.

The Fabrication of Experience

If this could be easily admitted for the experience of writing a book, which is, after all, a production, a creation, a construction, an invented event, how can one place in this fabricating key that which set off the book? How can one understand this first "experience," from which the author departs, as a *fabrication*? Our intuition would say the contrary; lived experience is considered to be original, authentic, and natural, whereas experience in a book is considered to be a copy, an imitation, a fabrication. However, Foucault gets rid of this difference by subtracting from the lived experience its original characteristic. But how — isn't it about the personal circumstances of life, the vicissitudes of singular, and therefore lived, original stories? How can one imagine that this is fabricated? But precisely that which is personal, if carefully considered, is not at all natural, much less exclusively personal, since the suicide attempts of a young homosexual inside an institution of academic excellence, where in the 1950s this sexual orientation within the conservative hegemony of the Communist Party, was still seen as a personal aberration, an anomaly or an infirmity, in any case as a deviation of conduct. This personal experience is less something that is "natural" or "personal," it is a fruit of historical, social, medical, psychological, psychiatric, institutional, and discursive fabrication. Moreover, the personal is thus the result of a fabrication which is entirely historical. The form of this experience of "madness," in a restricted sense of the word, can only be comprehended if it is not reduced to its private aspect, but returned to its historicity, which is precisely what the experience-book takes upon itself to elucidate, call into question, turn over, and explode. The experience, in this case, however thoroughly lived and authentic it may seem, cannot be naturalized, it must be historicized. That is to say, returned to the network of knowledge and power, which elucidates it, and (to formulate it in an even more paradoxical manner) that tell the

---

298. Michel Foucault *"Les confessions de Michel Foucault,"* Interview with Roger Pol-Droit, *Le Point,* 1 July 2004.

"truth" of this experience. Of course every problem, within this kind of posture, is that of the status of truth inside this fabrication, this experience, and of the status of truth embedded in the book that prolongs this experience. If a book, or even a book conceived as an experience, submitted itself to a previously supposed truth to be revealed, everything would be easily resolved. However, as Foucault says, an experience-book has a difficult relationship with "the truth," since this truth, implicated in an experience-book which does not depend on truth, but first and foremost tends to destroy it, is itself problematic.[299] Furthermore, if the book makes use of veridical documents, it is not only to attain a confirmation of truth through them, but above all else an experience "that permits a change, a transformation of the relationship we have with ourselves and with the world where, up to then, we had seen ourselves as being without problems — in short, a transformation of the relationship we have with our knowledge."[300] Therefore we could, or should read the *History of Madness* in this light: as an experience-book, which subverts our relationship with the truth that until then seemed to impose itself. Now, we insist, it is not the account of a personal experience, it is not a novel, it cannot be frugal with a certain regime of scientific, academic, or historical veridiction, under the penalty of losing all effect and effectiveness in the field of prevailing knowledge and power, yet if undertaken it is more with the intention of destroying truths that rule over this domain than of submitting to them. That is why Foucault's work cannot be bundled into an epistemological tradition which sees progress in the study of science, or the progress of a rationality, and it can be assumed that the *History of Madness* was written precisely in the countercurrent of this tradition, showing (in the case of a less, let's say, "hard" science, like psychiatry) to what degree the rationality that it flaunted was problematic. It is a method that operates from within, digging inside a regime of the circulation of knowledge, inside a regime of enunciation, revealing a gearing that problematizes the very thing that seemed to constitute the object of analysis and, why not say it, also the subject of such an analysis. Is this not what we confirm in the *History of Madness*? With the support of abundant documentation and an entire economy of historical demonstration,

299. *Ibid*, p. 84.
300. *Ibid*, p. 244.

the object Madness can be viewed as though it were pulverized, returned to its heteroclitic "construction," dispossessed of its naturalness and necessity, not of its reality, but of its inevitability, conceivable therefore not as a given, or a possible, but as an "impossible," constructed with elements derived from the most heterogeneous juridical, policing, or institutional registers, that are also legible through literary or iconographic material. The concern consists of restoring the genesis of a social perception produced at a determined historical moment, and accompanying the effects of segregation, expulsion, confinement, in the distance relative to the speeches and medical knowledge existing at that very time. Therefore, not only is the object explained by the conditions of its emergence, those being discursive, institutional, and archaeological, but also the subject of such "competent" discourse which subsequently emerged, the subject of knowledge, the subject that has little by little been constructed but also delegated to be occupied with madness, delegated to act upon such madness, occasionally freeing this madness from its chains, of treating it, disciplining it, silencing it, or making it talk. Thus, in this withdrawal, it is an entire gearing that continues to be revealed as having originated a specific object and a specific subject (of knowledge and of intervention), that in its presumably natural coupling continues to be "unscrewed." It is what can thus be called a critical history of thought, in which the status of a subject and of an object should not be taken as given, but on the contrary, should be remitted to their historical constitution, to the modes of subjectivation and objectification and their reciprocal relationship, according to certain rules and games of truth. Refusing, therefore, not only any specific anthropological universal — man, the madman, the delinquent, the subject of a sexuality — but equally refusing the exigency to make the analysis withdraw to the constituent, presupposed subject and final conditions of the entire analysis. And Foucault clarifies: "refusing the philosophical recourse to a constituent subject does not amount to acting as if the subject did not exist, making an abstraction of it on behalf of a pure objectivity. This refusal has the aim of eliciting the processes that are peculiar to an experience in which the subject and the object "are formed and transformed" in relation to and in terms of one another. The discourses of mental illness, delinquency, or sexuality say what the subject is only in a certain, quite particular game of truth; but these games are not imposed on the subject from the outside according to a necessary causality or structural determination. They open up a field of experience in which the subject and the object are both constituted only under certain simultaneous conditions, but in which they are constantly modified in relation to each other, and so they modify this field of experience itself."[301] When referring to his project of a history of sexuality, he insists: "It is a matter of analyzing 'sexuality' as a historically singular mode of experience in which the subject is objectified for himself and for others through certain specific procedures of 'government.'"[302]

Dislodgments

As is evident from Foucault's later formulations (and here we are already talking about his texts from the 1980s), we still see in his writings this theme of experience, but it continues in a much more reformulated manner. It is as if, when thinking the modalities of experience, the forms of experience, and the fields of experience, Foucault increasingly needed to join them to the processes of subjectivation and objectification, and their reciprocal relationship, within unique games of truth, having as a challenge a perpetual re-problematizing, without presupposing that it remain unaltered. "What blocks thought is admitting implicitly or explicitly a form of problematizing, and of searching for a solution that could substitute for that which is accepted. Now, if the work of thought has a meaning — different from that which consists the reformation of institutions and codes — it is to delve back into the roots whereby humans problematize their behavior (their sexual activity, their punitive practices, their attitude toward madness, etc.) The work of thought does not consist of denouncing the bad that secretly inhabits everything that exists, but rather of portending the danger that threatens everything habitual, problematizing everything that is solid."[303] One of the most difficult challenges

301. Michel Foucault, "'Foucault' by Maurice Florence," in *Aesthetics, Method and Epistemology,* trans. Robert Hurley, (New York: New Press, 1998), p. 462.

302. *Ibid*, p. 463.

303. Hubert Dreyfus and Paul Rabinow, "A propos de la généalogie de l'éthique: un aperçu du travail en cours," in *Michel Foucault. Un parcours philosophique*, (Paris: Gallimard, 1983), 325-326. Quotation taken from the French due to inconsistencies with the

in this task of incessant problematizing that increasingly occupies Foucault consists of getting rid of the humanist idea of a subject considered as origin or destiny. As he notes: "There are more secrets, more possible freedoms, and more inventions in our future than we can imagine in humanism."[304] When remarking on Marx's idea that man produces man, he clarifies that this can't be understood as though it were up to man to rediscover his fundamental essence, a mistake which is present in all of humanism centered on the idea of repression and alienation, rationality and exploitation, branding the image of an ultimately liberated man. In his essay on Blanchot's writing, already in 1966, Foucault conceived of language as an incessant murmur, which destituted the subjective source of enunciation as well as the truth of the enunciated, emphasizing the emergence of an anonymous position, free from any center or homeland, capable of echoing the death of God and of man. "Where 'it speaks,' man no longer exists." Much later, Foucault reiterates this position: it's not about rediscovering man, even through a so-called process of liberation, but "to produce something that doesn't exist yet, without being able to know what it will be."[305] Furthermore: this production of man by man is at the same time "the destruction of what we are as well as the creation of a completely different thing, a total innovation." Or more concretely: "Could it be that the subject, identical to itself, with its own historicity, its genesis, continuities, effects of its infancy prolonged to the end of its life, etc., would not be the product of a certain type of Power that is exercised over us in old juridical forms and recent political forms?"[306]

As can be noted by this small recurrence, however zigzagging it may be, the meaning of the word experience undergoes some important inflections. It's as if it acquired, throughout Foucault's theoretical career, new variables that were not previously explicit or had not even been initially thought, such as processes of subjectivation and objectification, games of truth, problematizing, government proceedings, not to mention his

English version of this interview.

304. Michel Foucault, *Technologies of the Self: A Seminar With Michel Foucault*, ed. Luther, Guttman, Hutton, (Amherst: University of Mass. Press, 1988), p. 14.

305. Foucault, "Interview with Michel Foucault," interview with Duccio Trombadori, in *Power*, op. cit., 275.

306. Roger-Pol Droit, *Michel Foucault, Entretiens*, (Paris: Editions Odile Jacob, 2004).

own genealogical focus, or the ethical framework within which they were being explained. But what most surprises whoever is willing to confront the logic of this development will find that this note, present at the beginning of Foucault's career, about the limit-experience, which seemed like a literary or lyrical babbling belonging to the 1960s, afterward dug up by more serious studies in the subsequent period, reappears at the end of his career but with an entirely different meaning. In an interview with Paul Rabinow in 1983, the year before his death, he compares the last move of his career to the first moment of his oeuvre in the following terms: "To study forms of experience in this way — in their history — is an idea that originated with an earlier project, in which I made use of the methods of existential analysis in the field of psychiatry and in the domain of 'mental illness.' For two reasons, not unrelated to each other, this project left me unsatisfied: its theoretical weakness in elaborating the notion of experience, and its ambiguous link with a psychiatric practice which it simultaneously ignored and took for granted. One could deal with the first problem by referring to a general theory of the human being, and treat the second altogether differently by turning, as is so often done, to the 'economic and social context'; one could choose, by doing so, to accept the resulting dilemma of a philosophical anthropology and a social history. But I wondered whether, rather than playing on this alternative, it would not be possible to consider the very historicity of forms of experience."[307] Let us dwell on this elaboration for a moment. From the outset, he thus confesses that he had the idea of studying the question of experience. At first, it meant studying experience within the psychiatric field. In other words, he gave himself the task of studying the experience of madness, or mental illness, or psychiatry. And if we consider the introduction to Binswanger's book, *Le rêve et l'existence*, we find a poignant portrait of this moment. In this commentary, he closely follows the experience of the dream and that of madness, with all of the phenomenological somersaults, in a completely pre-Foucauldian description, as a way of saying: where the experience of madness is taken as a given lived-experience, that is, autonomous and closed off to itself — without this

---

307. Michel Foucault, "Preface to the History of Sexuality, Vol II." in *The Foucault Reader*, ed. Paul Rabinow, (New York: Pantheon Books, 1984), p. 334.

lived-experience — this experience having always been related to psychiatric practice from which it is inseparable, or to any reference to knowledge (much less to prevailing powers), what this experience deals with is *a naturalized experience* and thus it is not *historicized*, wherein the very notion of experience is not elaborated, or problematized. This is what made him dissatisfied, as the writings indicate. He invokes two ways of resolving this difficulty. On the one hand, resorting back to a conception of experience as a "theory of the human being," on the other hand, invoking the "economic or social determinations" that marked this experience. Notice the alternative. He either invokes an underlying universality, "the human being" (phenomenology, in any case, an anthropology), or an exteriority of determination, "economic conditions" (Marxism). In any case, in this schism, the two paths remain separate. What is preserved is an anthropology, a humanism, a universality, or on the other hand, it is sociologized. It is philosophical anthropology on the one hand, and social history on the other. Now, philosophical anthropology is that which Foucault's first book, the one on Kant,[308] calls into question, foreshadowing *The Order of Things*. And the sociology of Marxist coinage is that which he rejects, even though he has been influenced by it, since, at bottom it leaves the idea of man intact, insofar as it presupposes it entirely. When asked about how this double influence, from Phenomenology and Marxism, operated in his career like an obstacle, he responds that people from his generation, as students, fed off of these two forms of analysis: one that referred back to the constituent subject, and the other that refers back to the economic in the last instance, to the ideology and to the set of superstructures.

It's where he refers to his exit from this impasse. Instead of returning to the constituent subject, let's set up the historic plot again. "But this historical contextualization needed to be something more than the simple relativization of the phenomenological subject. I don't believe the problem can be solved by historicizing the subject as posited by the phenomenologists, fabricating a subject that evolves through the course of history. One has to dispense with the constituent subject, to get rid of the subject itself, that is to say, to arrive at an analysis that can

---

308. Michel Foucault, *Introduction to Kant's Anthropology,* (Los Angeles: Semiotext(e), 2008).

account for the constitution of the subject within a historical framework. And this is what I would call genealogy, that is, a form of history that can account for the constitution of knowledges, discourses, domains of objects, and so on, without having to make reference to a subject that is either transcendental in relation to the field of events or runs in its empty sameness throughout the course of history."[309]

Experimentation

In some of his supplementary writings, under the pretext of allowing himself to express not exactly "what he thinks" but rather "what would be possible to think," Foucault goes even further. For example, when responding to a question about the function of theory as a toolbox, as an instrument, to be used even in struggle rather than as a system, he states (in the interview entitled "Powers and Strategies") that in writing responses to the written questions, that his manner of writing without revising — as an initial outpouring — was not due to a faith in the virtues of spontaneity, but rather to allow for his response to have a problematic character and let it be voluntarily uncertain. He adds this exquisite comment: "What I have said here is not 'what I think,' but often rather what I wonder whether one couldn't think."[310] Perhaps what we have here is something that could pertain to much of *Dits et Écrits*. Could these writings be an expression of what Foucault thinks, or an experiment of that which could be thought, in other words, at the threshold between the thinkable and the unthinkable? Therefore, it was not an expression of a self, or even the formulation of a consolidated perspective, but an experiment, like Nietzsche, who so often changed perspective in order to experiment, let's say, with the question what is thought capable of, so as to paraphrase a well-known author who asked himself what the body is capable of?

When describing his years of education, Foucault insists:

309. Foucault, "Truth and power," in *Power*, op. cit., p. 118.

310. Michel Foucault, "Power and strategies" *Power/Knowledge: selected interviews and other writings, 1972-1977*, ed. C. Gordon, (New York: Pantheon, 1980), p. 145.

Nietzsche, Blanchot, and Bataille were the authors who enabled me to free myself from the dominant influences in my university training in the early fifties — Hegel and phenomenology. Doing philosophy in those days, and today as well in fact, mainly amounted to doing the history of philosophy — and the history of philosophy delimited, on the one hand, by Hegel's theory of systems and, on the other, by the philosophy of the subject, went on in the form of phenomenology and existentialism. Essentially, it was Hegel who was the prevailing influence. For France, this had been in a sense a recent discovery, following the work of Jean Wahl and the teaching of Jean Hyppolite. It was a Hegelianism permeated with phenomenology and existentialism, centered on the theme of the unhappy consciousness. And it was really the best thing the French university could offer as the broadest possible mode of understanding the contemporary world, which had barely emerged from the tragedy of World War II and the great upheavals that had preceded it — the Russian revolution, Nazism, and so on. While Hegelianism was presented as the way to achieve a rational understanding of the tragic as it was experienced by the generation immediately preceding ours, and still threatening for our own, it was Sartre, with his philosophy of the subject, who was in fashion outside the university. Establishing a meeting point between the academic philosophical tradition and phenomenology, Maurice Merleau-Ponty extended existential discourse into specific domains, exploring the question of the world's intelligibility, for example, the intelligibility of reality. My own choices ripened within that intellectual panorama: on the other hand, I chose not to be a historian of philosophy like my professors and, on the other, I decided to look for something completely different from existentialism. I found it in my reading of Bataille and Blanchot and, through them, of Nietzsche. What did they represent for me? First, an invitation to call into question the category of the subject, its supremacy, its foundational function. Second, the conviction that such an operation would be meaningless if it remained limited to speculation. Calling the subject in question meant that one would have to experience something leading to its actual destruction, its decomposition, its explosion, its conversion into something else. [...] The experience of the war had shown us the urgent need of a society radically different from the one in which we were living, this society that had permitted Nazism, that had lain down in front of it, and that had gone over en masse to de Gaulle. A large sector of French youth had a reaction of total disgust toward all that. We wanted a world and a society that were not only different

[…] we wanted to be completely other in a completely different world. Moreover, the Hegelianism offered to us at the university, with its model of history's unbroken intelligibility […] [and] phenomenology and existentialism, which maintained the primacy of the subject and its fundamental value [… were] not enough to satisfy us. Whereas the Nietzschean theme of discontinuity, on the other hand, the theme of an Overman who would be completely different from man, and, in Bataille, the theme of limit-experiences through which the subject escapes from itself, had an essential value for us. As far as I was concerned, they afforded a kind of way out between Hegelianism and the philosophical identity of the subject.[311]

Genesis of the Subject

It is worth noting the shift that started in the 1960s. It went from an ontology of language to a critical ontology of the present, in which the dissociation of the subject was due less to a literary adventure (where language appears, man disappears, as Foucault said at the time) than referring back to a whole set of forces, apt to reinvent the relationship between subject and experience. Foucault states: "In a philosophy like that of Sartre, the subject gives meaning to the world. That point was not called back in question. The subject dispenses significations. The question was: can it be said that the subject is the only possible form of existence?"[312] It was as if at this time Foucault asked himself, echoing a question that had been put to him since the beginning of his career, but in a different way, would it be possible to dissociate the notion of experience from the notion of subject?

And the fact is that even his research on knowledge, which occupied ten years of his work throughout the 1960s, was not disconnected from this theme. It's as if he's reading it, at the end of his career, while establishing a difference between *connaissance* and *savoir*. While *connaissance* is a work that allows multiplication of cognizable objects, developing their intelligibility, comprehending their rationality, but preserving the fixity of the subject that investigates, *savoir* is a process through

311. Michel Foucault, "Interview with Michel Foucault," interview with Duccio Trombadori, in *Power*, op. cit., pp. 246-248.

312. *Ibid*, p. 248.

which the subject itself undergoes a modification through that which it knows, or from the work that it carries out in knowing. Thus, *savoir* both modifies the subject *and* constructs the object at the same time. It is in this sense that the entire archaeological sequence is not only a study about knowledge [*savoirs*], but about the emergence of certain objects, such as madness, or death, life, language, and simultaneously the emergence of certain subjects such as reason, life, language, production, etc. It is not merely the study of a dominion, but of an experience through which men are constituted as subjects, when engaging in the study of these very objects. It's a whole genesis of the subject that one may only see sketched out here, to be elaborated upon later, more closely, when referring to a set of forces, to anonymous strategies, to the field of power, to the forms of power, with the production of individuals, linked to their identity, as well as to the forms of subjection, which are, at the same time, modalities of subjectivation.

And all of this, in a third movement, will acquire a different layout, when it is no longer precisely a question of the relationship between a subject and an object, nor between subject and Power, but between the subject and itself, as ethical agent — a whole new continent opens up here, in this genealogy of the subject as subject of ethical actions.

The final lecture series that Foucault gave before his death provides us with a glimpse of this last development, published under the title, *The Courage of Truth*. Here he focuses on *parrhēsia* as his theme, truth-telling, or speaking-frankly. In this series of lectures it's not about asking oneself what truth is for the Greeks, or what makes it possible, or what true knowledge consists of. It's not a study on the possible formal conditions for truth, nor is it a study of epistemology. Rather, it is about thinking what implications truth-telling has for that which speaks, what transformations are brought about in the relationship with oneself and with others, therefore, what ethical mutations can be detected in this practice of truth-telling, or the speaking-frankly. Thus, what is at stake here, is a certain form of veridiction, which does not only constitute a discursive act, but implies a care of the self and a care of others, and therefore implies a mode of existence, in a manner of conducting oneself, a form of life. It's what Foucault calls an *Ethopoietic* dimension. Here we see, not so much an intersection between the dimensions of knowledge, of power, of the subject, but in a somewhat shifted way, the intersection between an order of veridiction, techniques of governmentality, and practices of the self. Foucault states, in his lecture, that it is what he always wanted to do.... Of course, we should be suspicious of this retrospective reading, always made to serve his present research. But here we cannot fail to see an important shift in relation to his previous research, that he himself recognizes, when noting how, when becoming interested in the relationship between subject and truth, in his first studies, his question was: from which practices and discourses did he try to speak the truth about the mad subject, or about the delinquent subject? This is the case for *The History of Madness* and *Discipline and Punish*. Or, "On the basis of what discursive practices was the speaking, laboring, and living subject constituted as a possible object of knowledge (savoir)?"[313] (Here we recognize *The Order of Things*.) Up until this point in the lectures, Foucault delineates a moment of his career. Afterward, he says, he no longer sought discourse in which one could say the truth about the subject, but "the discourse of truth which the subject is likely and able to speak about himself, which may be, for example, avowal, confession, or examination of conscience."[314] This brings us to the *History of Sexuality*. And from there, this theme that would bring him to a historical analysis of the practices of truth-telling about oneself, in this long sequence in which it is inserted into the theme of care for the self, of the practices of the self, of the culture of the self. It's the problem of the ethical constitution, or even ethical differentiation, in any case, of the constitution of ethical subjects.

Care of the Soul or Care of Life

Foucault contrasts two of Plato's writings, *Alcibiades* and *Laches*, even though in both there appears to be this need for speaking candidly, for a truth-telling, and for a courage to do so. In *Alcibiades*, since it is necessary to know how to care for the self, the question is posed "what is it really within the self

313. Michel Foucault, *The Courage of Truth*, trans. Graham Burchell, (New York: Palgrave), p. 3.

314. *Ibid.*

that needs to be cared for, what is the object of the care? Well, it's the soul. And what in the soul? The divine element that in it allows one to see the truth." There is therefore the care of the self, the soul, divine truth, and thus a whole direction that should end up at a metaphysics of the soul, or an ontology of the self (I). In *Laches*, indeed, it is necessary to care, to care for the youth, and teach them to take care of themselves, but what is it that is necessary to take care of, and what is it that is necessary to teach them to care for? What is the object of such care? Now, it's not the soul, but life, not *psyche*, but *bios*, in other words, a way of living. Thus the two directions in philosophy, philosophy as a *metaphysics of the soul*, as an *ontology of the self*, or philosophy as the elaboration of a certain form and *modality of life, life itself as ethical material*.[315] In this contrast there is something like a bifurcation, and what is at stake in the second modality is the *form that is given to life*. The emergence of life as object means that it is necessary to exercise an operation upon it, putting it to the test, submitting it to a screening process, to a transformation, etc. Therefore, instead of the contemplation of the soul, the stylistics of existence emerges, the visible figure that humans should give to their lives, with all the risk and the courage that it implies. It is not in search of the *being of the soul*, but a *style of existence*. Foucault insists on how throughout his career philosophy would have left this second way on the sideline, privileging the first, as if the care of the self that has life for its object, and the elaboration of a beautiful life, through a truth-telling, had been relegated to a second plane in favor of a metaphysics of the soul. Foucault's daring, not to mention his causticity, allows him to say: "if it is true that the question of Being has indeed been what Western philosophy has forgotten, and that this forgetting is what made metaphysics possible, it may also be that the question of the philosophical life has continued to be, I won't say forgotten, but neglected; it has constantly appeared as surplus in relation to philosophy, to a philosophical practice indexed to the scientific model. The question of the philosophical life has constantly appeared like a shadow of philosophical practice, and increasingly pointless."[316]

Until now we were sailing in somewhat calm waters, whether in the old world or in the philosophical world. Where

---

315. *Ibid*, pp. 126-127.
316. *Ibid*, p. 236.

everything gets complicated is when Foucault takes the example of cynicism to show how all of this becomes exacerbated. In order to make it the true life, according to the precepts that the cynics profess, in a type of jocose transvaluation of all values, life should be a different life, a radically different life, in total rupture with every code, law, institution, habit, including those belonging to philosophers. The true life is a different life, and should also, in its public, aggressive, even scandalous manifestation, transform the world, call for a different world. It is thus not the question of another world, according to the Socratic model, but that of a different world. Truth-telling, the care of the self, the care of others, the different life, the different world. There is, hence, a necessary inversion whose logic Foucault exhaustively scrutinizes, showing to what point within this supposed true life an alterity is insinuated, one that throws it back toward the world itself.

In the second to last class of his course, he defines the bifurcation at stake like this: "Metaphysical experience of the world, historic-critical experience of life: these are two fundamental cores in the genesis of European or Western philosophical experience."[317] Foucault never fails to stress that such *experience* occurs in this historic articulation between a regime of veridiction (*Savoirs*), a form of governmentality (Powers), a practice of the self (Subjectivation). If philosophy is a form of *experience*, supposing that the historical forms of experience produce different modalities of subjectivation, in relation to itself or in modification of itself, it's up to philosophy to "produce," as a way of saying, the subjectivation or desubjectivation that corresponds to it. It can therefore be asked, if in Foucault a transformation of the self is not equivalent, at times, to an abandon of the self, or, in other terms, if certain modalities of subjectivation detected or evoked by him would not imply different degrees of desubjectivation.

---

317. *Ibid*, p. 315.

SUBJECTIVATION AND DESUBJECTIVATION

At the beginning of the 1980s, Jacques Derrida traveled to communist Czechoslovakia, and after a journey of work-related meetings, he was arrested at the airport under the accusation of carrying cocaine. Of course, it was a procedure of political systematic intimidation, at an especially harsh moment of the regime. Liberated from jail thanks to direct intervention by Mitterrand, in the first class upon returning to the École Normale, on the Rue d'Ulm, he told of what he had spoken about with his Czech interlocutors, who were in general philosophers and intellectuals. They stated that in political resistance to the regime, deconstruction didn't help. They had difficulty dealing with deconstruction of the subject, at a moment in which what they needed, as opposition, was precisely to strengthen the subject squashed by repression. Now, we can imagine the enormous philosophical detour that Derrida had to take in order to explain that resistance and deconstruction were not only compatible, but were also even coinciding, in a more radical sense, since they questioned not only political representation, but also the subject that established it. It is unlikely that he convinced his interlocutors, seeing as the problem continues to thrive, at a moment, for example, in which something like the political subject of resistance is sought after. It's true, perhaps some intellectuals have given up on looking for the political subject, to speak of subjectivity, and perhaps they have even given up on speaking of subjectivity, in order to evoke processes of subjectivation.

Let us take, in contrast, an interview published in the magazine Vacarme twenty years later, where the Italian philosopher Giorgio Agamben is asked why, in his analyses, he privileges the plane of power so much, overlooking the subjects of resistance. What is the reason for this insistence on concepts like *homo sacer*, bare life, the concentration camp as a biopolitical paradigm, the state of exception, to the detriment of the resistance, reappropriations, to the gestures of reprisal, which would have more pragmatic relevance? Had Agamben forgotten about "our" biopolitics (those who resist), in favor of "theirs" (those in power)? In privileging major biopolitics, had he not sacrificed minor biopolitics? He answers that this difference, which used to be clear, has become foggy. Distinct domains, even antithetical, that in other moments could be lived as dichotomies, such as *bios* and *zoè*, form-of-life and bare life, political body and biological body, public and private, have today become so mixed up that it's not about claiming one of the poles against the other, as if it were possible to retreat behind an already overtaken border. The distinction between them is already not working. That is why, contrary to what you are charging me with, he insists, it is necessary to part from this indistinction of spheres: "It's from this uncertain terrain, an opaque zone of indifferentiation, that we should today regain the path of a different politics, of a different body, of a different speech. I wouldn't know of any other pretext under which I would renounce this indistinction between public and private, biological body and political body, *zoè* and *bios*. It is there where I should regain my space — there, or in no other place. Only a politics that parts from this consciousness could interest me."[318] Therefore, if the actors of concrete struggles, those that comprise the experience of the state of exception, such as the undocumented, AIDS carriers, drug addicts, the unemployed who call for a universal salary, barely make an appearance in Agamben's writings, and when they do appear, it is more in the form of objects than the form of subjects, it is because he sees a larger problem here, precisely that of the subject. Agamben is unable to look at them as given subjects, but rather inside a process of both

318. Giorgio Agamben, *Interview with Giorgio Agamben* by Stany Grelet and Mathieu Potte-Bonneville, (*Vacarme* 10, Paris, 2000).

subjectivation and desubjectivation at the same time. On the one hand, he reminds us that the modern State is a machine of decodification, which shuffles and dissolves classic identities. But, at the same time, it is a machine that juridically recodes dissolved identities. Therefore, while it desubjectivizes, it re-subjectivizes. Without citing Deleuze and Guattari, he seems to be very close to a recurrent idea in *Anti-Oedipus* — in other words, while capitalism deterritorializes, the State as well as the family, psychoanalysis, and the media reterritorialize. But let us stick to Agamben, before opening this plethora of directions. "Today, it seems to me that the political terrain is a type of bat-tle-field where two processes are carried out: both destruction of everything that was traditional identity — I say it without any nostalgia, evidently — and immediate resubjectivation by the State. And not only by the State, but also by the subjects themselves. It's what you evoked in your question," he says to the interviewer, "the decisive conflict takes place henceforth, for each one of the protagonists, including the new subjects of which you speak, in the terrain of what I call *zoè*, biological life. And, indeed, there is no other terrain: it's not about, I believe, returning to the classic political opposition that clearly sepa-rates the private and the public, the political body and the pri-vate body, etc. But this terrain is also that which exposes us to bioPower's processes of subjection. There is thus an ambiguity, a risk. It is what Foucault showed. The risk is re-identifying, investing into this situation with a new identity, producing a new subject, perhaps, but subjected to the State, and redirect-ing from early on, in spite of oneself, this infinite process of subjectivation and subjection that is precisely what defines bio-Power."[319]

It's a strong, categorical, seductive interview. As he does so often, Agamben helps us enter a problem with a key that seems to open all doors, but suddenly we see that we are locked in. Maybe because he is a thinker of the impasse, while Deleuze, to stick to a single example, takes the great lesson from Kafka's animals — what matters is not freedom, but rather finding an exit. Indeed, if we consider that conflict takes place in the field of life laid out as *zoè*, we have to agree with the consequence that Agamben indicates. Further taking into account the tem-poral extension he attributes to bioPower, making it reassemble

319. *Ibid.*

the Roman juridical figure of *homo sacer*, killable life, though not sacrificeable, without such a death constituting a crime. A juridical region, hence, in which the law is suspended — bare life. Extrapolating from the historical picture hung up by Foucault, as his scope, the shadow of bioPower has been cast upon us since Roman antiquity. Thus, all of us today would are still and even more subjugated to this condition of bare life inside a state of exception. Hence the growing difficulty in thinking a resistance that doesn't exactly start from this bare life, life reduced to its state of mere actuality, biological banality, be it that of the prisoners in Guantanamo, users of mental health services, those without documents, on the one hand, or from the optimized performance, genetic manipulation, on the other — all of which in a slightly abusive manner, perhaps, today is called biopolitics.

But what if we disagree on this point of departure, considering that it seems to stick to the perspective of Power? And if we pull ourselves away from this ontological primacy attributed to Power, and from the risk of a metaphysical essentialization, with its messianic counterpart? If we stopped seeing everything in the light of Power, wouldn't we also attain, as Didi-Huberman has suggested, the minimal images which used to seem blurry, or their flashes of counter-Power?[320] And if we dare to affirm that it's not in the field of *zoè* that this resistance takes place, it's not in the zone of bare life, understood as life reduced to its state of actuality, of indifference, of deformity, of powerlessness, of biological banality, but rather within the resistance that takes place within what Deleuze calls *a life*, that is, from a life conceived as virtuality, difference, invention of forms, and impersonal power, the contemporary cartography that consequently appears is different. Not catastrophist, but also not jubilatory — as if it were necessary to extricate oneself to a single time, on the one hand, the claustrophobic demonization, so as not to say paranoid, of an omnipresent Power, omniscient, omni-invasive, always joined by, in passing, a salvationist temptation,[321] but also it would be necessary to nuance the euphoria coming from the cult of inexhaustible power, maniacal or

---

320. Georges Didi-Huberman, *Survivance des lucioles*, p. 77.

321. As Jacques Derrida says, it deals with demystifying the apocalyptic tone, which is always done on behalf of a clearer, more luminous, and truer vision — "revelation": *D'un ton apocalyptique adopté naguère en philosophie*, (Paris: Galilée, 1983).

anxiolytic vitalism. It is important to refuse these two courses in order to attain a different plane. One could relaunch a hesitating and tactful experiment, departing from vital matter that we could call desire, with all its multiple runoffs and infiltrations, if this word were relieved of all of the virility that bioPower has marked it with, just like "fat-dominant health" which has seized.

If we accept taking this step, if we accept making this change of plane, the issue of desubjectivation and resubjectivation changes shape, and stops being seen merely from the point of view of Power itself. That is why Deleuze-Guattari never demonized capitalistic deterritorialization, or the desubjectivations coming from it, though they never ceased to criticize the Oedipal, signifying reterritorializations, the identitarian and compensatory resubjectivations. It's as if, from the outset, for the schizo figure, for instance, who became a conceptual persona, desubjectivation and resubjectivation were not a problem, were not his/her problem. Something else matters, lines of perception, blocks of intensity, paths of experimentation. On a broader scale, the issue is that collective assemblages of enunciation, creative lines of flight, the minor-becoming of each and every one, but also that of dead times, of exhaustion, of anti-production, of the body without organs — none of which redirects to the subject, or derives from it — on the contrary, they are positive processes of singularization, adjacent to those that occasionally produce collective subjectivations, temporary individuations, incorporeal universes, existential territories, even autopoietic self-references. They don't depend on, or reflect that to which they are opposed, or that from which they flee, the State, Oedipus, the Signifier, Capital, or the general equivalent. Therefore, from Deleuze and Guattari's point of view, this telescoping between a desubjectivation and a subjected resubjectivation is a false problem, since in the middle, in the emptiness or in this remnant that Agamben sees and where he deposits his hope or his messianism, from the very beginning Deleuze and Guattari see something different — neither a remnant nor an emptiness, but a type of excess — and I would be very prudent with this word, so as to not take it as a saturated plenitude, but rather as a complex virtuality....

But let's return to Agamben's commentary. Addressing the "care of the self," Foucault would have at the same time defended the right to "release oneself." A care of the self equivalent to a detachment of the self is a paradox that Nietzsche has already taken to the extreme. Thus Agamben's question following Foucault's footsteps: what would a practice of the self be that didn't correspond to a process of subjectivation, but found its only "identity" in a detachment of the self? "Is it necessary, as a way of saying, to sustain oneself at the same time in this double movement, desubjectivation and subjectivation. Evidently, it is a difficult terrain to sustain. It truly deals with identifying this zone, this *no man's land* that would be between a process of subjectivation and a contrary process of desubjectivation, between an identity and a non-identity." Both in the example of the AIDS carriers and the prisoners of Auschwitz, we would be facing a "subjectivity that would be the subject of its own desubjectivation." What would have interested the author at the end of the book entitled *Remnants of Auschwitz* is precisely the remnants, what remains between a subjectivation and a desubjectivation, a word and a muteness, this non-substantial space, this interval — it is as if here we had touched upon a new structure of subjectivity, not so much a principle, but a practice, that should worry about not relapsing into a resubjectivation that would be at the same time a subjection — the big risk. To be a subject, thus, at most to the extent of a strategic or tactical necessity, a useful principle in all domains where a practice of the self touches a zone of non-knowledge or desubjectivation, where a subject watches his own collapse or skims over his own desubjectivation. It's what a minor biopolitics would consist of, concludes Agamben.

None of this is without interest to us. As we said, Deleuze formulated a similar problem in the late 1960s, when he called for the domain of the impersonal, of the event, of pre-individual singularities as the only "subjective" line possible, not to say a-subjective, without there being any drama here; nor justifying before any egological or political tribunal, since upon this lay a new dimension of politics itself, he deserted the traditional frameworks of historical subjectivity. For example, a becoming, what is it? Desubjectivation, certainly, insofar as it drags given individuals out of their constituted identity, besides dismantling boundaries between human and non-human spheres, animal, vegetable, mineral, mythical, or divine. But from these imperceptible becomings are born larval subjects, multiple selves,

246

different subjectivations.... So, when Deleuze says, years later, that there is only one universal in politics, the minor-becoming of each and every one is a call for a simultaneous desubjetivation and occasional subjectivations, an approach already quite distant from identity, subjection, subjugation, not to mention the subject, or the subject of history, according to a dialectic of recognition and identity. As the introduction to *Difference and Repetition* says, in 1968: "A Cogito for a dissolved self. We believe in a world in which individuations are impersonal, and singularities are pre-individual: the splendor of the pronoun 'one.'"[322] Coherence of the impersonal Event or of crowned anarchy. Desubjectivation as a political-strategic, or agonistic procedure.

Life Capable of Conducts

Let's go back to Foucault. We can't ignore that the moment at which the theme of the care of the self appears in his work, in parallel emerges the thematization of governmentality, of liberalism, and of the transformation of the individual into an entrepreneur of the self. It is not by chance that in this context Power is thought of as action upon action, conduct upon conduct, in which the government is defined as "a set of actions upon possible actions" ("Subject and Power"). Power has as a tradeoff, or as a condition of possibility, the freedom of subjects. The government conceived as "structuring the field of eventual action of others" supposes a subject that corresponds to it, is correlated to it, or resists it. And indeed there is a turning, above all from *The government of the living*, toward a problematic of the subject. For it becomes clear that the conditions needed for the government to function is the construction of a relationship to the self, and it is precisely from this relationship that obedience is possible. It is the government's relationship to itself that is the means by which the government can operate. But contrary to similar practices from antiquity described by Foucault, as in Stoicism, where the technique of the self sought a dominion of the self, Christianity aims for humility, obedience, mortification, detachment, in short, a destruction of the form of the

---

322. Gilles Deleuze, *Difference and Repetition*, trans. Paul Patton, (New York: Columbia University Press, 1994), xxi.

self. There is a contrast between the dominion of the stoic self and the destruction of the Christian self, just like there is a distance between this destruction of the ego's vanity in Christianity and modern hermeneutics, which aims for the identity of the subject. In any case, this knot between life, the self, and Power does not only characterize primitive Christianity, but also the modern Western State, to the extent that it has integrated procedures of pastoral Power. Thus, it is about a form of Power that cannot do away with knowing "what happens in people's heads, nor quit exploiting their souls, forcing them to reveal their most intimate secrets." In other words, as Foucault says, "it is a form of Power that transforms individuals into subjects" and favors "everything that connects the individual to him or herself and thus guarantees submission to others." When the figure of the subject appears in Foucault's later work, it's not like a deviation from the biopolitical analysis, but is the culmination of the analysis of bioPower, this Power over life that passes through the subject, since this is the way through which Power monopolized life.

If the subject was previously thought of as an effect of the procedures of subjection, as the inverse of a process of subjection, as in a disciplinary society, this thesis is no longer sufficient, for it does not precisely explain "how" this mechanism creates subjects. Muriel Combes makes the instigating hypothesis that it is precisely to explain *how subjecting operates* that later on Foucault resorts to the techniques of the self, which, associated to the techniques of domination, would allow for undertaking "a genealogy of the subject in Western civilization," instead of relying on a "philosophy of the subject."[323] These techniques of the self are defined as those that "permit individuals to effect, by their own means, a certain number of operations on their own bodies, their own souls, their own thoughts, their own conduct, and this in a manner so as to transform themselves."[324]

If the techniques of the self seem to still obey the soul/body division, Combes notes that this division is not operational, if properly considered, as in the examples given by Foucault, since there are reversibilities. In any case, it's only out of these

---

323. Michel Foucault, *"Sexuality and solitude"* in *Ethics: subjectivity and truth,* ed. P. Rabinow, (New York: New Press, 1997), 175-184. *apud* Muriel Combes, *La vie inseparée: vie et sujet au temps de la biopolitique,* (Paris: Dittmar, 2011).

324. *Ibid*, p. 177.

techniques of the self that one can understand how a Power, even if disciplinary, produces subjects, naming that which the disciplines invest in, the body, desire, and thoughts. Thus, for Combes, in the end, there is neither soul nor body (despite the divisions in operation at every moment of history), but rather *subjective conducts*. If the techniques of domination aren't enough to account for the genealogy of the Western subject, it is because this link was missing, the techniques of the self, the way subjects are constituted, for it is this level, after all, that allows us to think the relationship between power and life, even and above all in the context of bioPower. To say it in a different manner: if in the analysis of the disciplines one could still consider the psychological subject as a type of effect of material incidence of Power upon bodies, the analysis of bioPower requires, in its relationship with life, the techniques of the self, the relationship of the self, mediation of the subject. It's because — and here I am closely following Muriel Combes — life, precisely, is no longer just the body, a life is not just biological, even if it isn't about saying that it is also soul, or spirit, or subjective. Life upon which the techniques of the self are focused is above all a *life capable of conducts*, a life susceptible to adopting diverse directions.[325] Life capable of conducts, here is a curious definition to think the object that bioPower focuses on: "When I was studying asylums, prisons, and so on, I perhaps insisted too much on the techniques of domination. What we call 'discipline' is something really important in this kind of institution; but it is only one aspect of the art of governing people in our societies."[326] Therefore, the techniques of the self are not specifically techniques of domination, nor do they proceed by subjection. They are in the passage between a modality of subjection to a modality of self-control, in the context of governmentality.[327]

325. Muriel Combes, *La vie inseparée*, p. 52.

326. Michel Foucault, "*Sexuality and solitude*" in *Ethics*, p.177.

327. None of this excuses us from considering this theoretical set in light of the injunctions of contemporary capitalism, such as Lazzarato did by postulating an "authoritarian" governmentality in a context in which the sovereign/disciplinary exercise is conjugated within a "security" society, in which the capitalistic axiomatic, in times of crisis, should be reassured by a State capitalism already distant from the pure neoliberalism that Foucault analyzed in his last courses, and for which he had precisely created the notion of governmentality. Cf. Lazzarato, *O governo do homem endividado*, to be released by n-1 publications.

Subjectivation thus appears as a modality of exercising Power over life, to the extent that it summons a work upon itself, this self understood not as a specific substantive, personological, or universal instance, situated behind the subject, or as an immutable nucleus, but as a relational potentiality, a zone of the constitution of subjectivity. The government being a Power that is exercised over "individual or collective subjects that have in front of themselves a field of possibility where several conducts, several reactions, and diverse modes of behavior can take place," as Combes says, Power's zone of consistency should be conceived more on the side of the subject considered as a field of possibility, a field of action for a multitude of conducts to invent than the side of "bare life." If Agamben had bothered to bring to the surface the difference between bare life and form of life, bare life should be conceived as a limit, a critical point, for a Power that is exercised as action over action "for life over that which a bioPower focuses is an informed life, a life capable of many conducts, and for this reason, always capable of insubmission."[328]

From this we can extract diverse consequences. If we don't start from bare life, in order to think bioPower, but rather from life capable of conducts, then a different horizon opens up. Even in the concentration camp, but also in the most brutal contexts of our contemporaneity, or in the most delicate, like in those populations to which were referred in the interview with Agamben, or in Deligny's work with those with autism, or in the psychotics of our day--hospitals, it's never about bare and raw biological life, or vegetative life, but about gestures, manners, modes, variations, resistances, as minuscule and unapparent as they may seem.

---

328. Muriel Combes, *La vie inseparée*, p. 52.

AFTERWORD

Various lines have been conjugated throughout this book. The relations between power and desubjectivation, ways of existence and erratic lines, crises and creation, life and exhaustion, among others. None of this can be thought of, today, without avoiding the contemporary biopolitical context and, more radically, the problematic of nihilism.

One may be surprised that a "European" problem, if not also to say a "Russian" one, such as nihilism, would worry us today in the "tropics," if such geophilosophy still preserves any meaning in such a globalized context. What is the interest in addressing this theme to such a hazy or depressing degree — is it not just a fad from the 19th century, which is already resolved? Now, what Nietzsche called "the most sinister of guests" doesn't seem minimally prone to dispense with its hosts, though having taken inaudible forms, and at times unrecognizable ones, that continually ask for new descriptions from one day to the next, as well as complements, and precisions. Thus, the almost redundant addendum that we dare include here, as an explanatory note in regard to the subtitle: that is, to call contemporary nihilism *biopolitical* — is our way of "updating it." In fact, over the past several years these two lines of research that have interested me, biopolitics and nihilism, have repeatedly been drawn toward one another, interweaving, reverberating, and referring to each other reciprocally. It was therefore necessary to further investigate this association.

The urgency of this task is due to increasing pusillanimity, in which a *biopolitical abasement and monitoring of life* obtund the *variability of perspectives, of modes of existence and resistance* that this context could provoke. There is a biopolitical stranglehold that demands gaps, as small as they might be, in order to reactivate our political imagination, be it theoretical, affective, bodily, territorial, or existential. Some of them were discussed in previous books, but time has shown that they would reclaim a conceptual amplification and new deviations.[329]

It's obvious that today precise forms of control, monitoring, expropriation, and intensification of "life," individual and collective, mental and corporal, bio-psychological and biophysical, sexual and behavioral, are everywhere, which at times has bestowed upon Nietzsche's interpretation of nihilism aggravated inflections and an unprecedented concreteness: for example, the negation of life operated as "production" of life, the negation of health brandished as "production" of health, the narcissistic reterritorialization or self-entrepreneurship comprehended as care of the self, to stick with just a few restricted examples. As if the change from repressive logic to the productive logic embedded in the exercise of power, in the way Foucault pointed out, has been unleashed. But this process has its opposite. If in its strict sense, nihilism refers to the historical-philosophical decline of a metaphysical matrix of the denial of life, Nietzsche claims that the same symptoms can be traced back to the "vital energies that are growing and cracking a shell." What are such vital energies in our biopolitical context? And how do we map them? The active destruction of ruling values and, above all, the means of the production of values, today, cannot form the economy of the biopolitical analysis. Since biopolitics, as Foucault defined it, is the management and control of the life of populations in a broad sense, compatible with what Deleuze called "control society," having as its lower limit the biologizing abasement of existence (bare life). Conversely, however, power and multitudinous expansivity (affective, subjective, collective) affirms itself as biopower. As such, it implies in the dissolution of certain forms of dominion — for example, the growing prevalence of the immaterial work, in replacement of the Fordist model, leads to a recomposition of class and new lines of conflict.

Both nihilism and biopolitics obey the logic of a Moebius strip, in a reversibility that is intrinsic to them — under certain conditions, they reveal their opposites. As if in both cases it were

329. Peter Pál Pelbart. *A vertigem por um fio: Políticas da subjetividade contemporânea,* (São Paulo: Iluminuras, 2000), or *Vida Capital: Ensaios de biopolítica,* (São Paulo: Iluminuras, 2003).

necessary to go to the limit of the process in order to turn it onto its back, or in other words, to reveal the force of the other side (outside) that from the beginning was there, virtually, exerting pressure. If the logic of both is assimilated to such a point, it won't be just by a structural homology. It is because biopolitics does not fail to be a sociohistorical, psycho-political, affective-subjective concretion of nihilism itself, understood as an escalation of the denial of life, that, however, carries, in its reverse, an affirmative element.

It was necessary to sustain the points where both Moebius strips, in a manner of speaking, cross one another and communicate. This implies assuming the equivocal and non-deterministic character in both cases, without letting it be engulfed either by somber and sinister colors that some interpretations of nihilism favor, or, on the contrary, by the effusively utopian tone that some interpretations of biopolitics instigate. Such a tension merely expresses the fact that one faces a complex entanglement of multiple fields of forces, traversed by concrete struggles on various scales, with all the reversibilities thus implicated.

For it is necessary to recognize the dangers of every approach that touches an abusive totalization, in which one imagines a closed System, of which would befit some kind of "leaving" — with all the powerlessness and paralysis that this idea implies. Or a History in relation to that which one imagines an "overcoming," which would postpone this great "turning". As David Lapoujade rightly noted, a system is never closed in Deleuze and Guattari, it flees by way of all its ends, and the whole time the system itself tries to contain, "repel, subdue this heterogeneity that undermines it from within." In this sense, "it is not about overcoming or reverting whatever it is, but of *turning it over* [...] walking on the other side, [...] the outside."[330]

To this extent it was necessary to resort to figures such as *disaster, exhaustion,* and *chaosmosis,* capable of revealing the points of a-foundation where there appear, paradoxically, and at the same time, the counter-movements (*to* nihilism and *of* nihilism, *to* biopolitics and *of* biopolitics). It is therefore impossible to speak of nihilism today without plunging into this complex and composed stew, where there appears — without any such psychologism — a bodily, material, affective, aesthetic, psychopolitical, micropolitical,

---

330. David Lapoujade, "Deleuze: política e informação," in Cadernos de subjetividade n10, São Paulo, (2010).

and biopolitical dimension, which through certain derangements or collapses reveals the heteroclitic components that ask for other assemblages, by way of a different "element" — a different *Yes*. These are the inflexion points that insinuate, at times imperceptibly, the counterblows that are eagerly awaited, but also in a spectacular fashion, public explosions that denounce the means of the production of sense and value that have decayed. To formulate it more precisely, we would say that it is not about producing an amalgamation of nihilism and biopolitics, but about experimenting with the biopolitical dimension of nihilism, and the nihilistic dimension of biopolitics, and the reverse of both. Only then can that which is depleted and that which is insinuated be revealed, through an outside force.

Considering this, what can be done in order to address the theme of "nihilism" refusing its substantivation or reification, assuming its infinite elusiveness? There is no response, but rather local tactics. One of the challenges, in any case, consists of refusing at each step a "nihilistic" reading of nihilism — with which we distance ourselves from the many available approaches, however consecrated they may be, which refer to the "history of Being," or to an anthropocentric dialectic based on notions of alienation, reappropriation, and authenticity. Both the auratic and the humanist solutions "solve" what escapes us, the lines of drift having been preferable to us — even when it does not "solve" anything. When recognizing the modesty of Deleuze's philosophical endeavor facing the question "what do you propose?", Lapoujade maintains with acuity that we still haven't grieved for "philosophy as State apparatus."[331]

As such, our suspicion regarding excessively totalizing readings remains, whether in the historical arc that returns to antiquity, or in the extensive range that encompasses all planetary space, sometimes resulting in a tonality of *a priori* aversion to contemporary complexity — which is already, let's say in passing, part of the symptom to be thought. As Deleuze says in a reference to Kostas Axelos' analysis that tried to conjugate Heidegger, Marx, and Heraclitus in order to think the "planetary" era: precisely when everything seems flat, when the earth has become smooth, and all the powers are determined by the code of technique, after all, it is in this apparently unidimensional state that nihilism has "the most bizarre effect: it returns the elementary forces to

---

331. David Lapoujade, "Deleuze: política e informação."

themselves in the raw play of all its dimensions, *liberating the unthought nihil in a counter-power which is multidimensional play.* Of the most unfortunate souls, it will no longer be said that they are alienated or tortured by the powers, but rather that they are shaken by the forces."[332] It's this irreverence facing a grave tone, solemn and lapidary that allows for the game to begin again ("it plays, without players"), avoiding the nihilistic captures — in short, freeing the thought of nihilism from the risk of turning into the nihilism of thought. Such a capacity of turning from the other side, of shaking the dusty consensus, of finding the counter-powers, the counter-attacks, the new stratagems, and also the new disorders that the supposed totalized order hid, already brings a different affective tonality whose effect should not be underestimated. Echoing Nietzsche, Deleuze insists that at times what matters more than the distinction between the true or the false, is the distinction between the heavy and the light, the deep and the aerial. Referring to a song by Charles Koechlin, for example, that renounces classical affirmations and romantic raptures, Deleuze notes at what point it becomes particularly apt to say "a particular disarray, a particular disequilibrium, even a particular indifference," and, besides that, "a strange joy almost like happiness."[333]

A book published recently by Georges Didi-Huberman adopts a similar direction, unquiet with the predominance of an apocalyptic tone that prevents us from seeing precisely that which survives, in a strange paradox where the discourse of denouncement, as lucid and "luminous" as it may be, helps to specifically obfuscate the existences that survive, with its discrete luminosity. Didi-Huberman states with reason: "It is one thing to call the machine totalitarian, it is another to hastily attribute to it a definitive victory and without partitions. Is the world really at such a totally enslaved point as they dreamed it — projected it, programmed it, and want to impose upon us — our current 'perfidious counselors?' Postulating this is precisely giving credit to that which the machine wants to make us believe. It's seeing nothing but the night or the obfuscating light of the projectors. It's acting like losers: it's being convinced that the machine accomplished its job without remnants or resistance. It's not seeing if not the *whole*. It's furthermore not seeing

---

332. Gilles Deleuze, "Fissure and Local Fires," in *Desert Islands*, org. David Lapoujade, (New York: Semiotext(e), 2004), 160.

333. *Ibid*, p. 158.

space — were it interstitial, intermittent, nomadic, improbably situated — from the openings, the possibles, the flashes, the *despite everythings*." Or still, taking up his beautiful image of the fireflies and the threshold of their visibility, he adds: "In order to know about the fireflies, it is necessary to see them in the present of their survival: it is necessary to see them dance in the heart of night, even though this night were swept up by some ferocious projectors. [...] Thus as there is a minor literature — as Gilles Deleuze and Félix Guattari showed with regard to Kafka — there would be a *minor light* with the same philosophical characteristics."[334]

Everything indicates that there is really a problem of "light" in thought. How not to submit to the "searchlight" of reason? Bergson said that light is in the world, not in the spirit that contemplates... It is possible that a regime of obscene luminosity, like what currently predominates, has unprecedented effects of obfuscation of the "bioluminescences" — white nihilism! Hence our more reserved mention of micropolitical experiments (of the order of "fireflies") that make for confusing testimonies, such as the chapter on the Ueinzz theatrical group, where "minor" modes of existence are approached and, to speak as Souriau, their "establishment" is thought.[335]

We can now return to the question that doesn't want to keep quiet. After all, from what are we so exhausted nowadays? It's necessary to imagine a cartography of exhaustion, as if it were a type of molecular symptomatology, as Nietzsche attempepted with nihilism, though from a mostly historic-philosophical perspective, but also a "psychological" one. Now, following Deleuze's trail, shouldn't we rethink exhaustion, nowadays, according to Beckettian categories? Perhaps this would allow us to face with less jolts the states of suspension, of bankruptcy, of Musil-esque mist, even of dissipation, whether individual or collective, and glimpse at the stirring up of words and consumption of images, vital stratagems, indissociable from the forces and humor that they express.

For my part, for whom all these authors, thoughts, winds and events constitute incessant sources of inspiration, I'm left

---

334. Georges Didi-Huberman, *Survivance des lucioles*, p. 44.

335. Étienne Souriau, *Les différents modes d'existence*, (Paris: Puf, 2009), presented by Bruno Latour and Isabelle Stengers, who clarify: "To Souriau, all beings must be established, both the soul and the body, the work of art and the scientific existent, electron or virus."

with the impression that they are also a clue, though a fleeting one, of a shift in progress. By whom? Of what? In which direction? We don't know. It is a collective cartography, unfinished, moving, from the inside out of nihilism — "cartographies of exhaustion" should be understood also in the genitive: exhaustion itself is the cartographer, as a manner of speaking. It's not about, therefore, knowing "who speaks," or "from what place one speaks," perhaps not even "of what" is spoken, but like Guattari suggested, "what speaks through us?"

REFERENCES

HOW TO LIVE ALONE

Presented at the 27th São Paulo Art Biannual, entitled *Como-viver-junto*, in 2006, curated by Lisette Lagnado.

THE BODY OF THE FORMLESS

Published in P. P. Pelbart, *Vida Capital: Ensaios de Biopolítica,* São Paulo, Iluminuras, 2003.

BARE LIFE, BEASTLY LIFE, A LIFE

Presented at "Um mergulho — Pensamento, Poesia e Corpo em Acção", organized by Vera Mantero in Lisbon, at the Festival Alkantara, in 2006, and also published in the online magazine *Trópico.*

POWER OVER LIFE, POWER OF LIFE

Published in P. P. Pelbart, *Vida Capital: Ensaios de Biopolítica,* São Paulo, Iluminuras, 2003.

EXCURSUS ON DISASTER

Published in P. P. Pelbart, *Da clausura do fora ao fora da clausura: Loucura e Desrazão,* São Paulo, Iluminuras, 2009.

THE COMMUNITY OF THOSE WHO DO NOT HAVE A COMMUNITY

Published in P. P. Pelbart, *Vida Capital: Ensaios de Biopolítica,* São Paulo, Iluminuras, 2003.

---

336. The following is a list of essays and presentations that have either been previously published or presented at various conferences. All of the texts listed have been reworked and revised for the present work. Other chapters in the present volume that are not mentioned in this list are being published here for the first time.

EXHAUSTION AND CREATION

Presented in the seminar "L'expression du désastre: entre épuisement et création," organized by Barbara Glowczewski and Alexandre Soucaille, at the Quai Branly Museum, in 2008. Partially published in "Desastres", *Cahiers d'Anthropologie Sociale* 07, Paris, L'Herne, 2011.

THE DETERRITORIALIZED UNCONSCIOUS

Presented in the seminar titled "The Guattari-Effect," organized by Éric Alliez in the ambit of the Center for Research in Modern European Philosophy, in Middlesex, 2008. Published in Multitudes magazine n°34, October, 2008, Paris and in *The Guattari Effect*, (ed) Alliez and Goffrey, London/NY, Continuum, 2011.

INHUMAN POLYPHONY IN THE THEATER OF MADNESS

Presented in "Poison and Play Workshops and Seminar,"on invitation by André Lepecki, in *Haus der Kulturen del Welt* in Berlin, in October 2011.

THE THOUGHT OF THE OUTSIDE, THE OUTSIDE OF THOUGHT

Published in *Rhizomatics, Genealogy, Deconstruction* (org. Constantin, Boundas), Angelaki, Routledge, London/New York, 2000.

IMAGES OF TIME IN DELEUZE

Published in P.P.Pelbart *A vertigem por um fio: Políticas da subjetividade contemporânea*, São Paulo, Iluminuras, 2000.

EXPERIENCE AND ABANDON OF THE SELF

Presented at VII Colóquio Internacional Michel Foucault, at Pontifícia Universidade Católica de São Paulo in 2011, on invitation by Salma Tannus Muchail and Márcio Alves da Fonseca.

SUBJECTIVATION AND DESUBJECTIVATION

Presented at *Exhausted subject, impossible community*, promoted by mollecular.org in Helsinki, Finland, 2011, under the coordination of Virtanen Akseli. Revisited at Colóquio *Transformações da biopolítica*, at PUC-SP, 2012, on invitation by Edson Passetti.